Praise for *Fruitless Fall*

"Past a certain point, we can't make nature conform to our industrial model. The collapse of beehives is a warning—and the cleverness of a few beekeepers in figuring out how to work with bees not as masters but as partners offers a clear-eyed kind of hope for many of our ecological dilemmas."

—Bill McKibben, author of *Deep Economy*

"Jacobsen reminds readers that bees provide not just the sweetness of honey, but also are a crucial link in the life cycle of our crops."

—Seattle Post-Intelligencer

"Written with a passion that gives this exploration of colony collapse disorder real buzz . . . Jacobsen invests solid investigative journalism with a poet's voice to craft a fact-heavy book that soars."

—Publisher's Weekly

"Rowan Jacobsen tells the fascinating—and alarming—story of honeybee decline with energy and insight."

—Elizabeth Kolbert, author of
Field Notes from a Catastrophe

"A passionate sequel to Rachel Carson's *Silent Spring*."

—New York Observer

"Although Rachel Carson famously warned us about pesticides causing a 'silent spring,' we now face a 'fruitless fall.' Jacobsen explains why with compelling lucidity, carefully documented facts, and a deep respect for the sophisticated and diligent honeybee."

—[illegible] (starred review)

"The apiculture industry now has its own Upton Sinclair—*Fruitless Fall* is an eye-opening, attitude-changing, and exceptionally engaging examination of America's most overlooked multi-billion-dollar industry."

—May Berenbaum, professor of Entomology, University of Illinois, and Chair, National Research Council Committee on the Status of Pollinators in North America

"In this densely woven account of waggle dances, almond trees, and confounded pathologists, Jacobsen tells the story of CCD: how it happened, the likely culprits, and its implications for the future of agriculture." ***—Seed***

"Intelligent, important assessment of a confusing phenomenon and its potentially catastrophic implications." ***—Kirkus Reviews***

"Rowan Jacobsen visited citrus groves in Florida and almond fields in California for his new book, *Fruitless Fall* . . . Jacobsen, who explains the science in accessible language, ends the book on a note of optimism: He's ordered another colony of bees."

—Boston Globe

FRUITLESS FALL

The Collapse of the Honey Bee and the Coming Agricultural Crisis

Rowan Jacobsen

BLOOMSBURY

New York Berlin London

Published by Bloomsbury USA, New York

All papers used by Bloomsbury USA are natural, recyclable products made from wood grown in well-managed forests. The manufacturing processes conform to the environmental regulations of the country of origin.

LIBRARY OF CONGRESS CATALOGING-IN-PUBLICATION DATA

Jacobsen, Rowan.
Fruitless fall: the collapse of the honeybee and the coming agricultural crisis / Rowan Jacobsen.—1st U.S. ed.
p. cm.
Includes bibliographical references and index.
ISBN-13: 978-1-59691-537-4 (hardcover)
ISBN-10: 1-59691-537-4 (hardcover)
ISBN-13: 978-1-59691-639-5 (pbk.)
ISBN-10: 1-59691-639-7 (pbk.)

1. Honeybee—Diseases—United States. 2. Colony collapse disorder of honeybees—United States. I. Title.

SF538.3.U6J33 2008
638'.15—dc22
2008026126

First published by Bloomsbury USA in 2008
This paperback edition published in 2009

3 5 7 9 10 8 6 4 2

Typeset by Westchester Book Group
Printed in the United States of America by Quebecor World Fairfield

CONTENTS

AUTHOR'S NOTE

Copyeditors of the world beware. The spelling of insect names in this book follows the rules of the Entomological Society of America, not *Merriam-Webster's.* When a species is a true example of a particular taxon, that taxon is written separately. Honey bees and bumble bees are true bees, and black flies are true flies. A yellowjacket, however, is not a true jacket. Entomologists, who have to read the names of bugs a lot more than the rest of us do, would appreciate it if we all followed these rules.

Prologue

FLORIDA, NOVEMBER 2006

LATE IN THE afternoon of November 12, 2006, Dave Hackenberg stepped into a Florida field of Brazilian peppers that should have been buzzing with honey bees and noticed that it wasn't. Hackenberg, a commercial beekeeper, had four hundred of his best hives in this particular beeyard. It was a mild day, sunny and 65 degrees, good flying conditions, and thousands of bees should have been zipping purposefully about on their nectar errands. But there weren't enough bees in the air for ten hives, much less four hundred.

Hackenberg didn't think much about it. His bees had been grooving on these Brazilian peppers—an invasive menace to Florida ecosystems but a nectar-rich boon to beekeepers—for weeks, but now a cold front had come to Florida and shut off the nectar flow. Hackenberg figured there were no bees in the air because there was no food to gather.

It's been forty years since Hackenberg, who owns one of the largest apiaries in Pennsylvania, let his bees overwinter in the Keystone State. The bees were some of the original snowbirds, making the late-fall trek to Florida starting in the 1960s. Honey bees can survive a Northeast winter, clustering in a ball in the middle of their cold hive, vibrating their wing muscles to stay warm, and living off their honey stores, but things are easier in Florida, where nectar flows much of the mild winter.

Hackenberg lit a smoker and approached the first hive. He'd been pleased with these hives when he'd dropped them off a few weeks earlier. They'd been strong, thick with bees and brood,[1] and with all the Brazilian peppers around he was sure they'd now be full of honey to get through the winter. It was a rare good feeling.

For the past two or three years, he'd had this nagging sense that something was wrong with his bees. He couldn't put his finger on what it was, but he knew what it wasn't: not varroa mites, the scourge of beekeepers everywhere, nor hive beetles, wax moths, or any of the other honey bees' pests. He knew the signs of colonies suffering those afflictions, and this was something different. Whatever it was, it was subtle. If he hadn't been watching bees most of his life, he'd have dismissed the feeling. But he knew bees, and sometimes his weren't acting right. They almost seemed . . . nervous.

He wasn't alone in his concern. In January 2005, his good friend Clint Walker, a major Texas beekeeper, had called him in distress. "They're gone, Dave," he'd said on the phone.

"What are, Clint?"

"My bees. They're dying." Two thirds of the Walker Honey Company's two thousand hives had suddenly collapsed.

Hackenberg had told Walker that he must have a mite problem. Over the past fifteen years, beekeepers have learned to blame everything on varroa mites. These pinhead-sized parasites, sometimes called "vampire mites," sink their fangs into bee larvae and

1. Brood are young bees in the egg, larval, or pupal stages.

adults, introducing diseases in the process. If left unchecked, they can wipe out a whole colony. Several chemicals have been developed to treat hives infested with varroa, but the mites have developed resistance to the chemicals at a faster pace. They caused horrific losses throughout the 1990s and still kill hundreds of thousands of colonies a year. But Walker didn't think mites were responsible this time. His bees had collapsed after feeding for a month in the West Texas cotton fields. "They must have done something different to the cotton this year," he'd told Hackenberg.

Hackenberg had heard enough weird stories from fellow beekeepers that in August 2006 he was one of a dozen beekeepers and half a dozen honey bee scientists who convened for a quiet meeting in Nebraska to discuss what was going on. They tossed around ideas—Were they trucking the bees too hard? Was some new disease or parasite in play?—but couldn't come up with anything that fit.

But here in the open fields of Ruskin, Florida, with the sun shining and a great nectar flow just completed, such concerns seemed distant. His essential optimism in full flower, Hackenberg pulled the cover off the first hive, smoked it to calm the bees, and pulled up the frames. Plenty of honey, nice honey. He replaced the cover and kept going, hive after hive, the relentless routine of the commercial beekeeper. Not until he'd smoked five palettes did it hit him that the yard was so quiet it was spooky. He turned to his assistant and said, "Glen, I don't think there's any bees in here."

Hackenberg yanked the covers off several more hives. No worker bees. Just a handful of young nurse bees clustered around the queen.

A knot began to form in his stomach. He ran from hive to hive, jerking covers off. They were all empty.

Moving faster now, dread dripping into his mind, he ignored

the covers and began tipping hive after hive to take a look at the open bottoms. Nobody was home. He thought he saw healthy brood, but he told himself he was just seeing things. Worker bees leave the hive every day to forage, but nurse bees stay inside to attend to the brood. They would never, ever abandon a hive full of healthy juveniles.

Of Hackenberg's four hundred colonies, all but thirty-two had collapsed. His first thought was, "What the hell did I do wrong?" When you are the steward for ten million little beings, and you spend every day over many years worrying about their health, nutrition, and happiness, you take it hard when they die.

Beekeepers blame themselves, a lot, and usually their first assumption is that they somehow haven't been diligent enough in preventing mites. But when mites infect a colony, dead bees are laid out in front of the entrance like a carpet. The brood chamber is full of mites, and plenty of dead mites litter the bottom of the hive. And Hackenberg didn't see any dead bees. He got down on his hands and knees and crawled through the yard, face inches from the ground, searching for the bodies that would at least tell him what the crime was. There were none. What the hell was going on? Whatever had happened to these bees, they'd been healthy enough to fly off and not come back.

Hackenberg is fifty-eight, with the grooved face that comes from forty-five years of working in the weather and worrying about bees. He's seen the business shudder through sweeping changes in that time, from the rise of monocrops and the advent of the migratory beekeeper, earning more money from pollination rentals than from honey, to the decimation of bee colonies in the 1990s by varroa. But never had he seen conditions like what he was staring at amid those Florida peppers. Dead bees, sure. Vanished bees? No, sir.

As Hackenberg knelt amid the lines of empty hives, he saw his own financial ruin. He didn't think about the August meeting in Nebraska, because that had been about nervous bees, not vaporizing ones. He didn't immediately think about Clint Walker's dying colonies in the Texas cotton fields either. What could any of that have to do with his Florida bees? No, Hackenberg still assumed that he'd screwed up somehow, that the problem was limited to him.

But he was wrong. As fall hardened into winter, beekeepers up and down the East Coast watched their hives go from bustling colonies to ghost towns in a matter of weeks, with no sign of why. The mysterious deaths soon spread across the country, then around the world. Hackenberg would lose two thousand of his three thousand hives, and some beekeepers would lose even more. The losses threatened an ancient way of life, an industry, and one of the foundations of civilization. By spring 2007, a quarter of the northern hemisphere's honey bees were AWOL.

Chapter 1

BREAKFAST IN AMERICA

I'M STANDING IN my kitchen on a July morning, serving up breakfast for my family. Honey-Nut O's for my son, almond granola for my wife and me, all piled high with blueberries and cherries. Wedges of melon, glasses of apple cider, and mugs of coffee on the side. It's a delicious breakfast, its colors, textures, and flavors a feast for the senses. And it wouldn't exist without honey bees. Take away the bees and we'd be left with nothing but wind-pollinated oats and maybe some milk to wet them.

Berries, cherries, melons, and apples are all fruits, you see, and fruits are special. Almonds and other nuts are simply the large seeds inside fruits. (Almonds are in the family of stone fruits, like peaches and plums, and do have a fruit around them, but it's inedible. With a peach you eat the flesh and discard the nut; with an almond the reverse.) Coffee beans come wrapped in fruit jackets, too. Even many of the foods we think of as vegetables—cucumbers and tomatoes and peppers and squash—are fruits. And fruits, unlike true vegetables, or meat, or just about anything else we eat, want to be eaten. Nature has designed them—with a little help from human plant breeders—to be as eye-catching and irresistibly delicious to animals as possible.

And they are. No matter how many rungs up the industrial food chain I sit, no matter how far removed from my primate roots, I still react to the dazzling sapphire of a ripe blueberry in a satisfyingly primitive way. My mouth waters, my hands reach, and I am its slave. My nine-year-old son, a full-fledged frugivore, will hurry past cakes and cookies to get to a plate of pink, juicy watermelon.

The plan, which is certainly working on us, is that the animals eat the fruit and unwittingly spread the plant's seeds around—a major challenge for an immobile life-form. It's an ancient covenant, one that has served them and us well, and one that's still fairly obvious, since not so long ago we primates were playing a significant role in the process.

But there is another covenant, equally essential and much easier for us to overlook because it rarely involves large creatures. We've done a spectacular job of ignoring it across all levels of society, with catastrophic consequences that are only now beginning to hit home.

The basic story of plant life, familiar to every grade-schooler, is that the plant grows and has a flower, and the flower turns into a seed-bearing fruit, and the fruit falls to the ground, where the cycle starts all over again. In the common imagination, the process happens all on its own. The fruit is the event. The flower is nothing really, just the herald of the fruit. Eye candy. Growing up, I don't think I even connected the flower and the fruit. Flowers grew along roadsides—daisies and hawkweed and Queen Anne's lace. Fruit came from the supermarket. They were two things trees and weeds produced, not necessarily related.

But, of course, flowers are not there to please landscape artists. They are supremely functional, and their function is sex. Flowers' purpose is to swap genetic material with other individuals of the same species and reproduce. When that happens successfully, a fruit grows out of the flower.

No flower, no fruit. It's that simple.

The presence of a flower doesn't guarantee fruit. Most flowers have male and female parts. The anthers—the long filaments with pads on the end—hold grains of pollen, the plant equivalent of sperm. To make a fruit, that pollen needs to be carried to the stigma, the central column that is the female receptor. From there, it can combine with the ovule—the plant equivalent of an egg—in the ovary (usually hidden within the flower). A seed is born, and fruit is soon to follow.

Some flowers can use their own pollen to fertilize their ovules, but this doesn't accomplish the gene mixing that is the whole point of sexual reproduction, so most can be fertilized only by the pollen from a different individual. The trick is to get the pollen from one flower to another. A few of our food plants—primarily corn, oats, and the other grains—use wind to do the job. Make vast quantities of powdery, flyweight pollen, cast it to the winds, and cross one's metaphorical fingers. It's like direct mail, or Internet spam: You need to send out a million if you hope to get a single hit. When your car is caked in yellow pine

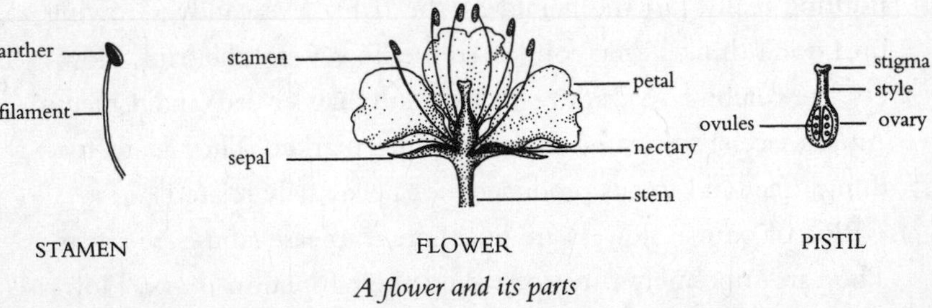

A flower and its parts

pollen, or your nasal passages are swollen with ragweed pollen, you can be sure that a wind pollinator is broadcasting.

Direct mail is pretty wasteful, so most of our food plants rely on courier service instead. Somebody picks up the pollen package from one flower and delivers it directly to another flower of the same species. Most birds and mammals aren't going to fit this bill; they are way too big to handle sand-sized grains of pollen. Insects, on the other hand, are perfect.

For 150 million years, insects have served as sexual handmaidens to the flowering plants. Most plants on earth today can't reproduce without them. Of course, they aren't doing it out of the goodness of their hearts. It takes a bribe. Protein-rich pollen makes good health food, but nectar—energy-rich sugar water contained in tiny wells in most flowers—seals the deal. The bugs visit the flower to drink the nectar and in the process brush against the sticky pollen grains, which become attached to them. When the bugs fly to the next flower for more nectar, some of the pollen is transferred to the new stigma. Wham, bam, thank you, ma'am.

Thousands of insect species feed on nectar and pollen. Some 80 million years ago, one group of them, the bees, made it a specialty. Of the twenty thousand species of bees, only one has become a true artisan of nectar, developing a worldwide human culture around itself. That insect is *Apis mellifera*, the honey bee. And how this one life-form wound up shouldering so much of the industrial food chain on its tiny back is one of the subjects of this book.

When we think of productive human-animal partnerships, we tend to think of the dog or the horse. The dog can't lay claim to more than improving our quality of life, plus a bit of guard duty and seeing-eye work, but the horse brought agriculture, not to mention transportation, to a whole new level. Yet fossil fuel technology relegated the horse to country fair sideshows. The same cannot be said about the honey bee. In fact, as industrial agriculture has come to dominate world production, and as exotic crops were grown on new continents, it has been forced to rely more and more heavily on middle-aged men with their wooden boxes of bees and tin smokers. This is an astonishing Achilles' heel for industries increasingly devoted to high-tech solutions.

It's also quite wonderful. To witness an orchard full of bees merrily nuzzling flowers and packing honey into the hive—"on the flow," as beekeepers say—is to feel that all is right with the world. We may not get food from flowers, as bees do, but at some primordial level, we share the same tastes. We are attracted to the same shapes, scents, and colors. We may not be able to "get" a fly or a dung beetle, but we get a bee.

And we admire them. The techniques bees have developed to help in their mission (dancing, navigation, pheromone communication), the extraordinary array of products they make (honey, propolis, wax, royal jelly), and the amazing social structure of the hive are all signs of an estimable intelligence wholly unlike the human variety and well worth comprehending. Bees can do things no other creature can.

For now, suffice it to say that plenty of varieties of insect are capable of pollinating the blueberries stippling my son's cereal (even the black fly, pariah of the Northeast, contributes), but only honey bees come in convenient, mobile boxes of fifty thousand and have a passion for hoarding concentrated nectar in astonishing quantities. This passion has given us the natural miracle of honey, but it also means that a hive of honey bees can cross-pollinate twenty-five million flowers in a single day. Try plucking solitary black flies or hummingbirds out of the air and exhorting them to do the same. Honey bees are the most enthusiastic, best-organized migrant farmworkers the planet has ever seen, and today the majority of U.S. bees spend the year traveling the country on the backs of flatbeds, fertilizing America's crops.

But why do we need them? Didn't these crops exist before rent-a-pollinator?

The reason you need migrant workers of any kind is because no one local will do the job. In many human communities, there aren't enough locals left to work the crops. With insects, it's the same. A vast monocrop of California almonds leaves no natural habitat where wild insects could live. If a New Jersey blueberry farm is hemmed by suburbs, it's probably out of the three-mile range of any local, stationary honey bees. If flower sex is to happen in such landscapes, bussed honey bees are the only option. Large-scale agriculture can no longer exist without them.[1]

It used to be that beekeepers were the ones begging farmers to let them set their hives in a field or grove. An acre of apple blossoms is a windfall for a honey bee colony. The farmer got his apples fertilized, and the beekeeper fed his flock and got his honey. Everybody won. Usually no money changed hands. For years, however, due to a complicated mix of factors that we'll explore in later chapters, honey bee populations have been crashing in Europe and America, while the acres of crops needing pollination have expanded. The free market kicked in: Too many crops and not enough pollination equals farmers desperate to get some honey bees in their fields and willing to pay for it.

The whole situation snuck up on us. A century ago cranberry growers were already observing that their yield doubled if a hive

1. In systems thinking, this increased reliance on fewer and fewer supports is a classic characteristic of any developing system, and leads to the collapse of resilience—a term you can file deep in the back of your brain, because you won't need it again until chapter 9.

was nearby, but for most of human history hives have always been nearby. In Europe up through the nineteenth century, a hive or two was kept on every farm. Many old stone houses still have niches in their outer walls for beehives. Pollination was plentiful.

When Europeans settled the New World, they brought apple trees with them, but, removed from their Old World habitats and pollination partners, many of the trees fared poorly. In settlements that also imported honey bee hives, however, apple trees took off—so successfully that most people assume they are native (as American as apple pie). Fortunately (for both the settlers and the apple trees) honey bees were popular with the colonists. They had been introduced to Virginia by 1622 and Massachusetts by 1639,[2] and had covered the East Coast (by swarm or human transport) before long. A British officer in the Revolutionary War wrote that in Pennsylvania "almost every farmhouse has 7 or 8 hives of bees." George Washington kept hives at Mount Vernon in 1787. By then, people were already forgetting that bees hadn't always been on the scene, though Thomas Jefferson tried to set the record straight: "The honeybee is not a native of our country . . . The Indians concur with us in the tradition that it was brought from Europe, but when and by whom we know not. The bees have generally extended themselves into the country a little in advance of the settlers. The Indians, therefore, call them the white man's fly, and consider their approach as indicating the approach of the settlement of the whites."

2. And probably St. Augustine, Florida, many years earlier. St. Augustine, the oldest city in the United States, was settled by the Spanish, who, being good Catholics, brought bees on all their conquests to keep their churches in candles. We have no ship's log, however, to prove the St. Augustine theory.

Both the white men and the bees kept coming. Washington Irving's book *A Tour on the Prairies* includes his account of an 1832 honey hunt in Oklahoma, about as far as honey bees had advanced at that point:

> It is surprising in what countless swarms the bees have overspread the Far West within but a moderate number of years. The Indians consider them the harbinger of the white man, as the buffalo is of the red man; and say that, in proportion as the bee advances, the Indian and buffalo retire. We are always accustomed to associate the hum of the bee-hive with the farmhouse and flower-garden, and to consider those industrious little animals as connected with the busy haunts of man, and I am told that the wild bee is seldom to be met with at any great distance from the frontier. They have been the heralds of civilization, steadfastly preceding it as it advanced from the Atlantic borders, and some of the ancient settlers of the West pretend to give the very year when the honey-bee first crossed the Mississippi. The Indians with surprise found the mouldering trees of their forests suddenly teeming with ambrosial sweets, and nothing, I am told, can exceed the greedy relish with which they banquet for the first time upon this unbought luxury of the wilderness.

As settlers spread across the continent, they did so in partnership with the honey bee, whose omnivorous tastes allowed a multitude of European and Asian fruits and vegetables to thrive. The New World was to their liking. The pioneers, having little concept of pollination, probably never questioned why their European crops flourished in the New World. They just happened to have the bees around for honey. They had unwittingly brought a particularly European fertility with them.[3]

At times, the ignorance was so astounding that it's a wonder American agriculture didn't collapse under the weight of its own stupidity. Well into the twentieth century, many parts of America believed that bees *robbed* plants of their vitality. Utah even passed a law in 1929 banning the import of honey bees into the state because they "took the nectar required by the alfalfa blossoms to set seed."

This misinformation persisted despite Easterners having long observed that fruit was choicer and more abundant in areas near hives. John Harvey Lovell's 1919 book, *The Flower and the Bee*, describes hives being placed in cranberry bogs, just as they are today, and even in cucumber greenhouses. "Without bees or hand-pollination, not a cucumber would be produced." For apples, he describes an eerily familiar scene as he explains why wild bees are not sufficient pollinators:

> With the planting of orchards by the square mile, their number became wholly inadequate to pollinate efficiently this vast expanse of bloom. This difficulty is met by the introduction of colonies of the domestic bee. No other insect is so well adapted

3. To look back on old photos of these pioneers, hauling their hives by horse-drawn wagon, literally sitting on top of the hives, is to gain an appreciation for how tough they must have been. To put it mildly, rickety wagons, horses, and bees are a combustible combination. As M. G. Dadant warned in his 1919 guide, *Outapiaries and Their Management*, "If it is necessary to haul with wagons and horses, too much caution against having trouble with escaping bees and consequent stinging cannot be taken. Immediately any trouble is encountered, teams should be unhooked and gotten away from the angry bees until all is quiet."

> for this purpose. In numbers, diligence, perception and apparatus for carrying pollen it has no equal. In orchard after orchard the establishment of apiaries has been followed by an astonishing gain in the fruit-crop; and today it is generally admitted that honey bees and fruit culture must go together.

And so they have. By allowing planting patterns that could never exist in nature, and adapting to a wide variety of environments, the honey bee has been something of a landscape architect of the American pastoral, remaking the countryside in its own vision. Farmers worried about land and water and sun, but they never had to think about the bugs that would set their fruit. After World War II, as machinery and pesticides enabled farms to expand from family operations into vast enterprises, rented honey bees became indispensable to many farms.

What was a nice little sideline in the 1960s became the chief source of income for many commercial beekeepers by the 1990s. Fertility is at a premium. No beekeeper is eager to truck his bees around the country, but as world honey prices disintegrated in the face of cheap Chinese competition, beekeepers found that they couldn't survive on honey alone. Pollination filled the gap—first locally, then farther and farther afield as beekeepers confronted a choice between a migratory business and no business at all.

America didn't invent migratory beekeeping. Egyptians followed the bloom up and down the Nile thousands of years ago, floating their hives on barges. Europeans used the Danube, mules, and their own backs, always seeking to extend the season. But only in America did tractor trailers and five-thousand-mile circuits become commonplace.

Then, in fall 2006, the corroded bottom finally fell out of the

American beekeeping barrel. A mysterious syndrome began wiping out honey bee colonies from coast to coast. The number of hives, which had been at 6 million during World War II, and 2.6 million in 2005, fell below 2 million for the first time in memory. Soon the syndrome had a name as vague as its cause: colony collapse disorder. By the time the media got wind of the syndrome, it was just called CCD.

When California's almond groves began blooming in February, CCD was raging. As growers scrambled to find enough bees, pollination fees exploded, from $50 per hive in 2004 to $150 per hive in 2007. Almond pollination alone now generates more than $200 million in annual revenues for beekeepers, while the entire U.S. honey crop itself is worth just $150 million.

As with the cost of oil, those spiraling prices portend an impending shortfall. When beekeepers in Florida are paid to load their "six-legged livestock" onto flatbeds and truck them thousands of miles to pollinate California almonds in February, Washington apples in March, South Dakota sunflowers and canola in May, Maine blueberries in June, and Pennsylvania pumpkins in July, the system hovers on the edge of breakdown. Today there may no longer be enough bees to pollinate our crops no matter what the incentive.

Europe has many more small-time beekeepers than America, and distances are shorter, so much less long-range trucking of bees takes place. And it's unclear whether Europe's bees are suffering the same afflictions as America's bees. What is clear, however, is that they are collapsing, too, as are bees in Canada, Asia, and South America. The system is broken everywhere.

It's a system we've taken for granted. Because nature always looked after it, we have been as clueless and complacent about the realities of plant reproduction as a child who thinks that storks bring new babies. We assumed it just happened, and would go on happening. If the crops bloomed, fruit would follow.

We can no longer count on that, and there are no options other than bees. Every almond in my granola was started by a bee. Every apple pressed for my son's cider was the work of multiple bees. All the berries, cherries, and melons were serviced by honey bees. Even my coffee came from beans produced by bees in Panama. Then, obviously, there is the honey in my son's cereal. Without bees, our breakfast would be depressingly bland.

What about the milk in my granola? Sure, it came from a cow, which last time I checked didn't need pollinating, but what was that cow eating? In this case, the cow came from Monument Farms, in Vermont's Champlain Valley, where it grazed all spring and summer on clover and alfalfa—two bee-pollinated species of forage vital to many dairy operations.

Our dinner wouldn't fare much better. All the cucurbits—cukes, zukes, squash, pumpkins—will be crossed off the menu if honey bees disappear. True, an indigenous bee—the squash bee—is even better at pollinating cucurbits than honey bees are, but how's your local squash bee population doing? Don't know? Neither does anyone else.

Dessert would be eighty-sixed. The cacao trees that make chocolate are pollinated by rainforest flies—species that may also be in steep decline. Mangos and most other tropical fruits are fly- or bee-pollinated. In 2008, the ice-cream maker Häagen-Dazs recognized that it was dependent on honey bees for everything from almonds (Rocky Road) to cherries (Banana Split)—about half its flavors in all. And don't forget the cream, produced by clover-foraging dairy cows. The company donated $250,000 to honey bee research and launched a new flavor, Vanilla Honey Bee, to promote the cause.

All in all, nearly one hundred crops—the ones I've mentioned, plus pears, plums, peaches, citrus, kiwis, macadamias, sunflowers, canola, avocados, lettuce, carrot seeds, onion seeds, broccoli, and many more—rely on bees for some or all of their pollination. In fact, 80 percent of the food we put in our mouths relies on pollination somewhere down the line. If your beef is pasture-fed, chances are the cattle were eating insect-pollinated plants. Don't forget cotton, one of the biggest oil and textile industries in the South, which recently was forced for the first time to rent hives to ensure a bumper crop.

I make a cup of mint tea and stir a dollop of wildflower honey into it. On impulse, I treat myself to a spoonful of the honey straight up. Standing there with musky perfume molecules bounding around my sinuses, I understand wildflower honey as flower essence, one of the small miracles of nature. Its robust and spicy flavor outclasses the bland honey found in every supermarket. This pound of honey is a distillation of the nectar of two million blossoms, a snapshot of a moment in the life of a meadow. People like to speak of the *terroir* of wine, but no food or drink bares its provenance so nakedly as honey. "You can't eat the view," rural Vermonters like to say, but when I taste that spoonful of honey, and the combined efforts of millions of flowers and thousands of bees burst in my mouth with untamed flavors, I have to disagree.

What were those particular wildflowers? Hard to say, but since the honey came from a local beekeeper, they probably resembled what I see in my fields through the kitchen window. I step outside. The sun is burning off the last of the morning fog; it's going to be a July scorcher. Already the gardens are humming with the bustle of the world. Hummingbirds duel for bee balm rights, while bumble bees land on the small bee balm flower petals and stick their proboscises inside, looking like clowns trying to pull magenta hats over their heads.

As I walk through waist-high fields, a dozen wildflowers are on offer. No honey bees are around, but a variety of other insects work their traplines. Yellowjackets probe the red clover, while moths resembling coppery house flies nuzzle the bedstraw. Furry, orange-rumped bees disappear into tubes of milkweed flowers. If I shift downward in scale an order of magnitude, another world opens up: flowers so small I hadn't been able to pick them out of the background hue. Tiny golden bees burrow in the lilac-petaled oregano, and white flies no bigger than gnats hover like a fine mist over the first goldenrod of the year.

I'm fortunate enough to have two acres of meadows surrounded by forested hills rolling for miles in every direction, interrupted by occasional red barns and black-and-white cows. It's the kind of landscape that used to dominate America, but is now so rare that city dwellers arrive on tour buses to see it for themselves. A good landscape for bugs: plenty of undisturbed land, no pesticides, lots of blooming things. It's why the property's apple trees continue to bear lots of fruit in the absence of managed honey bees. It's why so many wild plants still thrive on this patch of land.

Of the 250,000 species of plants that share our world, three quarters rely on wild pollinators to reproduce. Wherever you live, look around and see a world engineered by these pollinators. Then look around and see a world in distress. Honey bees may have been filling in for wild pollinators to bolster our agriculture, but they can't do much for the other 249,900 species of flowering plants. That's up to the native bugs. And while evidence is hard to come by, many of these species are failing under the triple threats of habitat loss, pesticide poisoning, and exotics.

It's not as if no one saw this crisis coming. Forty-five years ago, Rachel Carson warned that new pesticides and insecticides would lead to silent springs when no birds would sing. People listened, and DDT was banned. But she also warned of falls in which "there was no pollination and there would be no fruit." Beyond honey bees, *Silent Spring* worried about the demise of all native pollinators:

> Man is more dependent on these wild pollinators than he usually realizes . . . Without insect pollination, most of the soil-holding and soil-enriching plants of uncultivated areas would die out, with far-reaching consequences to the ecology of the whole region. Many herbs, shrubs, and trees of forests and range depend on native insects for their reproduction; without these plants many wild animals and range stock would find little food. Now clean cultivation and the chemical destruction of hedgerows and weeds are eliminating the last sanctuaries of these pollinating insects and breaking the threads that bind life to life.

The entomologist Stephen L. Buchmann and the crop ecologist Gary Paul Nabhan amplified Carson's warning in their 1996 book, *The Forgotten Pollinators*. They predicted fruitless falls unless our land-use patterns changed fast. But few people paid attention. Songbirds generate lots of sympathy; bumble bees, fig wasps, and moths do not. Today, nobody knows how our native pollinators are faring; the studies haven't been completed. What little evidence exists suggests that they may be in a free fall, the implications of which surpass even the honey bee crisis. That potential catastrophe will be the focus of the last chapters of this book.

How strange to live in a world where the very fecundity of the earth is in doubt. We tend to think of our farms as burgeoning places, with fruits and vegetables almost spontaneously springing from the soil, but we are creeping awfully close to a postfertile era. In the Midwest, grain farmers must cake their fields with chemical fertilizer if they expect anything to grow. On both coasts and everywhere in between, farmers must import honey bees to provide the fertilization their area can no longer guarantee. Twenty-five years ago, in her novel *The Handmaid's Tale*, Margaret Atwood described a dystopian world where most of the population was barren and fertile young handmaids were purchased by families to provide reproduction. An equally skewed arrangement has existed in our fields for decades.

But now even the handmaids are dying.

Chapter 2

HOW THE HONEY BEE CONQUERED THE WORLD

IN THE COASTAL mountains of Mediterranean Spain, near Valencia, lies a cave known as Barranc Fondo. The cave has hosted modern man for thousands of years, and likely sheltered Neanderthals for tens of thousands of years before that. Festooned in black and ocher pictographs, it bears witness to that most basic of human preoccupations: food. In addition to game animals, Barranc Fondo depicts a dramatic honey hunt from more than 6,500 years ago. A half-dozen figures climb a rope ladder up a tall tree to a cavity buzzing with bees. As a crowd of onlookers cheers them on, one of the honey hunters has slipped from the ladder and, arms flailing, is plunging to earth.

Honey hunting has always been dangerous, yet that's never stopped human beings. In hundreds of pictographs across the planet, from Europe to Northern Africa, Zimbabwe and South Africa, India, throughout Indonesia, and even in Australia, the basics rarely change: a bee cavity in a cliff or tree, ropes, honey hunters, torches, gourds or baskets to catch the bounty, and around all, a cloud of furious bees.

It's an old, familiar story. The lure of a substance almost preter-

Barranc Fondo cave art

naturally pleasurable. The willingness to endure hardship, pain, and absurd risks, even death, if it means a chance to partake of the bliss. Some people view humans' fascination with honey as the first stirrings of the culinary imagination. I see it as proto-addiction.

With good reason. Put yourself in the mind of a hunter-gatherer in the new Iberian forests sprung in the wake of retreating glaciers of the dying ice age. You subsist on a diet of game, fibrous leaves and roots, and occasional fruit. Not fat, juicy cultivated apples, either. The sweetest thing you have ever tasted is a sort of wormy crab apple. And then you reach into a tree hollow and scoop out a handful of golden, liquid delight.

Well, I'd be hooked, too. If your idea of honey is the bland, cooked sugar alternative that comes in little plastic bears, then you might not understand. But taste a spoonful of raw, unfiltered wildflower honey and you'll get it right away. Plants have spent millions of years developing flowers, and the nectar at the base of flowers, to be as irresistible to animals as possible. It's part of the exchange of favors that is their reproductive strategy. Nectar averages about 16 percent sugar, as sweet as fruit juice, and it has no purpose except to lure pollinators. Bees gather the nectar and concentrate it in the hive, evaporating water with their wings and bodies until it reaches about 70 percent sugar and has ripened into honey.[1] The honey carries some of the original plant flavors, as well as new ones formed by the bees' alchemy. The end-product of that original floral beckoning, honey is distilled desire. True, *Homo sapiens* was never the intended target, but throughout our evolution we've held on to that sweet tooth. It's a habit we've never kicked.

In fact, we can be pretty sure we know just what that honey hunt was like, because in isolated pockets of Indonesia and Malaysia, the honey hunt lives on virtually unchanged.

Honey hunters have many ways of finding "bee trees." The classic method is to capture a few bees in a box or hollow reed while they're at a flower or drinking from a spring. (Honey bait can be handy.) Then you let one go. It, presumably, makes a "beeline" for the hive, and you run like hell after it as long as you can, trying not to twist an ankle or smack into a tree. Once you lose sight of that one, you let another go, and once again the chase is on. If you have enough bees, and don't kill yourself, you'll make it to the hive. A more elegant variant requires just two bees and a compass. You let one bee go and mark its bearing. Then you move a few hundred yards away, in more or less a perpendicular line from the direction the bee flew, and let a second bee go, marking its bearing. The point where the two bearings intersect should mark the bee tree.

Most wonderfully, African honey hunters follow a bird known as the honeyguide. This sparrow-sized bird has the taste for honey-

---

1. Honey is to nectar as maple syrup is to sap.

comb but not the arsenal to plunder it. So it seeks out humans, chirps excitedly at them until they follow it, and leads them to the cache, feasting on the leftover spoils.

Because the same caves and trees host multiple generations of bees, ropes and ladders were erected long ago on the best bee trees. Still, picture yourself working an aerial trapeze with no net and a swarm of stinging insects intent on destroying you; honey hunting is not for the faint of heart. It would be impossible if not for smoke, the ancient ally of honey hunters and beekeepers alike. Smoke pacifies bees. No one is entirely sure why. It may prevent bees from detecting each other's alarm pheromones—messages transmitted via scent.

To drug the bees, honey hunters make a fire at the base of a bee tree, then, for safe measure, they carry torches up the ropes and smoke the bottom of the hive. This makes the difference between a lethal barrage of stings and only ten or twenty "love bites." Then, using a sharpened stick made of bamboo or some other lightweight material, they stab the hive and carve off the comb, lowering the chunks with rope to their assistants on the ground. A good hive can yield hundreds of pounds of honey.

Doesn't this destroy the hive as well? Yes. Bees can rebuild if they have the resources and the weather is gentle; if not, they're toast. And it's one reason why, in most places, Paleolithic honey hunting gave way to beekeeping as soon as humans decided to quit rambling and settle down.

The first attempts at beekeeping were probably as simple as relocating hives to a more convenient spot. Why bother trekking all the way to the bee tree when you could cut off the branch with the bees in it and bring it home? That's what people did. And they've been keeping bees, and moving bees, ever since.

The first human-constructed hives were variations on the

theme of the hollow tree. Dried mud or clay pots in India, wicker baskets covered in clay in Egypt, Greece, and Rome, coiled straw skeps insulated in cow dung in Medieval Europe.[2] In 2007, archaeologists in Israel unearthed the oldest beehives ever found. Thirty intact hives made of straw and clay were discovered in the center of the ruins of the city of Rehov, which thrived around 900 B.C. "Urban beekeeping" is not a new phenomenon. When the Bible refers to Israel as the "land of milk and honey," it isn't being figurative.

For the European honey bee, all went to hell for a while after the collapse of the Roman Empire, and throughout the Dark Ages the best beekeeping was practiced by monasteries. Northern Europe had a tradition of upright "log hives," in which the bees were often killed before honey and wax were extracted. Eastern Europe and Russia favored forest beekeeping (find a bee tree, mark it to stake your claim, pay off the local landowner, then deal harshly with any animals, human or otherwise, that try to muscle in on your territory).

All these beekeeping operations involved ripping apart the hive to get the honey, leaving the bees to put all their resources into building new comb. Even if they survived the winter, it would be a long time before they had excess honey again. Getting around that dilemma would fall to the Reverend Lorenzo Lorraine Langstroth, who on October 31, 1851, had one of the more jaw-dropping eureka moments in history. Nothing in beekeeping was the same after Langstroth's neurons fired off their thought bomb, but to fully appreciate the "Langstroth revolution," first we need to appreciate the genius of the hive.

---

2. These bell-shaped skeps, which were often built into niches in abbey walls and houses, remain iconic bee motifs.

Honey, I'm Home!

Of the twenty thousand species of bees on earth, only a handful make gobs of honey, because only a handful have complex urban societies. Most bees are solitary or, like bumble bees, live in simple underground "villages" of perhaps a hundred individuals. Bumble bees do make honey—a honey that nature writer Bernd Heinrich, for one, claims is superior to honey bee honey—but only enough to fill a few tiny "honeypots" in their grass-covered nests, which larvae feed from. They produce wax but use it only to build their honeypots and a few chambers for brood. They don't build comb, and almost all members of a bumble bee colony, including the old queen, die in the fall. Only the virgin queens disperse to mate and look for underground nests where they can hibernate through the winter before starting their own colonies in the spring.

Bumble bees are rugged frontier types, amazingly self-reliant and personally formidable, yet uncooperative. As soon as their colony reaches a certain size, workers will start eating the queen's new eggs unless she guards them. Honey bees are individually unimpressive but loyal and regimented. Conflict is exceedingly rare. Bumble bees are Gaulish villagers; honey bees are the Roman legions.

While bumble bees and some solitary bee species can fly at temperatures below freezing, honey bees don't like to fly when it's below 60 degrees Fahrenheit. Nor will they fly in rain. They start relatively late in the morning (compared with other bees) and stop early in the evening. A friend of mine who is an apple specialist refers to them as union workers—if several conditions aren't met, they'll shut it down for the day. However, like many a union, that team spirit has resulted in tremendous success.

That success begins with the hexagon—the building block of the hive. To make the leap to highly social insects who could live in groups of tens of thousands, bees needed efficient infrastructure: Instead of using their wax-making skills to form individual, artisanal honeypots and brood cells, why not combine forces to make factory-scale nurseries and warehouses? The hexagon proved the perfect form for this. Triangles and squares also fit together in endless repetition, but hexagons use less wax to cover the same area and better accommodate the round larvae. Hexagons are basically circles that fit together with no gaps.

A natural beehive consists of a hundred thousand or so wax hexagonal cylinders, constructed back-to-back and hung in panels facing each other, with aisles in between just wide enough for an adult bee to access them. Imagine library shelves laid out vertically instead of horizontally, where the patrons pull themselves up and down the shelves to get to the books they want. (This is easier if you have six legs and weigh a tenth of a gram.) These hexagonal cells are used to store not books but food and brood.

In the tropics, where honey bees evolved, there's little impetus to move this operation indoors. Just as humans in the Amazon or the Florida Keys will sometimes forgo walls on their dwellings, so bees in Africa, Malaysia, and other warm regions will hang their comb from exposed tree limbs, cloaked by a crawling veil of bees.

About two million years ago, in Africa, a branch of honey bees decided to give up veranda living. *Apis mellifera* moved indoors, usually to a dry tree hollow or rock crevice, and weatherproofed the place by sealing off any cracks with propolis—caulking resin they gather from tree buds—leaving only a small entrance at the base of the hive. Initially, this probably offered more protection, but it had an unintended benefit: It allowed them to expand beyond the tropics. To colonize Europe, honey bees had to deal with a little thing called winter. Instead of hibernation (the standard mammal and reptile solution), or migration (birds and butterflies), or generational death (most insects), they opted for a rather humanlike "keep the home fires burning" approach. They brought the tropics with them, staying metabolically active through the winter and leaning heavily on those honey stores.

When fall turns bleak and the last flowers disappear, a colony will stop raising brood, cluster together in the middle of the hive, shivering constantly, with the precious queen in the warm center, and wait out the dark days by eating sugar and snuggling together. (We Vermonters do much the same thing.) To make heat, they vibrate their wing muscles. A steady rotation from the inner cluster to the surface ensures that nobody freezes.

And it works. In the depth of a northern winter, when the outside temperature drops to 20 below, a honey bee cluster will maintain an Africanesque, honey-powered 95 degrees Fahrenheit in the center. Only about half the bees survive, the rest succumbing to old age and harsh conditions, but that's enough to keep the brood warm once the queen starts laying again in late winter as the colony gears up for the spring bloom.

With this move indoors, honey bees were at last primed for their partnership with humans: We give them more nesting cavities (in the form of beehives) than they could ever hope for in nature, and they give us more honey than our hunter-gatherer forebears could ever imagine. In the process, *Apis mellifera* became a more gentle and manageable creature as beekeepers chose to work with the most docile and productive colonies. The bee that helped Europe prosper was a far cry from its African roots. The wolf had become a collie. It's this agreeable European honey bee that convinced humans to transport it around the globe.

Of course bees aren't attempting a bribe when they convert

nectar into honey. They're simply condensing their food into the smallest, most shelf-stable form possible. Sugar draws moisture. Pack anything in sugar and it will dehydrate, as will the microorganisms that cause food to spoil. Corned beef and lox benefit from this curing process, and so does honey, which also contains a touch of hydrogen peroxide, a natural by-product of the ripening process. The jar of honey on your shelf is antiseptic and could outlast you. It makes a superb wound dressing and is useful for embalming the organs of mummies, should the need arise.

Millions of years before humans discovered how to make sugar syrups, bees had aced the test, inventing the ideal preserved, high-energy, vitamin-rich food. They store it in their honeycomb cells and cap it with wax, like jars of preserves in an endless pantry. A single hive can make hundreds of pounds of honey in a good season, yet the living occupants of that hive weigh only a combined ten pounds. They need those stores for the same reason we have grain silos—to get through the lean times, which, for a honey bee, can be long indeed.

How often, over the course of the year, are flowers blooming where you live? In New England or northern Europe, the window is depressingly short. A few tiny flowers in early April, then crocuses and daffodils, then in May the apple blossoms kick in and things really get rolling. By August, however, just three months later, the choices are already spotty: goldenrod, joe-pye weed, purple loosestrife (a recent invader), and not much else. Asters in September. From mid-October through March, nothing. For a bee, no flowers means no food. It's hard to believe bees could survive in such an environment, but they do. New England farmers need to make hay while the sun shines. Honey bees need to make honey—enough by August to power the entire colony all fall and winter.

Even in the tropics, *Apis mellifera*'s original home, the blooming isn't continuous; most flower species tend to bunch around cooler and moister seasons. It isn't unusual for blooms to be scarce for weeks at a time. In Florida, for example, once the Brazilian pepper is done in November, it's slim pickings until the citrus blooms in early spring. And even when blooms are plentiful, heavy rains can prevent bees from flying at all. Hives lose a little weight most days of the year.

And so they must gather nectar as fast as they can, whenever they can, and store it in staggering quantities. And that super-concentrated sugar, with its druglike ability to flood the human brain with dopamine, has spurred us into all sorts of creative endeavors.

Which brings us back to Lorenzo Langstroth.

Lorenzo Lorraine Langstroth, Yalie, Congregational minister, beekeeper, bipolar eccentric, sat in his Ohio study on October 31, 1851, "pondering," he wrote, "as I had so often done before, how I could get rid of the disagreeable necessity of cutting the attachments of the combs from the walls of the hives." If he could only make his combs more removable and his hives more reusable, Langstroth knew, he could stop destroying hives and bees every harvest and have a truly efficient enterprise on his hands. But how to do it? No matter what style of hive you presented to the bees, they quickly built out wax comb wherever possible and sealed up the small spaces with propolis, effectively gluing all parts of the hive together. Then it hit him:

"The almost self-evident idea of using the same bee space as in the shallow chambers came into my mind, and in a moment the suspended movable frames, kept at a suitable distance from each other and the case containing them, came into being. I could scarcely refrain from shouting out my 'Eureka!' in the open streets."

Bee space—the 0.3-inch-wide aisle bees leave between their combs—was Langstroth's epiphany. He knew that bees standardized this space, no matter what. He envisioned a file-cabinet-style hive, with each hanging file, or frame, being exactly wide enough for a two-sided sheet of honeycomb and exactly one bee space apart from the next frame and from the surrounding box.[3] Theoretically, the bees would build out their comb but leave a bee space so that any frame could be lifted out of the hive, the wax caps removed and the honey harvested, and the empty comb returned for restocking, without disturbing any of the other frames or ruining any comb.

He was right. And it changed everything. Within a decade, the Langstroth hive had swept the United States. In another decade, it was standard throughout the world. And it has endured with only minor improvements ever since.

It seems remarkable that not a single individual, in the previous eight thousand years of beekeeping history, hit upon this idea. It looks obvious in retrospect, but then so do a lot of revolutionary ideas. Langstroth's eureka moment saved an ungodly amount of honeycomb; and bees, freed from the torture of cranking out tons of wax every year to fix their comb, started cranking out unprecedented amounts of honey instead. Beekeeping became a more attractive profession.

One race of bee made things especially attractive. In the 1840s, a Swiss army captain noticed that the bees across the border in Italy were particularly gentle and industrious. They made tons of honey, rarely stung, and were prolific breeders. He acquired a

3. He used a wooden Champagne case for his prototype, a celebratory touch.

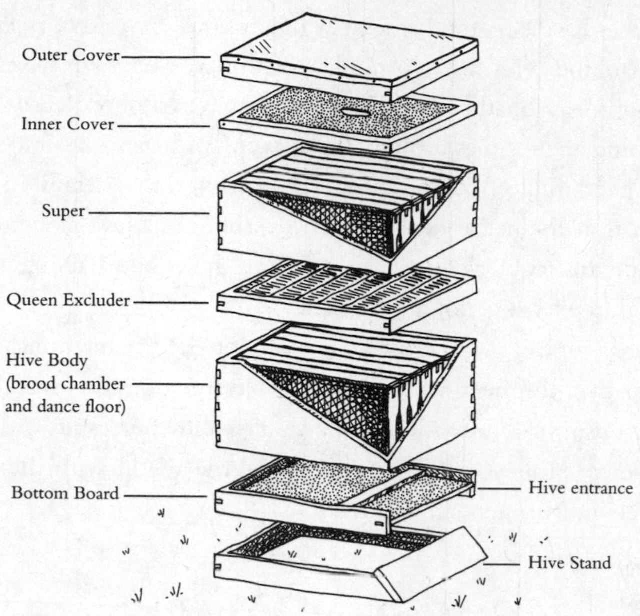

The modern Langstroth hive

colony and began spreading the word. Soon a book appeared—*The Italian Alp-Bee; or, The Gold Mine of Husbandry* and the craze was on. Lorenzo Langstroth acquired his first colonies around 1861 and immediately began advertising "Italian Queens" in *American Bee Journal* (half price for "Ministers of the Gospel"). By 1900 the Italian honey bee was the bee of choice in Europe, the Americas, Australia, New Zealand, and even Japan. Breeders have continued to coax those desirable qualities out of the bee, and today's Italian bee, which dominates the industry, is as mellow and fruitful as any in history.

We humans are quick to pat ourselves on the back for our clever manipulation of nature, but, if you'll allow me a Michael Pollan moment, I'd say the manipulation goes both ways. I see the human–honey bee partnership as a classic example of coevolution.

The bees have benefited at least as much as we have. By "furnishing mankind with the two noblest of things, which are sweetness and light," as Jonathan Swift put it, they have bamboozled us into spreading their genes around the planet. And they did it fast. It took bees millions of years to hammer out the details of the pollination-for-nectar deal with flowers, but just a few thousand to get humans to break our backs building hives and hauling them around in exchange for a little sugar.

Sure, you can say that we were conscious of the relationship in a way that the bees weren't, but evolution doesn't care about consciousness or intention, only results, and the results are unequivocal: Honey bees have conquered the world with the help of their human general contractors.

Diary of a Young Bee

A honey bee colony is a bristling and formidable intelligence. Notice I use the singular. With honey bees, most of the intelligence lies in the colony, not the individual. So asking "How smart is a honey bee?" is like asking "How smart is one of my brain cells?" They don't live independently, and aren't meant to. Yet with its hive mind and evolutionary adaptations, a honey bee colony is capable of accomplishing sophisticated and complex tasks that put many "higher organisms" to shame.

Harvard University naturalist E. O. Wilson considers the social insects—bees, wasps, termites, ants—to be the most successful group of animals on earth. They're small, so we don't pay much attention, but Wilson points out that in some forests ant biomass alone is four times the biomass of all vertebrates put together. "This then is the circumstance with which the social insects challenge our ingenuity: their attainment of a highly organized mode of colonial existence was rewarded by ecological dominance, leaving what must have been a deep imprint upon the evolution of the remainder of terrestrial life." They aren't just fascinating; they rule. "When reef organisms and human beings are added, social life is ecologically preeminent among animals in general."

Yet that social intelligence may be exactly what is being undermined by colony collapse disorder. Bear with me while I take you deep into the life of the hive and mind of the bee. To understand what's gone wrong with honey bees, it helps to appreciate how they interact when everything is going right.

Of the fifty thousand bees in a full hive, more than forty-nine thousand are sterile female "worker" bees. Well-named, they do all the work of the colony—foraging, comb construction, defense, nursing, you name it. The one thing they don't do is reproduce.[4] That's left to the queen bee, who lays her body weight in eggs each day (up to two thousand) and must be fed constantly. Because the queen mates with multiple males from other hives, most of the workers are half-sisters.

4. In a darkly poetic development, once it's clear that a bee larva isn't destined to become a queen, her ovaries produce a poison sac and stinger. Make love or war, but not both. One in ten thousand worker bees does manage to maintain a functioning ovary and lay eggs, but since she's never been fertilized, the eggs will be drones. In any case, the other workers, devoted to their queen, quickly notice the rogue eggs and destroy them. On the other hand, if the queen should die, and no new queens are on the way, suddenly those drone-laying workers come in handy. The colony is doomed, but at least the drones, carrying the colony's genetic uniqueness, can be sent far and wide like lifeboats leaving a sinking ship.

Occasionally the queen lays an unfertilized egg, which becomes a male, known as a drone. These few hundred members of the colony lead lives so much like a certain stereotypical human male that comparisons are irresistible. They have big heads and stout bodies. They hang around the hive all day doing essentially nothing. They don't forage, don't feed the kids, don't even build anything. They wait for the females to bring them food. And the females do. Other than grub, their only interest is sex. Every so often, they "go out for a while" to hang with males from other hives and chase after virgin queens. If they catch one, they don't come back.[5] If they don't catch one, they return to the hive and free food, but even the workers' philanthropy has limits. Drones are basically flying sperm, so once mating season is over, they're truly useless. When the weather cools in the fall and hive resources get scarce, the workers evict the drones from the hive, and they soon freeze.

All functioning societies place a premium on the next generation, and so it is with bees. Kids are raised in the safe lower center of the hive, pollen (baby food) conveniently at hand around them. Honey (adult food) is stored in the upper chambers. This is convenient for beekeepers, too, because it means that honey can be harvested from "supers"—the upper drawers of the file cabinet—without disturbing the brood in the lowest drawer. (To ensure this separation, beekeepers use a "queen excluder": a narrow passage dividing the lower chamber from the upper ones, through which worker bees can squeeze but not the larger queen, who must lay all her eggs below.)

Kid bees have things pretty cush. They begin life as white,

---

5. More on that gory story later.

pinhead-sized eggs, laid one per hexagonal cylinder by the queen. From the moment they hatch, they are lavished with protein-rich royal jelly—the bee equivalent of mother's milk—made from digested pollen by nurse bees, whose sole job is to staff the nursery. The crescent-shaped larvae grow quickly, doubling in size twice a day, and after six days they practically fill their chambers.[6] The nurses then seal the chambers with wax caps so the larvae can pupate in peace. The wax is fat from the nurses' own bodies, exuded from pores in little wafers. They soften up the wax wafers by chewing on them and adding saliva, much as you might soften a piece of gum, then molding them to cover the brood cell.

Alone inside her cell, the kid bee can get down to the serious business of transformation. She spins a cocoon around herself, like a butterfly, and three days later emerges as a fresh, fuzzy adult bee. Her first task is to chew through her nursery wax cap so she can join the hive. Once there, she gets no coming-out party. Instead she cleans herself up, has a snack, then gets to work.

Now, put yourself in the mind of this newly hatched "house bee." In many ways, her life is not so different from the life of the newly adult human. Day 1, you are ready to enter the workforce, but you have few skills. Your first job is to clean up the cell you just emerged from. After that you spend about half your time in the menial task of cleaning other cells. The rest of your day is spent eating, resting, and looking for a better job. Around Day 4, you find work: day care. You nurse the brood, squirting royal jelly from your head into their cribs. Your peers who show a building

6. Picture an 8-pound newborn growing to 16 pounds her first afternoon, 32 pounds the next morning, and 128 pounds the day after that. You can see why so many adult bees are involved in the food service profession.

aptitude may start constructing new wax comb. A few get assigned to the queen's retinue, charged with the precious tasks of bringing her food and carrying her waste out of the hive.

Around Day 10 things pick up. A wizened forager bee comes scrambling through your section of the hive, trembling all over and twitching her legs. "We need receivers!" she yells. "We've hit a clover gusher and there's no one to unload!" (The foragers don't store nectar themselves; they look for somebody in-house to hand it off to so they can get back out to the nectar flow ASAP.) It seems simple enough. You'll still be a house bee, but those days of cleaning and raising the little brats are finally over.

You make your way to the excitement of the hive entrance, where forager bees are returning from all over the wide world with a steady stream of pollen, nectar, and water. As soon as they land, they bustle around, calling, "Somebody take this, somebody take this." You watch for a while, then work up your courage, approach a forager who's almost bursting at the seams with nectar, tap her with your antenna, and say, "Please, ma'am, I'll take it." Relieved, she unrolls her proboscis and drains her entire tank into you. You slosh back into the hive with your cargo, find an empty cell, unload your nectar into it, then spend the rest of the day pumping that nectar in and out of your mouth, evaporating its water in the process and adding enzymes that convert the sugar in the nectar from crystally sucrose to syrupy fructose. When the water content has dropped from the original 70 percent to about 40 percent, you and your colleagues start fanning your wings to pass maximum air over the nectar, reducing it like a good sauce. When the water content drops below 20 percent, it is honey. You cap it with a nice wax seal and go back to the entrance for another load.

A week later, you're still enjoying life as a receiver bee, but those tantalizing glimpses of the fields outside the hive have got you curious. One day you work up your courage, walk out the hive entrance, and give your wings a practice buzz. Before you realize it, you're off the ground and floating around. This isn't so hard after all! You take some mental snapshots of your surroundings, then scoot right back inside where it's safe. Over the next few days, you take more orientation flights, each one a little farther out, memorizing the landmarks around the hive.

Then it happens. It's early morning, and things have been slow. It rained all day yesterday and no one was flying. You and your colleagues completely caught up on your honey ripening, so, with nothing to do, you rested to conserve energy. Suddenly, a forager has her legs on *your* shoulders and is shaking you awake! "The apple blossoms!" she shouts. "Nectar's coming fast and furious! All hands to the flight deck right now!"

"Me? But I've never foraged."

"Now's the time! Get going, kid."

So you head for the "dance floor," flustered with excitement. The dance floor is a section of comb, just inside the hive entrance, where the returning foragers do their waggle dances and other worker bees hang out, looking for a mission. You join the spectators, pushing your way through the crowd until—yes!—here comes a waggle dancer right past you, waggling her butt from side to side with urgency to tell everyone about her new find. You watch for a bit, noting the angle of her dance, which tells you what direction to head, and how long it lasts, which tells you how far to fly. There's no doubt what she found, because she is bloated like a water balloon and just reeking glorious apple perfume from every pore. "I've got it!" you shout, and you hop into the conga line behind her, shaking your butt, too. A few others join in as well, then you all scramble to the hive entrance.

The others set off, following the same angle from the sun as the forager indicated in her dance, and you zip off right behind them. You count how long you're supposed to fly . . . should be about here . . . nothing at first . . . then there it is, like a big white-pink firework: an apple tree in full bloom. Your comrades are already there, so you fly in, single out a flower, and land on the petals. Ultraviolet lines on the petals point to a little well down at their base, from which an irresistible smell is emerging, so you follow the lines, unroll your proboscis, stick it into the well like a straw into a milkshake, and, *ahhhh* . . . sweet bliss.

You fill your "honey sac," a bladder in your abdomen that can be filled or unfilled using a special hydraulic pump in your head. But you don't digest all that nectar. It's all for one and one for all in the beehive, so once you've gorged on enough apple blossoms that you'd drip nectar if squeezed,[7] you fly, sputtering like an overloaded helicopter, back to the hive. At the entrance, you squirt the contents of your honey sac into the waiting mouths of receiver bees—young up-and-comers who remind you of you at that age, way back last week. Sometimes, after a great score, you're so excited about your awesome flower patch that, after unloading your nectar, you just can't contain yourself—you scoot over to the dance floor and waggle your butt. Sure enough, other bees leap into line behind you, following your dance, then zip off toward your flowers. Go team.

So it goes for about three weeks. Your twenty-one days of life in the hive as a house bee are mirrored by three weeks on the range, foraging. You get better and better at it, flying dawn to dusk, until changes start to set in. Those gossamer wings show more and more wear. You're feeling kind of creaky. Diseases are creeping through your gut. One day, you land on a fall aster, but

7. On slow days, bee researchers do this for fun.

your legs just don't seem to be working. You try to take off, but instead your wings fold, you fall to earth, and die.

Wise Beyond Their Years

That's the bee's-eye view of life in the hive. It gives a pretty fair account of the events in a typical bee's life, as well as the decisions she faces. Now let's pull back, look at the same events from the human's-eye view, and try to understand how remarkable coordination and intelligence—we might even say wisdom—can arise from thousands of individual bees making their own decisions with little knowledge about what's happening elsewhere in the hive. Think about it: fifty thousand individuals, and *no one is in charge.*[8] A human company of fifty thousand employees would be rife with territorial middle managers, each overseeing twenty employees and reporting to a supervisor, who reports to her supervisor, and on up the hierarchical tree all the way to the CEO. Pooling information and power in the hands of just a few people allows for quick, unilateral decisions, but it also means one incompetent executive can bring down the whole enterprise.

Bees, on the other hand, manage to precisely calibrate their food intake, nest construction, and other needs by following a "wisdom of the crowd" philosophy. There's no centralized decision making, just the order that naturally emerges from thousands of workers making unselfish decisions. "Unselfishness" is the key. If those forty-nine thousand sterile workers are to pass their genes onward, they have to do it through Mom. The "survival of the fittest" genetic competition that is a hallmark of

8. People used to think the queen was in charge, but she's more of an egg-laying slave.

most evolution doesn't quite apply to honey bees. Members of a hive don't compete with each other; they're all in the same boat.

This has allowed evolution to establish a network of communications and feedback loops enabling a honey bee colony to make enlightened decisions that couldn't be made by any one member. A lot of these abilities are explained in Thomas Seeley's brilliant and pellucid book *The Wisdom of the Hive.* The feedback loops are made possible because of the division of labor between forager bees and receiver bees. It would be a waste of the experienced foragers' time to have to take every load of nectar high into the hive, find an empty cell, and process the nectar into honey, so that labor falls to the receivers. To efficiently bring as much food into the hive as possible, a colony needs to maintain a perfect balance between foragers and receivers. Too many foragers creates a bottleneck at the hive entrance, with foragers waiting to unload their cargo. Too many receivers means bees hanging around the hive doing nothing when they could be out gathering food.

Bees calibrate this balance through their famous dances. The "waggle dance" recruits more fliers. The "tremble dance" recruits more receivers. A third signal, "shaking," encourages inactive bees to start foraging. Here's how it works:

Say a scouting forager hits an orange tree that is just pumping out nectar. She sucks up a full load and races back to the hive. Immediately she looks for a receiver bee to take her nectar. What she does next depends on how long this takes. If receivers are falling all over themselves to get her nectar, and she can unload in just a few seconds, then there must be a shortage of foragers. She heads to the dance floor and does her waggle dance for the spectators, running up and down the comb while wiggling her butt and buzzing. The angle she runs from the vertical (remember, all comb, including the dance floor, is vertical) corresponds to the angle from the sun of the path that will lead straight to the orange tree.[9]

The duration of the waggle dance tells other bees how far to go—loosely, three quarters of a mile per second of waggling. Spectator bees aren't choosy about which waggle they'll follow; they usually jump right in with the first waggle dance they see, following in the conga line for a few rounds to make sure they've got the coordinates before heading out. So the more repetitions of a waggle dance, the more recruits a dancer will get, and sure enough, repetitions correspond to how valuable the find is. An orange tree will get more repetitions than a few tufts of clover, and a near orange tree will get more than a far orange tree. It's also relative; the same orange tree can be a front-page feature if it's the only thing blooming for miles, or a yawner if it's in the midst of a gallberry explosion. Waggle dance repetitions can vary from one (barely worth telling another bee) to one hundred (turn out the whole hive!), with anything over twenty being a real find.

You know the feeling. Say you are out for lunch alone and you blunder into the best Sri Lankan restaurant in Manhattan. You stuff yourself on curry and street hoppers, then hustle back to the office. You tell all your coworkers, write Zagat's, and soon the place is bustling with activity. If, on the other hand, the food is lukewarm and greasy, you might mention it to only a few people, or no one. This is Manhattan, after all, there are ten thousand

9. Brightness seems to play a role, too. The horizon is brightest directly below the sun and directly opposite it, and darkest in the two perpendicular directions. If you place a polarized filter over a hive entrance and rotate it, you can make the bees start off in the wrong direction for a particular waggle dance, though they'll quickly correct it once they leave the polarized zone.

restaurants to choose from. You can do better. Soon, the place has disappeared.

Now, in my town of Calais, Vermont, which has a grand sum of zero restaurants, things would be different. In the unlikely event that I'm hiking the back roads and chance upon a just-opened Sri Lankan restaurant, well, even if it's a little on the greasy side, I'm gonna waggle my ass off to everyone I meet.

Just like the restaurant scene in any city, honey bees find floral hot spots through word of mouth—a beautifully efficient barometer of quality.

But wait a minute. How can bees "know" how excited to get, especially those fairly new to foraging? Is that raspberry patch a once-in-a-lifetime find or a daily staple? Since they are genetically distinct, couldn't one bee get more excited, and thus do more waggle dances for goldenrod, while another waggles more for fall asters? And might one bee simply waggle more than another in general, and thus get more recruits to some sites that aren't all that good?

Well, yes. In one of the most charming experiments in *The Wisdom of the Hive*, Seeley tracked the waggling tendencies of ten individual bees. First the bees were given a feeder filled with weak sugar syrup, then Seeley swapped it for a [illegible] trated syrup. The bees' individual responses [illegible] map. One bee (labeled BB) accounted for a full [illegible] waggle dances produced by this group, while an[illegible] tributed only 5 percent. OG, like a jaded restau[illegible] times didn't bother waggling at all. Even the su[illegible] stirred OG to a mere thirty waggle runs of excit[illegible] ber BB was doing for the lousy stuff. ("I had t[illegible] lunch; it was *so good!*") The good stuff made BB completely lose her cool and waggle more than one hundred times.

This genetic variability seems like it could screw up a hive's ability to make good use of its resources, but it averages out over thousands of bees. Sure, BB may get a bunch of recruits to follow her to her supposed find, but then those underwhelmed recruits will come back and report that the place wasn't so exciting after all: They won't waggle. By then perhaps BB will be back in the hive, sleeping off her Big Mac attack, and the wildfire of overenthusiasm will have burned out.

Hives need a few BBs around, because when food is scarce, a Big Mac really is a great find; and they need a few skeptical OGs, who recruit only to the best joints, for when food is plentiful. A wide bell curve of excitement allows the hive to respond wisely to a constantly changing nectar supply.

Less than 10 percent of foragers dance at all when returning to the hive. It takes a pretty darned good nectar flow and an eager receiver. If the time to find a receiver is between twenty and fifty seconds, that means the troops must be well deployed. The forager will unload, clean up, maybe get a snack, then head back to her flower source alone. If the flower source was really lousy, she'll stop foraging altogether for a while and switch to some in-hive task instead. In the thousands of foraging returns that Seeley watched, he never saw a bee go straight from foraging to the dance floor to find a new target.

If it takes more than fifty seconds to find a receiver, this means a lot of nectar must be coming back to the hive and there aren't enough receivers to handle it. Our forager will give up on finding a receiver and instead plunge into the depths of the hive, doing a tremble dance. She jerks spastically from side to side, spinning in random directions, her two forelegs held aloft and shaking. She trembles for, on average, half an hour, covering a lot of territory inside the hive—which she needs to do, because the only way to get a message to another bee in those dark, congested quarters is to be very close to it. It doesn't matter whether she knows she is sending a signal with her dance, or whether the stress of not finding a receiver triggers her spasms; either way, the message gets through loud and clear: NEED MORE RECEIVERS. Nurse bees and comb builders who have never received before heed the call and head for the hive entrance.

If our forager passes a waggle dancer, she'll buzz at her and sometimes even head-butt. *Stop recruiting flyers, you idiot! We've got too many already.* Sure enough, waggle dancers who hear a tremble dancer's buzz or get head-butted tend to stop dancing and return to foraging alone.

With these two built-in behaviors, the waggle dance and the tremble dance, a honey bee colony is able to constantly adjust its rates of nectar acquisition and processing to make best use of what the flowers are providing. When a scout bee finds a new nectar flow just beginning, she'll make a beeline for the hive, waggle her findings, and bring ten recruits back with her. If the flow is a gusher, those recruits will waggle when they return, each bringing a new posse. This is how one bee sniffing your peonies in the early morning turns into a hundred-bee orgy by noon. If those hundred foragers have trouble finding receivers, they'll tremble to produce new ones before returning to the peonies. On the other hand, as the peonies get Hoovered dry, those bees will first stop waggling up new recruits, then eventually quit that mission altogether. It takes only hours for a colony to abandon a weakening flow for an improving one.

But how do foragers know to start foraging in the first place? The answer is the third type of signal foragers send: the shake. If a honey bee returns from a great discovery and can't find anyone waiting on the dance floor, waggling would be pointless. Instead, she'll plunge into the hive, put her legs on resting bees, and shake them into action. Sometimes she'll shake two hundred bees, many of them young bees that have never flown before. Any shaken bee is stirred to go to the dance floor and get her flight plan.

Seeley tracked one bee in a colony that had found no food for days. He then placed a feeder of sugar syrup nearby. The bee's first ten return trips from the feeder consisted of shaking signals to wake her comrades. Then, as more bees crowded the dance floor, she switched to a mixture of shaking signals and waggle runs for her next fifteen trips. After that, she did only waggle runs.

Protein Power

Ask a school kid "What do bees eat?" and she'll say, "Honey." She's right, but that's only half the story. Bees also collect pollen—the most vital food for the colony. Like nuts and seeds, pollen is full of complex, top-quality nutrients: mostly protein, plus fats, vitamins, and minerals. Honey is a doughnut for breakfast; pollen is a spinach and garlic omelet.[10]

The carbohydrates in honey make great fuel, which is why a forager bee eats little else. Like a marathoner, she needs to "carb load" so she can fly all day long. Protein is the building block for all animal bodies; once a worker bee is built, she needs much less. You and I need protein to repair damage to our bodies, but worker bees, who live only a few weeks, don't come with a maintenance plan; when they break, they don't get fixed.

A baby bee, on the other hand, needs lots of high-quality protein to grow. Famished from day one, it makes its needs known like babies everywhere—it cries. Only, being a bee, it doesn't use an auditory cry but instead an olfactory message using what's

10. It's also tasty stuff. Clover is my favorite.

known as "brood pheromone." The format is different, but the content is the same: *I'm here, feed me*. Over the five and a half days of its larval development, it will increase in size 1,300 times. That's a lot of protein. And it can come only from pollen.

Like nectar foragers, pollen foragers do a waggle dance to announce a good discovery. Usually about a quarter of the foragers in a colony will be concentrating on pollen collection. Some individuals specialize in pollen while others prefer gathering nectar, though they flex with need. A few bees will even gather nothing but water their entire careers.

The mechanics of pollen collection work differently than nectar collection. Since it's a solid, it can't be pumped into a honey sac. Instead, it sticks all over a bee's hairy body.[11] She then uses her legs to brush these grains into saddlebags made of curved hairs on each of her back legs, where the grains are packed into "loaves."

If you watch bees returning to a hive, you'll see many with bright orange or yellow bling-bling on their back legs. Because pollen arrives in this form, it doesn't require the labor-intensive tanker routine of nectar. Instead, pollen foragers head directly into the hive, deposit their pollen loaves in a cell near the brood chamber, puke up a little nectar to hold everything together, pack it in with their heads, beg a nibble of food from a nurse bee, and quickly return to the flowers or the dance floor. They don't get receiver-bee feedback. Instead, they judge the colony's need for pollen based on the taste of their food. If it's full of protein, there

---

11. Sometimes bees don't even need to rub against pollen. As they fly, wings beating furiously, bees generate an impressive static charge, like a balloon rubbed against a fuzzy sweater. When they land on a flower—*zap!*—the charge goes off and the pollen grains leap off the anthers and cling to the bee.

The honey bee

must be plenty of pollen to go around. If it's mostly sugar, that's a sign to gather more pollen.

Foragers bring all the pollen into the hive, but they don't eat it or feed it to the brood directly. They can't. Pollen, built to withstand long, hazardous voyages, is as impenetrable as a space capsule. It comes encased in a silica (glass) shell, with just one tiny hatch to let the sperm out at the appropriate time. Honey bees lack the digestive enzymes to pop open these capsules, so they let bacteria do it for them. That upchucked nectar that helps glue together the packed pollen encourages the growth of lactic acid bacteria, like those that turn milk into yogurt or indigestible straw into nutritious silage. The bacteria work their way into the pollen, break the glass capsules, and release the goodies. This fermented pollen, known as bee bread, is much more nutritious, digestible, and mold-resistant than raw pollen.

Nurse bees, the young adults of the colony, eat the bee bread, then use those nutrients to produce royal jelly through glands in their heads called hypopharyngeal glands, which are the bee equivalent of mammary glands. (They aren't called nurse bees for nothing.) Like breast milk, royal jelly is an easily digestible liquid protein suspension that provides numerous health benefits. It's rich in vitellogenin, a protein that bolsters immune defense, reduces stress, and is a powerful antioxidant that prevents wear and tear. The beekeeper Randy Oliver calls vitellogenin the "Fountain of Youth for the Honey Bee."[12]

The primary measure of a colony's health is its vitellogenin reserves. And since vitellogenin is synthesized from nutrients found in pollen, the health of a colony is its pollen supply. But bees don't store hundreds of pounds of pollen the way they do honey. They'd rather convert it into more bees. Most of the colony's protein supplies are stored within the bodies of the nurses and brood.

Queens get the most royal jelly. That's all they ever eat. In fact, they're the perfect demonstration of just how vital vitellogenin is to the health of the colony and the life span of the individual bee. The queen bee's vitellogenin-intensive diet allows her to live two to three years, instead of the six weeks of a worker. Every fertilized egg is a queen bee by default, and if fed buckets of royal jelly, will develop into one. Only by cutting off that vital supply of vitellogenin-rich food after a few days and capping the cell can the nurses short-circuit the development process and produce sterile workers who live only a few weeks.

Of all the bees in the hive, the foragers—the oldest workers—get the shortest end of the stick. They are fed the least royal jelly, and can't produce their own because their hypopharyngeal

---

12. If this "Fountain of Youth" talk has you wanting to try some royal jelly yourself, you're not alone. It's been a popular, if unproven, health supplement for years and is prized for cosmetic uses. Gathering royal jelly from hives is incredibly labor-intensive, which makes domestic royal jelly prohibitively expensive. The world supply comes from China.

glands have atrophied. With little vitellogenin in their bodies, they experience reduced immunity and enhanced aging. The drop in vitellogenin levels that occurs about three weeks into adulthood may actually be a chemical signal that initiates foraging behavior.

Responsibility to regulate the colony's protein falls to the nurses. If protein is scarce, they stop feeding it to the foragers. Then they'll start cannibalizing new eggs and younger brood, recycling that protein. If things get really tight, they'll follow behind the queen and eat everything she lays. It's another aspect of the perfectly calibrated wisdom of the hive. When protein levels drop and the nurses get hungry enough for it, they can't resist eating the most convenient source—eggs. By doing so, they ensure that only as many bees hatch as the colony can support.[13]

In late fall, as the days grow shorter and colder and the last flowers wither, the queen stops laying. The last batches of bees to hatch—who would normally gorge themselves on pollen, convert it to royal jelly, and become nurses—have no one to nurse. Instead, they get to keep all the "Fountain of Youth" vitellogenin in their bodies. And they need it. These are the winter bees. Unlike the foragers, who burn the candle at both ends and live just a few weeks, winter bees' main job is simply to survive until spring. Buoyed by all that immunity-enhancing, antioxidizing, life-expanding vitellogenin, they live for months, clustered in the hive, holding on until the days lengthen, the queen starts laying, and they can at last pass that vitellogenin to the new brood before ending their careers by becoming the first foragers of spring.

---

13. The system has its limits. If a colony is out of pollen, nurses will cap the older larvae a day or two early, cutting off their food supplies and forcing them to pupate. When these bees hatch, they'll be small, weak, and less capable.

The Great Divide

One last task a successful bee colony must perform also relies on the wisdom of the crowd. When a colony outgrows its quarters, and conditions are right, it will swarm. About half its members—twenty thousand or so bees, including the queen and a few hundred drones—set off in search of a new home. It's classic asexual reproduction, an organism splitting in half to form two distinct individuals. In preparation for swarming, the colony will leave behind some queen cells—special chambers that curl off the main comb and contain queen larvae—so that the old hive will have a new queen just a few days after the exodus. People tend to panic when they see a black thunderhead of bees on the move, but swarms have neither honey nor home to defend and rarely sting.

Overcrowding and floral abundance are prerequisites for a swarm. Until recently, most people assumed the decision to swarm was made by the queen. But in 2007, researchers observed the older workers caucusing and then giving signals to the rest of the hive, even "piping"—making tiny tin-horn sounds—at the queen to tell her to fly. Like everything else in the hive, swarming is a group decision.

It's a risky prospect for bees, leaving behind a sure thing and hoping to set up shop, lay eggs, raise brood, and gather nectar and pollen ASAP, but reproduction is always a necessary risk. One bad rainstorm can eliminate an exposed swarm, as can a protracted rain after they have colonized a new hive but not yet stored food. Which is why bees improve their odds by swarming when food is plentiful and weather mild—typically, on a late-spring sunny day.

Pre-swarm, scout bees head hither and yon, then report back to headquarters about any promising new cavity, doing a variation on the waggle dance. Again, the challenge is that the colony must decide which scout's site is best (based on size, entrance location, direction of entrance—south is good—and so on) when (A) no one is in charge, (B) none of the scouts have seen each other's sites, and (C) communication is fairly limited and any one scout might be more excitable than another. The evolutionary solution is that, unlike foragers, scout bees don't continue recruiting to their site. They do their dance, then hit the showers. A stronger waggle dance will send more recruits to the site, but if those recruits are unimpressed, they won't recruit others to it. Over many scouting flights, and many novice scouts, the law of averages takes hold and the best site gets the most supporters. The swarm is on.

Swarming is all well and good for bees, but it's a disaster for the beekeeper, who loses half a hive to every swarm. The remaining bees will build back up and aim to be at full strength by fall, which is necessary to survive the winter, but they often won't have a drop of honey to spare, nor will they be strong enough for pollination work. So beekeepers do everything they can to prevent swarming, primarily by adding supers—boxes of empty frames—to the top of burgeoning colonies. They also divide their hives before the hives get the notion to do it themselves. Splitting hives temporarily reduces their honey production, but it also adds a colony and is the main way beekeepers build their apiaries. Beekeepers try to strike a balance between production hives and expansion hives. Getting the bees to stick around, stay healthy, and play nice is an imperfect science, but that's the nature of apiculture. Rather than a domesticated species, eager for human contact, bees are more like a divine force, and beekeeping often resembles a form of supplication.

Sometimes that supplication takes strange forms. The U.S.

Department of Defense, for example, is experimenting with using bees to find land mines. What is a bee but an elegant little invention for tracking down distant aromas? Her knack for interpreting all the information flowers are transmitting, remembering numerous pinpoint locations, and communicating this information to other members back at headquarters is what keeps a colony going. With her one-milligram brain, she may be no Einstein, but as insects go, she's an amazing learner. Unlike most bugs, bees will change their behaviors in response to conditioning, like Pavlov's dogs. Give a bee some sugar syrup along with a puff of odor, and after only a few repetitions you can elicit the same response using just the odor. Flowers figured this out millions of years ago. And bees are incredibly good at detecting those odors. They have 170 odor receptors in their antennae, compared with just 62 for fruit flies and 79 for mosquitoes.[14]

A bee will track down any odor she's learned to associate with food. Jerry Bromenshenk, an environmental chemist and entomologist at the University of Montana with an aggressively original mind, has trained bees to find all sorts of chemicals, mostly pollutants. In the 1980s, Bromenshenk used his bees to track arsenic, cadmium, and fluoride pollution in Puget Sound to its source, a smelting plant in Tacoma.

Searching for land mines is a pretty lousy job. Dogs often get stuck with the task of sniffing out the explosive chemicals in the devices, but dogs take a long time to train, can't cover much

14. On the other hand, bees have only 10 taste receptors, while fruit flies and mosquitoes each have around 70. Bees don't need as many because they are one of the few life-forms that works cooperatively with its food. A lot of taste is devoted to screening for toxins, but bees trust flowers and don't bother.

ground, and tend to get blown up. Bees, on the other hand, are such adaptable learners that they can be trained in two days by putting a little explosive by-product in their food. They can cover vastly more territory than dogs and never get blown up.

They also don't linger long over the land mine once they realize they're getting shafted on the food. Which is where the lasers come into play. Lasers beamed across minefields will bounce off bees clustering over the mines. A computerized map can be made showing the locations of the mines. In experiments, bees detected mines with 97 percent accuracy and missed just 1 percent—the same rate as human minesweepers.[15]

I tell you all this not so that you'll bring a hive of bees instead of a metal detector on your next beach vacation but to emphasize what a colony of honey bees really is. It's a superorganism that thinks quickly, adapts constantly, and depends on wisdom to survive. We humans tend to think of wisdom as a top-down procedure. A powerful mind gathers information, measures it against the lessons of accumulated experience, and makes a rational decision. But really, wisdom is not a process but an outcome; it's the ability to live well, to anticipate and be prepared, to avoid disaster, to navigate troubles. It can come through experience and pattern recognition—"Last time I ate those red berries, I got sick"—or it can come through instinct and feedback loops, as it does with bees. Either way, it's a process of trial and error, of learning from

---

15. Bromenshenk couldn't tell me much more than that. "We are very restricted in what we can say about this. The military and State Department don't want the technology exported to certain foreign governments who might use the information for other purposes. As such, we're under a general information sanction." Clearly his partnership with the Department of Defense included a course in military speak.

mistakes. One method emphasizes the individual's role, while the other relies on genes and evolution. Our species tends to recognize only the former method, but nature seems to favor the latter.

The downside of this communal wisdom is that you don't have to kill bees to destroy a colony. Anything that affects bees' memory, learning, senses, appetite, digestion, instincts, or life span can be enough to throw those feedback loops off course. Skew enough of them, and the beautiful mathematics of the hive break down.

Chapter 3

COLLAPSE

THE FIRST THING Dave Hackenberg did after discovering his empty hives in November 2006 was to load the deadouts—colonies that have collapsed—onto a ten-wheeler flatbed and truck the whole mess to his shop in Dade City, where he could at least extract the honey and salvage the frames. He called Jerry Hayes, Florida's state apiarist, and reported the problem. Hayes suggested it was probably varroa mites—always the mites. Everything about modern beekeeping must be seen in light of varroa. The desperate practices, the shell-shocked psychology of the beekeepers, only makes sense when you understand what varroa has done to their bees.

Picture going through life with a tick the size and shape of a kettle stuck to your back. Now picture two or three of them glommed onto you, their fangs sunk in and drinking deep. Pretty horrific? Well, now picture those giant ticks abandoning you and attaching themselves to your children.

This is what life is like for a bee colony infested with *Varroa destructor.* The mite (same class as spiders and ticks) came from the Far East, where it has always parasitized *Apis cerana*, the Asian honey bee. But sometime in the twentieth century it made the leap to *Apis mellifera*, which had been brought east into Siberia, then worked its way back west with *Homo sapiens*' help, hitting Europe in 1976.

Honey bee imports had been banned in the United States since 1922, when Congress passed the Honeybee Act to prevent foreign diseases and parasites from entering the country. Everyone hoped the embargo would also protect the States from varroa. It did—until 1987, when, to the shock of the beekeeping community, the first varroa paratroopers somehow landed in Florida. A quarantine was placed on Florida bees, but migratory beekeepers in the state, fearing just that, had already trucked their bees out in the dark of night. In a single year, varroa was everywhere.

Varroa has killed millions of honey bee colonies. In the decade after its 1987 coming-out party, it put one quarter of the professional beekeepers in the country out of business. As an example, in 1995 Pennsylvania's population of bee colonies dropped from eighty-five thousand to twenty-seven thousand, primarily because of varroa. Things got so bad that in 2004 the Honeybee Act of 1922 was waived so that emergency bees could be airlifted from Australia to replenish American hives. Even in the CCD plague of 2006–07, as many colonies died from varroa as from CCD.

Varroa mites don't always kill bees outright. They don't have to. Instead, they weaken the bees, and the carefully orchestrated hive dynamic collapses.

The mites feed by sucking the blood of bees. They'll suck on adults, but most of their feeding and all of their reproduction takes place in the brood chambers. A pregnant adult mite will scramble into a cell with a larva, slide under the pool of royal jelly in the cell, stick up a little snorkel appendage to breathe, and stay perfectly quiet for days, avoiding detection until the cell has been capped. Then it goes to work.

The mite climbs out of the goo, sticks its fangs into the helpless but juicy larva, and sucks away. Then it lays some eggs in the chamber, and those hatch, feed on the larva's blood, mate with each other, and get ready to scramble out once the cell is opened and find their own chambers to start the cycle all over again.

All that sucking on the brood doesn't necessarily kill it, but it does it no favors. The open puncture wounds are like a red carpet for all sorts of bacteria, fungi, and viruses. The resulting adult bee is often malformed, malnourished, and crippled by disease.

A particularly insidious effect is that varroa-sucked bees don't always develop their hypopharyngeal glands—the ducts in the head that produce royal jelly. If bees' hypopharyngeal glands don't develop properly, they can't make baby food. So the first generation of bees to hatch after a varroa infestation may seem functional, but when they quickly take over the nursing duties of the colony, they malnourish the next generation (which is also getting drained by varroa). Malnourished bees are shorter-lived, which is a problem for summer bees but deadly for winter bees, which are tasked with making it through six months. Most varroa-infested hives collapse over the winter.

Treating varroa is hard. How do you kill one arthropod (the mites) without killing the other (the bees)? Like chemotherapy, any poison you introduce into the hive to kill the mites is likely to weaken the bees. The hope is that once the mites are gone, the bees will recover. But cancer cells don't evolve; mites do. In the early 1990s, a mite treatment called Apistan was introduced. It consisted of plastic strips impregnated with fluvalinate, a pesticide known to be relatively benign. Beekeepers hung two strips in each hive and the strips slowly off-gassed, killing the mites. It worked wonderfully for a few years, eliminating *almost* all the mites in a hive. Yet those somewhat resistant survivors quickly bred together and produced highly resistant offspring, and within a very short time Apistan was ineffective. Mites 1, Beekeepers 0.

Beekeepers seem to be allergic to doing things by the rules. When the strips stopped working, some beekeepers decided that if a little didn't work, maybe a lot would. Since fluvalinate was fairly nontoxic, they skipped the strips entirely, bought Mavrik, a liquid formulation of fluvalinate designed for "nonfood uses"—ornamentals, building perimeters, ant mounds—soaked shop towels in it, and tossed those into the hives. Though illegal, these megadoses are still used today. In any case, it didn't take the mites long to build even higher tolerances. Hives continued to die. Mites 2, Beekeepers 0.

In 1999, with the beekeeping industry on its knees, a new treatment called CheckMite was introduced. The clever name was the best thing about it. CheckMite used coumaphos, an organophosphate, among the most toxic chemicals on earth. CheckMite hammered varroa for all of a year before the mites again developed resistance. Mites 3, Beekeepers 0.

For the past decade, beekeeping has been one long scramble to stay ahead of the mites. Beekeepers rotate Apistan and CheckMite, hoping that one or the other will affect their particular mites, hoping for *only* 15 or 20 percent winter losses, but in reality both treatments are fairly ineffective and no savior is on the way. Part of the problem is the treatment schedule. CheckMite is so dangerous that it can't legally be used while bees are making honey, giving the mites free rein all spring and summer. The idea is that you wait until you've pulled your supers of honey in, say, October, and then knock back the mites until the following spring. But in temperate regions the fall is too late to treat because the winter bees have already emerged in September. Weakened by varroa, they don't make it through the winter. Sometimes the mites don't even leave fingerprints because they are killed by the chemicals in the fall—too late to save the hive.

Varroa now spans the globe, with the exception of Australia and Hawaii. It isn't going away, ever. But it's been around for decades, so it can't explain the 2006 surge of CCD deaths. Besides, mite counts have been no different in collapsed colonies than in healthy ones. Make no mistake, varroa is a nasty villain that makes everything harder, but in this case it can't be the lone gunman.

Dave Hackenberg already knew that. He'd checked. If anything, there were fewer mites in the deadouts than in the healthy hives. Whatever this was, it wasn't *Varroa destructor*. Jerry Hayes took "Hack's" word for it. Then he admitted that he'd recently met a Georgia beekeeper who'd lost 75 percent of his hives. Still, Hayes had no reason to suspect anything new was afoot.

Nor did Hackenberg. He didn't know the same disaster was striking beekeepers everywhere and was going unreported. Beekeepers speak of the stigma of losing hives. Your colleagues assume you have a condition known as PPB—piss-poor beekeeping. Why bother reporting it?

Yet the more Hackenberg watched new hives sicken and die, the more he became convinced that this was different. He began to recognize patterns. The young bees that were left in the hives just didn't act right. They wouldn't cluster, wouldn't eat, wandered aimlessly around the honeycomb.

Even stranger than the bees' behavior was that of the usual hive predators. A hive of honey is the Holy Grail of energy caches. It represents the combined food production of hundreds of millions of flowers, harvested by countless bees and processed into about a hundred thousand ready-to-eat calories. That lure is irresistible to many creatures, from wax moths to bears, and the only deterrent is the fifty thousand stingers bristling in the hive. Take away those stingers, and robbers, especially other bees, quickly move in to ransack the goods.

But not these hives. Across the field from Hackenberg's four hundred hives were a hundred belonging to another beekeeper. Those bees showed no signs of dying or disappearing, but they also didn't come robbing; they stayed away as if the hives were somehow repulsive. Wax moths will move into an abandoned hive and immediately start feasting on the larvae and pollen—the protein. But wax moths on Hackenberg's collapsed hives started on the outside and kept to it, avoiding the center of the hive altogether.

That caught Jerry Hayes's interest. "When you see wax moths not move in, or just move in on the periphery and stay on the outside, you say, what's going on? What is repellent here? You'd think first it may have been a pesticide that is repellent, then you think maybe it's some fungus spores. That's when we start examining bees and comb to see if there's any commonality."

Hackenberg was only beginning to piece this together when he received a call from a major South Carolina beekeeper asking him if he had any bees to sell. This was weird—the guy shouldn't have needed bees at that time of year—but Hackenberg wasn't in a position to worry about other beekeepers. He simply replied that he had nothing to sell. "My bees are dead."

The man sounded interested and began asking questions. Hackenberg described his symptoms—the absence of dead bees, the abandoned brood and honey, the nervous behavior and the repulsed hive robbers. There was silence on the other end of the line. Then the weary Carolina voice drawled, "Well I'd say you and me was in the same boat."

As Hackenberg watched more of his bees sicken and disappear

a week later, he decided he'd better find out what the hell was going on. He loaded his deadouts back on his flatbed and made the long drive to Pennsylvania, where he delivered a few to Dennis vanEngelsdorp, Pennsylvania's state apiarist.

When vanEngelsdorp checked the internal organs of the dead bees under the microscope, what he saw looked like an infinitesimal World War I battlefield. Everywhere was shiny, pockmarked ruin. The bees' guts, which should have been white, were stippled brown with infection. Their sting glands had blackened—a melanization last reported fifty years ago in connection with rare fungal infections. VanEngelsdorp found deformed wing virus, black queen cell virus, and many more. The bees didn't have one disease. They had them all.

Meanwhile, Jerry Hayes was doing his own experiments on Hackenberg's bees. He took some that were near death and isolated them in a Petri dish in an incubator. Within forty-eight hours the bees had fungus growing out of their mouths and anuses.

The immune systems of Dave Hackenberg's bees had collapsed. The comparison was obvious. They had something akin to bee AIDS. But what on earth was responsible? And why had it hit Hackenberg's bees in particular?

VanEngelsdorp didn't have a chance to make much progress on the first question before he got an answer to the second: There was nothing special about Hack's bees. He'd been the first to come forward, but across the United States that November and December, his colleagues lined up to report the same story: collapsing colonies, missing bodies, lots of brood and honey left behind, and a disaster in the making.

It's normal to lose some bee colonies over the winter. Cold weather and lack of food mean that an attrition rate of 5 percent or so has always been expected. Since the introduction of the varroa mite, the number has gone up. Today, a 17 percent winter loss is "normal." But the ferociousness of this new syndrome was something new. Healthy-looking colonies were losing all their adult bees in two weeks. As reports flooded in, Pennsylvania was the first state to survey its beekeepers. Nearly a quarter were experiencing the new symptoms, and they had lost an average of 73 percent of their hives. Even the beekeepers not suffering the new disorder averaged 25 percent losses. Of Pennsylvania's 40,000 hives, about 15,000 had died.

The story was the same from California to New York. Half the hives in the country were fine, the other half experienced freakish losses. Overall, perhaps 800,000 of the 2.4 million colonies of honey bees in the United States collapsed that winter. Thirty billion bees dead, and no one knew why.

Canada felt it, too. In the winter of 2007, 35 percent of Ontario's bees died.

In Europe the situation was also dire. France, Spain, Portugal, Italy, Greece, Germany, Poland, Switzerland, Sweden, Ukraine, and Russia lost as much as 40 percent of their bees over the winter. South America was devastated. Thailand, South Korea, and China suffered heavy losses.[1]

Of his 3,000 original colonies, Dave Hackenberg still had 1,300 in January good enough to load onto flatbeds and truck to California for the almond bloom, the single biggest event in the commercial pollination year. The vast almond groves of California's San Joaquin and Sacramento valleys serve as something of an unofficial beekeeper convention each January, when half the beehives in the country are trucked in to stay warm before pollinating the trees in February. California almonds are big business. The seven

1. Global food prices surged 37 percent during the same period.

hundred thousand acres in production pump out over a billion pounds of almonds a year—82 percent of the world supply—and sell for more than two billion dollars, making almonds the most financially successful crop in California, better even than grapes.

But every single almond requires a bee to pollinate it, and in February 2007, almond growers found themselves scrambling to find those bees. In previous years, it was just a question of how much pollination fees would hurt their bottom line. Now, it was a question of whether they had enough bees to make the world's almonds.

They did. Just barely. Over a million hives packed the groves. A lot of them were weak, so it took virtually every available hive to do the job, plus thousands of colonies flown in from Australia, but the almond growers survived.

Which is more than can be said for many of the bees.

Dave Ellington runs several thousand hives out of Minnesota. In the spring of 2007, the sixtieth anniversary of his family's company, he had them on a nectar flow in Texas and discovered that he had a CCD problem. "We had bees that we took to California that crashed and never went into the almonds. Those bees came back and we bought brood and put that in. On the thirtieth of March we put in two frames of brood and we gave 'em corn syrup. We went home for a couple of weeks and came back on the thirtieth of April to go through them bees, and when you opened that box up, there was two full slabs of brood, there was foundation drawn out, there was honey in that hive, there was the queen, and there wasn't a hundred bees in that box. What in the heck is going on? Hive after hive after hive. What did I do wrong? What did *we* do wrong? It's springtime in Texas, for crying out loud! It's the best time for gathering pollen and nectar. And those bees went right down the tube."

Of the 1,300 hives that Dave Hackenberg sent to California, only 600 returned to Pennsylvania. He was financially ruined. After forty-five years in the business, he had to borrow half a million dollars to buy new queens and equipment and start rebuilding his colonies.

By May, Hackenberg and Ellington and other beekeepers who weren't completely wiped out breathed a sigh of relief. Milder weather and plentiful blossoms strengthen the bees. This is the time bee colonies gather nectar and pollen, lay eggs at full speed, and build up after their winter losses. Most signs of colony collapse faded in the summer of 2007, giving beekeepers a chance to take stock, do a little research, try to figure out what the hell had just happened to them, and do anything possible to prepare for the following fall.

Would CCD return? If so, that might be the final straw. "This is a small industry," Jerry Hayes told me. "I know the beekeepers. I know their families. I know their kids. I know what they go through. These guys can't take any more."

The best hope for beekeepers lay in finding the villain—and coming up with a solution—fast. Dennis vanEngelsdorp and a number of other leading scientists formed the Colony Collapse Disorder Working Group at Pennsylvania State University and began testing their leading theories immediately.

Chapter 4

WHODUNIT

HOW FITTING IT would have been if the culprit had turned out to be cell phones. That rumor, one of the first to gain legs after the media seized on the CCD story in 2007, jibed with a lot of people's misgivings about an overly wired world. The environmental writer Bill McKibben summed it up perfectly: "I don't think anyone really has a clue as to what's going on, but if it turns out to be cell phones, it's the greatest metaphor in the history of metaphors. Starving the planet in pursuit of one more text message with your broker seems the very epitome of going out with a whimper, not a bang."

The theory: Electromagnetic radiation emitted by cell phones tweaks bees' antennae or brains and impairs their navigation abilities. They fly away from the hives, get confused, their GPS units go down, and they run out of gas in Fargo. The seed for this theory came from a 2006 German study of the effect of phones on bees. The media did the rest. A typical headline: "Are Mobile Phones Wiping Out Our Bees? Scientists Claim Radiation from Handsets Are to Blame for Mysterious Colony Collapse of Bees."

But wait a minute. Had the scientists actually claimed any such thing? For starters, "Can Electromagnetic Exposure Cause a Change in Behaviour?" wasn't a study of *cell phones* at all. The researchers, Wolfgang Harst and Jochen Kuhn, had taken the bases of *cordless* phones, like those found in most homes, stuck them right in the bottom of half of their experimental hives, and fired them up. The bees in the hives with the phones acted a bit funny, as indeed you or I might if the phone kept ringing and no one was there. Overall, the bees exposed to the radiation from the cordless bases made 21 percent less honeycomb than the nonexposed bees. In a second experiment, the researchers trapped twenty-five bees from each of four colonies (two phone-exposed colonies, two normal ones), carried them a half mile from the hives, released them, and counted how many bees made it back to the hives within forty-five minutes. In the normal hives, sixteen and seventeen bees made it back in time, averaging about twelve minutes. In one exposed hive, six bees returned, taking on average around twenty minutes. In the other exposed hive, not a single bee returned.

Clearly something creepy is going on here, but it's a mighty leap from a transmitter directly in a hive to a long-distance bath of cell phone radiation—as the horrified authors were quick to point out. "We cannot explain the CCD-phenomenon itself and want to keep from speculation in this case," Kuhn wrote in an e-mail message. "Our studies cannot indicate that electromagnetic radiation is a cause of CCD." His graduate student added, "If the Americans are looking for an explanation for colony collapse disorder, perhaps they should look at herbicides, pesticides and they should especially think about genetically modified crops."

Indeed. Genetically modified (GM) crops got their share of the CCD blame and were a more rational explanation than cell phones. After all, some of the CCD hot spots, like the Dakotas, have terrible cell phone coverage but are blanketed in genetically modified corn and canola.

GM corn has had the genes of a naturally occurring soil bacterium called *Bacillus thuringiensis* (Bt) inserted into its DNA. It produces Bt in all its cells. Since Bt is toxic to insects, this is like pumping a natural pesticide throughout the plant.[1] Countless activists have decried Monsanto for developing Bt corn, but I can see the appeal. Why spray crops with a pesticide that washes into the soil and groundwater when you can simply have the plants manufacture it themselves? Organic farmers have used Bt for years as a natural insecticide. So I can understand Monsanto's thinking. Then again, I can understand Dr. Frankenstein's belief that it might be useful to reanimate the dead; it's in the practice that things get messy.

Corn is a wind-pollinated plant. It has no use for insects and doesn't bother making nectar. It does, however, have that delightful tassel of protein-rich pollen on top. Bees will collect corn pollen and feed it to their brood. What might all that Bt be doing to the next generation?

Not a darn thing, say the scientists. The map doesn't fit. Lots of CCD cases have been reported in states with no GM crops, and some of the most corn-intensive states, like Indiana and Nebraska, have no reported CCD cases. Quite a few studies have been done on the subject, most showing no Bt effect on honey bees, including one U.S. Department of Agriculture study that fed Bt corn pollen to bees for thirty-five days and found them very chipper at the end of the study. In a four-year study,

1. Lots of plants produce natural pesticides. The nicotine in tobacco is one. More on that in the next chapter.

researchers fed the Bt protein to honey bees at ten times the level they could ever encounter in a field. Again, the bees came through with flying colors. Consider Europe, where colonies are collapsing rapidly despite a ban on GM crops.

As tantalizing as the cell phone and genetic engineering leads were, they didn't pan out. But that didn't stop them from getting serious attention in both the mainstream and alternative media. CCD took hold of the collective imagination in a way no one could have predicted.

Bees have always fascinated people. The industrious, cooperative mentality. The wondrous products they make. The black and yellow stripes. The way they play nice with people—usually. And, of course, the story had legs because it hit people where they live: This wasn't just about honey bees; this was about our *food!* But the real reason why shy and obscure entomologists suddenly found themselves on *Nightline* was that the bees had not just died; they'd *disappeared.* Every major newspaper in the United States, Canada, and Europe ran stories about "the mystery of the disappearing bees."

It was a classic whodunit, with all the savory elements: mysterious deaths, missing bodies, end-of-the-world ramifications, and no shortage of culprits. Fingers pointed in all directions, including some strange ones. The Christian Newswire pointed out that Revelation 6:6 states, "Then I heard what sounded like a voice among the four living creatures, saying, 'A quart of wheat for a day's wages, and three quarts of barley for a day's wages, and do not damage the oil and the wine!' " Since grapes and olive trees don't need bee pollinators, according to the Newswire, this was clearly a prophecy anticipating CCD, with obvious conclusions: "Grape and olive oil production will only be minimally impacted by Colony Collapse Disorder while much of the fruit, vegetable and nut production will be severely reduced resulting in famine. These end time biblical prophecies are coming to pass within our own lifetimes demonstrating once again that the Word of God is true and to be trusted."

You didn't need to believe in the Rapture to feel that something was out of whack in our ways of growing food and relating to the natural world. As the story evolved, it began to say as much about civilization's guilt and hopes as it did about entomology.

Microwave towers got some attention, as did alien abduction. More credibly, global warming raised its head. Were the bees getting broiled by warming temperatures? Daniel Rey, who keeps four hundred hives in Uruguay, thinks so. According to Rey, Uruguay lost 50 percent of its bees in 2007, which was actually an improvement on 2003, when *all* the honey bees in Uruguay died and the beekeepers had to restock their hives with imports from Argentina and the United States. Rey believes Uruguay's bee problems, which began in 1989, are related to the ozone hole perched more or less directly over Uruguay. People in Uruguay now commonly suffer from sun-sickness, so why not the bees? Rey's, which used to work from sunrise to sunup, like bees everywhere, now take a siesta from about eleven A.M. until five P.M. A blistering drought now parches Uruguay every summer, which is probably weakening the bees even more than the ozone hole. Bees can take heat—they evolved in Africa, after all—but drought vaporizes their food supply. Yet Uruguay has also embraced a pesticide-intensive agriculture in recent years, so, just as in the United States, no shortage of scoundrels exists.

For a while, organic beekeepers believed they were immune. Sharon Labchuk, an environmental activist in Prince Edward Island, wrote a message that was posted on many beekeeping Web sites and e-mail lists: "I'm on an organic beekeeping list of about

1,000 people, mostly Americans, and no one in the organic beekeeping world, including commercial beekeepers, is reporting colony collapse on this list. The problem with the big commercial guys is that they put pesticides in their hives to fumigate for varroa mites, and they feed antibiotics to the bees. They also haul the hives by truck all over the place to make more money with pollination services, which stresses the hives."

Yet I've spoken with organic beekeepers who "did everything right" and still had mysterious losses. Jerry Bromenshenk (the guy using bees to find land mines) made an extensive survey of beekeepers and found no such bias. "Colony collapse disorder does not play favorites. It doesn't care if you migrate, don't migrate, if you're a small beekeeper, medium-sized beekeeper, large beekeeper, or one of the world's largest beekeepers. It doesn't care whether you're a good beekeeper, middle-of-the-road beekeeper, or one of these guys who basically throws his bees out and hopes that they'll do well. Once you see it happen in your operation, don't feel bad if you can't fix it. Because so far, nobody can fix it."

Bromenshenk also pointed out a major hurdle to solving CCD: "The absence of dead bodies is one of the really strange symptoms of this thing, and it's also one of the things that makes it very hard to figure out what it is, because you can't do an autopsy if you don't have a body. The bees that we really ought to see are the ones that have disappeared."

Varroa mites were an obvious suspect. But they didn't make bees fly off and disappear. Perhaps the miticides beekeepers used to fight varroa were involved? Since the chemicals have been used, the life span of many queen bees has been cut in half. Yet without the chemicals, hives don't survive at all.

What about malnutrition? Bees evolved to eat pollen and concentrated nectar, yet lately many of them were living on a diet of high-fructose corn syrup so that they could keep pollinating crops in places where little food was available. Might that be a problem long-term?

Yet all these suspects had been factors for years. Something new had sent bee populations off a cliff. A virus? A parasite? A pesticide? The scientific community batted all these ideas around. And came up with nothing. "Researchers have picked through the abandoned hives, dissected thousands of bees, and tested for viruses, bacteria, pesticides, and mites," said the *Los Angeles Times* in a typical piece. "So far, they are stumped."

Everyone's best guess was that a pathogen was involved, because CCD seemed to be transmissible. Put healthy bees in dead CCD hives (or a dead hive on top of a good one) and they died, too. Further evidence came from Dave Hackenberg, who happened to know of a cobalt radiation facility just thirty-five miles from his Florida shop. There are two such facilities in the United States, one in California and one in Florida, which irradiate agricultural products by the truckload. Hackenberg asked if the local facility would zap a few of his deadouts. It did, and when he put bees into those hives, they did fine. By summer 2007, eight months after Hackenberg's original CCD discovery, he'd irradiated 80 percent of his hives and stocked them with new Australian bees, which were doing better than any hives he'd seen in years. They were thriving, making lots of honey. In particular, they weren't suffering the queen losses of recent years.

The hives Hackenberg hadn't irradiated weren't faring so well. They were already dwindling, and Hackenberg had no illusions they'd make it through the next winter. He'd tried requeening[2] them, but it made no difference. He was resolved to letting them die, irradiating the deadouts, and filling them with new bees the following spring.

Was the radiation killing a pathogen that was causing CCD? Not necessarily. If you put AIDS patients in a sterile environment, they'll do better because their immune systems won't be challenged, not because something in the air is causing AIDS. A sterile environment will always be gentler on an organism with a collapsed immune system.

A good whodunit needs numerous suspects, which the CCD mystery had, but it also needs a charismatic detective who nails the evildoer dead to rights. The story seemed distinctly lacking in that element until Dr. W. Ian Lipkin, an acclaimed researcher from Columbia University and a rock star of high-tech genetic sleuthing, stepped into the fray and announced he was taking the case.

Lipkin hunts viruses. Like a detective, he parses a crime scene, examining every scrap of evidence to discover who was in the vicinity at the time. If the same suspect is on the scene of enough crimes, you have a likely culprit. But Lipkin works entirely on the level of genetics, using some of the most sophisticated gene devices in the world. It was Lipkin who discovered that some very sick people in New York in 1999 were actually suffering from a little-known virus called West Nile. If there was some

---

2. When an old queen starts to lose her stuff, beekeepers catch her, kill her, and drop a younger, faster model into the hive. A queen that is unrelated to the workers in a hive will be killed if she's introduced directly, so the trick is to use a queen cage—a little plastic chamber with a candy plug in the entrance. The workers start eating the candy, and by the time they break through to the queen, they've been smelling her queen pheromone for days and are more likely to accept her as their new monarch.

new pathogen rampaging through honey bees, Lipkin was the one who could find it.

As luck would have it, the entire honey bee genome had been sequenced just a few months before CCD struck in 2006. Lipkin took frozen bees from four collapsed colonies—plus samples from two healthy colonies, as a control group—ground them up with liquid nitrogen to make bee slurpees, and sequenced all the material. That produced strings of genetic code—Gs, Cs, As, and Ts—millions of letters long. After blocking out the sequence that was the honey bee genome, he was left with sequences that belonged to various parasites, viruses, fungi, bacteria, and so on coexisting with the bees. It's a bit like playing an impossibly massive word-search game, circling HONEYBEE, VARROA, and other key words amid the sea of letters. Mystery sequences can be identified by matching them against a massive international database of organisms.

After Lipkin circled the sequence for every organism known to be at the crime scene, he was left with a few surprise appearances. One, in particular, turned up in most genetic word-searches of colonies that had collapsed. Inspector Lipkin had his man.

The media treated Lipkin's investigation with the breathless anticipation of a hotly followed murder investigation. Hints were dropped ahead of time, and the *Wall Street Journal* reported that Lipkin "says he has identified the cause of the honeybee plague," but nobody spilled the goods until the discovery could be announced in *Science* and at a corresponding September news conference attended by all the networks and major newspapers.

The suspect, Israeli acute paralysis virus (IAPV), a honey bee virus first identified in Israel in 2004, was found in twenty-five of the thirty samples taken from CCD colonies, but only one of the twenty-one samples from healthy colonies. In addition to the

CCD colonies, it was found on bees imported from Australia and in royal jelly from China.

The cloud of suspicion fell particularly heavily on Australia, as the *Science* paper explained: "All CCD operations sampled used imported bees from Australia or were intermingled with operations that had done so. Importation to the United States of bees from Australia began in 2004, coinciding with early reports of unusual colony declines."

Bingo. Remember that Honeybee Act of 1922, which was waived in 2004 because of imperiled honey bee numbers? The need for more beepower had been so urgent, particularly for almonds and other pollination duties, that it overrode all precautions. Virtually everyone sensible objected at the time, pointing out that the domestic industry couldn't take one more introduced problem. Remarkably, the Animal and Plant Health Inspection Service (APHIS) not only ruled that it was okay to go forward with the imports, but also decided *no* inspections or quarantines would be necessary because no honey bee diseases or parasites that didn't already exist in the United States were known to exist in Australia. Besides, the Australians would be doing inspections on their end.

Well, as Mark Brady, president of the American Honey Producers Association, put it to me, "Since when does the United States rely on other countries to safeguard its products? That's like letting the Chinese inspect their toys for us." After APHIS's 2004 decision, Jerry Hayes told APHIS that he was going to quarantine any Australian colonies coming into Florida until he got a cycle of brood out of them, just to be safe. He was told that if he did that he'd be sued by the government for disrupting international trade. Somebody really wanted those bees here.

And now it sure seemed like IAPV had come in with them. The timing was perfect. The *Science* paper by Lipkin and the

CCD Working Group summed it up: "The prevalence of IAPV sequences in CCD operations, as well as the temporal and geographic overlap of CCD and importation of IAPV-infected bees, indicate that IAPV is a significant marker for CCD." The researchers acknowledged the contradiction that Australia was one of the few places on the planet not suffering from CCD, but they postulated that perhaps the Aussie bees had evolved to live with it. They also took pains to differentiate between "significant marker" and "cause." Maybe IAPV didn't cause CCD, but rather CCD knocked out bees' immune systems, letting IAPV go wild. Like maggots feasting on the remains of corpses they hadn't killed, it would show up in all the collapsed colonies.

As far as the media were concerned, however, "significant marker" became guilt by association. Press coverage gave most of the general public the belief that the whodunit was solved. IAPV was to blame, but Australia was the real villain for sending us its nasty, diseased bees.

A few people objected right away. The beekeeper James Fischer wrote a piece for *Bee Culture* magazine, arguing each point of the *Science* paper, and concluded: "I'd like to apologize to the beekeepers of Australia for the public bashing they are about to endure due to the groundless accusations made in this paper."

He wasn't exaggerating. It took Senator Bob Casey of Pennsylvania all of four days to fire off a letter to the secretary of agriculture calling for him to "temporarily suspend the importation of Australian honeybees until it can be definitively determined that these bees are not linked to CCD" and to "consider measures such as quarantines and increased testing that can be taken to mitigate the effects of the Australian honeybee colonies already present in the United States." The American Honey Producers Association followed suit three days later with a letter to APHIS, "writing on an urgent basis to request that APHIS immediately suspend the importation of all honeybees, including queens and packaged bees, into the United States . . . A recently published, peer-reviewed study by university, government and private sector scientists suggests a strong link between the serious condition known as honeybee Colony Collapse Disorder ('CCD') and the importation of honeybees."

Throughout the beekeeping community, a ban on Australian imports seemed a foregone conclusion—until APHIS refused to close the border until more evidence was in, causing an uproar.

Yet once the CCD Working Group's sizzling press conference was over and cooler heads started working, it became apparent that many facts didn't fit. The Aussie bees couldn't have evolved to live with CCD, because many of the beekeeping operations that had collapsed, as the *Science* paper had made clear, were stocked with imported Australian bees.

And what about Canada, which had been importing Australian bees since 1987? Canada suffered fewer CCD cases than the United States, so it couldn't possibly be as simple a matter as importing diseased Aussie bees. Besides, Canada bees came into the United States all the time, so anything that was in Canada twenty years ago would have reached the States long ago. Meanwhile Europe, which didn't import Australian bees, had no shortage of collapsing colonies.

Just what was IAPV, anyway? Ilan Sela, the Israeli researcher who first identified it, described its symptoms as shivering wings, paralysis, and death just outside the hive. The giant red flag you see rising before you waves conspicuously over the fact that these symptoms don't remotely match those of CCD. The *Science* paper acknowledged this and offered another hopeful explanation:

"Although the shivering phenotype is not reported in imported Australian bees or in CCD, differences in IAPV pathogenicity may reflect strain variation, co-infection, or the presence of other stressors such as pesticides or poor nutrition." In other words, maybe IAPV turned into something else in America that caused completely different symptoms. Or maybe something else in America (pesticides? poor nutrition?) made IAPV manifest in a completely different way.

A major blow to the Aussie theory came in November 2007, when researchers sampling bees that had been frozen in USDA labs as far back as 2002 discovered the presence of IAPV . . . as far back as 2002—well before the Aussie bee importation began. Australia was off the hook. Now that they knew IAPV's genetic code, everywhere researchers looked for it, whether into the past or across the ocean, they found it. It sure seemed less like a new invader and more like another worldwide bee disease that had been waiting for humans to develop the technical skills to recognize it. The CCD Working Group admitted as much in a follow-up letter: "Indeed, the fact that IAPV has now been found in the US, Australia, Israel and China (royal jelly samples) means that the virus may already be globally distributed."

Australia felt that maybe the researchers should have thought of that sooner. "Someone owes Australian beekeepers a big apology," said the country's federal agriculture minister, Peter McGauran, "but we won't hold our breath waiting for it." Denis Anderson, Australia's leading bee pathologist, was even harsher, claiming the data right in the *Science* paper showed that a fungus called *Nosema ceranae*, and not IAPV, was the cause of CCD. "But it was overlooked as the cause due to lack of experience and knowledge of general bee pathology on the part of the researchers," Anderson said. "This can't reflect well on a journal such as *Science* and its selection of referees."

Nosema? Where did that come from?

Well, that's what a lot of people wanted to know. Like varroa, *Nosema ceranae* originally afflicted the Asian honey bee and at some point made the leap to the European honey bee. The fungus infects bees' digestive tracts and destroys their epithelial cells (the lining of the gut), which bees use for digestion. Bees with nosema, unable to absorb nutrients, die of starvation. It was first spotted in Europe in 2006, making many Europeans suspect it was the scourge of their dying bees. In Spain, where colony deaths with classic CCD symptoms had exploded in 2004, nosema was found in virtually all bee samples dating back to 2003, but was rare before that. IAPV, on the other hand, was found in just one collapsed colony.

In early 2007, researchers at UC San Francisco had discovered nosema in CCD bees and announced it might be the cause. *Not*, said the USDA Bee Research Laboratory in Beltsville, Maryland, because it had already spotted *Nosema ceranae* in frozen U.S. bees dating to 1995. To be certain, it checked nosema spore levels in ten different bee operations suffering from CCD. The beekeepers had treated their bees with fumagillin, the standard nosema treatment, and it had worked: spore counts were very low in the hives. Yet the hives were still dying. At least in these particular hives, nosema wasn't doing the killing. The USDA lab also checked for varroa in collapsing hives and didn't see much of it.

The only thing everyone could agree on was that CCD must require a combination of triggers. Maybe a pathogen caused CCD only when bees were weak. This was the position taken by the *Australian*, which decided to turn the knife, pointing out that "unlike Australian colonies, US hives are stressed by poor nutrition, pesticides and parasites. As well, hives are trucked long distances to pollinate crops, reducing bee fitness."

Canada piled on. IAPV has been found on both coasts there, but the *Toronto Globe and Mail* published an article titled "Is the Bee Virus Bunk?" It quoted Mark Winston, a respected Canadian bee scientist, as saying that IAPV was "only a minor character in a larger tragedy. The real crisis ahead is . . . 'agricultural collapse disorder,' the impact of bee farming itself."

The CCD Working Group kept insisting IAPV was somehow involved. A closer look at the data determined that there were at least three distinct strains of IAPV. One, prevalent on the West Coast, was genetically identical to the IAPV in Australia, and probably *had* come in with the Aussie bees. Another East Coast strain is the one that's been around since at least 2002, so there must have been a completely separate introduction of that one from God knows where. To make things even more complicated, the two IAPVs in the United States were significantly different in genetic sequence from the original IAPV from Israel. And the U.S. strains seem to be quickly mutating, like the flu, meaning they may surprise us in the future.

In any case, our old friend Jerry Bromenshenk had his own set of data showing IAPV was not a significant player. Bromenshenk had teamed up with Charles Wick, an engineer who had designed a machine for the U.S. Army that could detect new viruses. In the era of germ warfare, the Army thought it might be a good idea to have that kind of machine around. The machine depends on the fact that each virus has a distinct size, and that viruses are some of the smallest things out there (about one hundred times smaller than a bacterium and ten thousand times smaller than a grain of pollen). If you make your bee slurpee and strain out all the larger particles, you can spray what's left into a tube where lasers count the number of particles of each size. (At least, you can if you have one of Wick's machines, of which there are six in the world.) You don't have to know what you're looking for. Deformed wing virus (DWV) is 20.9 nanometers (nm) in size, so you know every 20.9 nm particle is DWV, but you might find a lot of particles of a different size and know you've got some new, unidentified virus.

And that's just what Bromenshenk's team found: *fourteen* viruses in all, including two mystery viruses that were 25 and 33.4 nm in size and turned up in some, but not all, CCD hives. Could these be involved? Or were they just other viruses that had been lurking in bee populations forever? IAPV appeared in just 10 percent of the CCD samples, and none of the Australian samples, so according to this data it doesn't seem to be a cause or even a good marker. No virus was common to all CCD hives.

Really, the important piece of information from both groups' high-tech sleuthing is the discovery that all honey bees are suffering extraordinarily high disease loads. Bromenshenk's team found a 27.9 nm virus in many healthy hives. Kashmir bee virus was in all thirty of the CCD samples in the original IAPV study, and sixteen of the twenty-one healthy samples. Nosema was in virtually every sample. Sacbrood virus and DWV and acute bee paralysis virus were present. These were sick bees, even the "healthy" ones. The AIDS metaphor fit. But so far that was the only thing that did.

While most people in America believed the CCD case was solved, and quickly tuned out, professional beekeepers greeted the IAPV announcements with a collective raspberry, pointing out that it didn't do one thing to solve their problems. James Fischer, the beekeeper who'd apologized to Australia, observed that the diminutive *Science* paper had more authors (twenty-three) than paragraphs (fourteen).[3] As a breakthrough, it was about like announcing that the reason people get snuffly and achy every fall is because of a virus called influenza. It might be true, but it doesn't change anything. We've yet to create effective treatments for most viruses in people; we'll never have them for bees. Even spending the money to get the tests to see which viruses their bees had was unthinkable for most commercial beekeepers, considering their emaciated profit margins. The lack of a clear course of action was evident in the CCD Working Group's advice to beekeepers about how to act on this information: "Maintain healthy colonies. Keep varroa levels low. Keep nosema levels low. Supply supplemental nutrition when need be."

In other words, get some rest, stay hydrated, have some chicken soup.

In truth, commercial beekeepers hadn't put much stock in the virus theory from the beginning. Dave Hackenberg and his colleagues were on the front lines. They'd been comparing notes for years, figuring out exactly when and where their bees were getting sick. And they were pretty damn sure they knew exactly what was causing colony collapse disorder.

3. It's a great line, but not quite fair. The supporting data was in a supplemental paper. In truth, the CCD researchers heroically pulled together the funding and talent to study CCD in record time, often working pro bono. They are smart, hardworking, and dedicated. Their only mistake was trying to oblige the media and the beekeeping industry by offering instant answers instead of waiting five years until the air had cleared.

Chapter 5

SLOW POISON

CONSIDER THE DILEMMA of the pesticide manufacturer. Your goal is to make a chemical that is toxic to life. Yet it can't simply scorch all life, because the chemical kisses plants. You need a substance that kills pests but not plants. Yet the crop you protect is ultimately going to be fed to animals. You need to kill the right animals without killing the wrong ones. The art of the pesticide, therefore, lies in exploiting some basic biological differences between insects and humans.

The old-school approach focused on dosage. Organophosphates like Malathion and Diazinon are plenty capable of killing us, but not in the trace amounts left after they've been washed off the crops. About fifteen years ago, with little fanfare, a pesticide revolution replaced this archaic approach. A new group of pesticides called the neonicotinoids came along. Neonicotinoids mimic nicotine, a natural insecticide plants have been manufacturing for eons to discourage munchers. Tobacco is the nicotine king, of course, but tomatoes, potatoes, and green peppers also make small amounts.

Neonicotinoids are nerve poisons. They bind to receptors designed for acetylcholine, the neurotransmitter that neurons use to communicate with each other and with muscles. When these receptors are stuffed with neonicotinoids instead of acetylcholine, they quite literally get their signals crossed. Nerves fire when they shouldn't, while legitimate messages can't get through. Disorientation, short-term memory loss, and loss of appetite are some of the first signs of an acetylcholine breakdown, followed by tremors, spasms, and eventually paralysis and death. In people, Parkinson's and Alzheimer's are two diseases marked by inadequate acetylcholine reception.

The neural pathways of insects are far more susceptible to neonicotinoids than are those of mammals.[1] So while neonicotinoids give insects chemically induced cases of dementia within an hour, they have virtually no effect on us and are eliminated from our bodies within forty-eight hours. Perfect! Crops can be soaked in neonicotinoids with no worries. And they are. With annual sales of 560 million euros, and the approval for use on 140 crops in a hundred countries, imidacloprid, the most popular neonicotinoid, is now found in many of the bestselling pesticides in the world.

And it's not just for crops. If you put Advantage on your pet, you're using imidacloprid. Perfect again, because it will kill fleas without killing Fido, no matter how much of the stuff he licks up. If you put Merit on your lawn or golf course, you are using imidacloprid, which will kill soil bugs without killing cats, dogs, toddlers, or duffers. A stroll through Wal-Mart will turn up plenty of imidacloprid, sometimes in unexpected products. Look for all-in-one flower care that promises protection from insects, as well as any kind of grub treatment that offers "season-long

1. Think, for instance, how many cigarettes you've been able to smoke without once falling down on the floor and twitching. In fact, strangely, smokers are only half as likely to get Parkinson's as are nonsmokers.

protection." At least seven neonicotinoids are used in the United States and Europe, with imidacloprid the dominant player. The amount to cover an acre sells for twenty dollars in the United States, but in China it is just two dollars.

Sometimes it turns up in places you'd never expect. The U.S. Forest Service recently embraced imidacloprid in its desperate battle against the woolly adelgid, an aphid-like insect from Asia laying waste to eastern hemlocks from South Carolina to Maine. The adelgid, which sucks sap from the base of hemlock needles, kills trees within a few years of infestation and is expected to drive the eastern hemlock into extinction if it can't be curbed. Now thousands of hemlocks are having the soil around their root systems injected with imidacloprid. The insecticide travels throughout the trees, killing woolly adelgids and any other insect that might happen to suck on a hemlock. Essentially, many square miles of Great Smoky Mountains Park are now infused with the stuff.

Part of the reason for imidacloprid's success is that it is a *systemic* insecticide. It infiltrates the plant and manifests itself throughout the plant's tissue: stems, leaves, roots, everything. Bugs nibble on the plant, bugs die. It can't be washed off by rain. Often, it doesn't even need to be sprayed on the crop. Just soak the seeds in imidacloprid (the company will sell them to you this way), let them grow, and the mature plant will be chock-full of the stuff.

You can see why this seems like a blessing. Plant your treated seeds and you don't have to spray drifting clouds of toxins into the air and water. You don't have to reapply after every rainfall. Farmers love this. And it's hard to argue with the notion that neonicotinoids are an improvement over traditional pesticides. The Environmental Protection Agency is trying to phase out the organophosphates because they are so noxious. (More so than

DDT, although they don't persist in the environment nearly as long.) Switch to a systemic neonicotinoid and everybody wins!

Except, of course, the bees. A new pesticide that targets insect neurotransmitters and manifests in bee food is not exactly a blessing for them.

Then again, the threat of pesticides to honey bees is nothing new. Most insecticides will kill any bug. It used to be easy to spot the kills: A crop duster swoops low over a field, spewing streams of white mist behind it. Millions of bees turn up dead in the field, the beekeeper screams and asks for damages, usually to no avail. An awkward situation, to say the least. "The beekeeping industry has always been the ugly stepsister of agriculture," says Jerry Hayes. As bees performed the thankless task of pollination, they were taken for granted and frequently poisoned.

After a few decades of this dance, farmers and beekeepers improved their communication. The farmer would hold off spraying until the bees had done their job, or at least inform the beekeeper that spraying was imminent. Slowly, bee kills chalked up to pesticides went down to a third of what they used to be. Still, Eric Mussen, a honey bee expert at the University of California at Davis, estimates that 10 percent of bee deaths are due to pesticides. Many colonies get caught in the chemical crossfire.

But the new generation of systemics changed the game. They can't be removed while bees do their job. Bayer Corporation (yes, the aspirin guys) claims this isn't a problem. Its studies show that very little imidacloprid—just 1 or 2 parts per billion (ppb)—makes it into pollen or nectar, so the amount that bees eat and take back to the hive is insignificant.

Not everyone agrees. Shortly after CCD hit, Maryann Frazier, a Penn State entomologist who specializes in the effect of pesticides on honey bees, told me, "There's a lot of controversy about how much of the neonicotinoids gets into pollen and nectar. If you ask Bayer, they'll say very little. We're not convinced of that." In 2007 she and her team began the most comprehensive study of pesticides in bee colonies ever undertaken.

A study by Italy's University of Udine found that corn seeds coated with imidacloprid dripped the pesticide through the fan drain of the seed drill as they were planted. In fact, the paper filter used in the experiment was pink with Gaucho, a European brand of imidacloprid. Flowers bordering the fields had residues as high as 124 ppb the day of planting, and still 9 ppb three days later.

It's true that even these levels of imidacloprid won't *kill* honey bees. But what about those communal traits? Could sublethal doses of imidacloprid change bees' behavior, undermine the wisdom of the hive, and trigger CCD-like symptoms?

That's just what a number of studies have found.

In a 2001 study by Italy's National Institute of Apiculture, bees were allowed to drink from feeders containing nectarlike sugar solutions laced with varying amounts of imidacloprid: 0 ppb, 100 ppb, 500 ppb, and 1,000 ppb. The bees were trapped in cages, tagged, and observed to see if they returned to the hive. Nearly 80 percent of the control bees (who fed on no imidacloprid) returned to the hive within 2 hours, and about 90 percent returned within 24 hours. Of the bees that fed on 100 ppb imidacloprid, only 57 percent made it back to the hive within 2 hours, while another 27 percent straggled in within 24 hours.

And what about the bees who fed on stronger solutions of imidacloprid? "Bees treated with 500 ppb and 1,000 ppb completely disappeared both from the hive and from the feeder within 24 hours after the treatment. In fact, during the following days, none of these bees was seen, dead or alive, either in front of the hive or at the feeding station. Probably they were not able to return to the hive and died somewhere in the field."

Yet it's not as if imidacloprid killed these bees outright. They were all able to fly out of the cage after it was opened—though it took some longer than others. On average, the control bees flew off almost immediately, the 100 ppb bees took 10 minutes to leave, the 500 ppb bees took 45 minutes, and the 1,000 ppb bees took a full 75 minutes to escape. They also showed what the study authors call, understatedly, "anomalous flying behavior": "They often fell in the grass and their flight direction was not toward the hive. Treated bees seemed to be disoriented, and that could be the cause for their disappearance."

Yeah, it could. The pattern seems clear. Give bees a little bit of a nerve poison known to cause disorientation and short-term memory loss, and many of them have trouble getting home. But, like frat boys sleeping off a bender, they eventually revive and make it back within a couple of hours. Somewhere between 100 and 500 ppb, however, things get serious. So blitzed they can hardly find their way out of an open cage, the bees crash to the ground, eventually firing up their wings and heading blindly into the world like a drunk driver careening down the interstate.

Other studies in Italy, France, and the U.K. have confirmed the sublethal effects of imidacloprid. One study found that bees sequestered in a hive and fed 500 ppb imidacloprid virtually stopped moving or communicating with other bees for a few hours, but then shook it off and returned to normal—further support that the bees that flew off stoned on imidacloprid died not directly from the chemical but because they couldn't find their way home and died of exposure.

Colony survival depends on bees' exceptional learning abilities.

Dose bees with imidacloprid, however, as several experiments have proved, and their basic learning response is impaired; they can't make the connection between odor and food. Autopsies on these bees revealed brain damage.

Bayer doesn't argue much with these studies. Its assertion is that negligible amounts of imidacloprid make it into the pollen and nectar that bees feed on. Bayer's own studies found less than 1.5 ppb imidacloprid residues in sunflower nectar and pollen, and less than 5 ppb residues in corn and canola pollen, and its lab studies determined that it would take at least 20 ppb to produce a sublethal effect on honey bees—though the company admits other researchers have come up with numbers ranging from 6 to 48 ppb.

Why so many studies on imidacloprid? Because in 1994, the year Gaucho was introduced in France, French honey bees mysteriously began to disappear. What began as 1.5 million bee colonies had dropped below 1 million by 2001. A Bayer scientist's own description of the event rings eerily familiar: "The incidents are characterized by the occurrence of apathetic, immobilized bees, which tend to aggregate on the ground outside the beehives. Furthermore, bees are trembling and beehives get depopulated due to disorientation of foraging bees. Affected bees are attacked by guardian bees at the hive entrance. Morphologically, the abdomina of affected bees appear blackish and shiny. Usually, approximately one third of the bees of a colony show these symptoms. On the colony level, the malady results in severe bee losses without apparent mortality, and a strongly decreased yield of honey."

It's CCD by any other name, though the French came up with a catchier one: mad bee disease. And their fingers were pointed directly at sunflowers, a honey bee favorite, which had recently become the first crop to embrace imidacloprid on a large scale. In January 1999, after initial studies found small residues of imidacloprid in sunflower pollen, and with incensed French beekeepers protesting in the streets of Paris, France's Agricultural Ministry issued a two-year nationwide ban on the use of Gaucho as a sunflower seed treatment and commissioned a round of studies.

In 2001, the Agricultural Ministry admitted that the studies to date showed no conclusive link between Gaucho and dying bees. Then, in a move that would never fly in the United States, it decided to extend the pesticide ban for two more years anyway, citing the precautionary principle. Imagine the EPA saying to Monsanto, "We have no evidence that your bestselling product is causing problems, but we're gonna ban it for two years, just to be safe, while we do more studies."

Not that there wasn't reason for apprehension. A 2002 survey of pollen samples throughout France found imidacloprid in an astounding 49 percent of the samples—the most for any insecticide. In just a few years, low levels of the new chemical had managed to pervade the French countryside.

At the order of the Agricultural Ministry, a comprehensive epidemiological study to determine the risks of imidacloprid was undertaken by the Comité Scientifique et Technique, a committee formed by the Pasteur Institute, the National Center of Scientific Research, and the Universities of Caen and Metz. In 2003, the 108-page report concluded: "The results of the examination on the risks of the seed treatment Gaucho are alarming. The treatment of seeds by Gaucho is a significant risk to bees in several stages of life." Shortly thereafter, the Gaucho ban on sunflower crops was made permanent.

Seething, Bayer responded with studies showing no connection between Gaucho and the honey bee crash. The company pointed out, fairly enough, that mad bee disease hadn't improved since the 1999 ban. Maurice Mary, spokesman for the French beekeepers union, shot back: "Since the first application of Gaucho we have had great losses in the harvest of sunflower honey. Since the agent is staying in the soil up to three years, even untreated plants can contain a concentration which is lethal for bees." Furthermore, the beekeepers pointed out that since the initial ban on sunflowers, Gaucho had become widely used on corn, so even if the sunflowers weren't getting the bees, the corn was.

In a follow-up report, the Comité Scientifique et Technique agreed: "Concerning the treatment of maize-seeds by Gaucho, the results are as alarming as with sunflowers. The consumption of contaminated pollen can lead to an increased mortality of caretaking bees, which can explain the persistent bee deaths even after the ban of the treatment on sunflowers."

Apparently the French beekeeper's union has better lobbyists than its American counterpart, because in May 2004 France's minister of agriculture announced he was banning Gaucho for corn, too. For good measure, he banned six other insecticides containing fipronil, another systemic.

Did Bayer get a raw deal? It's hard to say. Although the description of CCD symptoms sounds like a slam-dunk conviction for imidacloprid, there is plenty of evidence in the other direction, too. France remains the only country to have banned imidacloprid and fipronil, yet its bees are doing no better than those elsewhere in Europe, where imidacloprid is still widely used.

In 2000, Canadian honey bees in Prince Edward Island and New Brunswick suffered their own collapse. Since imidacloprid had been introduced the year before and was already being used to control potato beetles on 90 percent of the potato crops in this spud-rich area, it immediately took the blame. Bees don't visit potato flowers, but they do forage on canola, clover, and sunflower fields in the same areas. Could imidacloprid be leaching from the soil and contaminating those flowers?

No, according to a University of PEI study carried out the following year, which found plenty of imidacloprid in soil samples but virtually none in flowers, nectar, or pollen. Another study in Argentina found no side effects in a bee colony allowed to feed on Gaucho-treated sunflowers. The bees made lots of sunflower honey and were thriving seven months later.

And what about the fact that Dave Hackenberg's irradiated hive boxes fared better than his non-irradiated ones? Doesn't that indicate that something biological is behind CCD? Doesn't that exonerate pesticides? Well, not necessarily. First, many pesticides break down when hit with strong radiation. (Sunlight is enough to degrade imidacloprid.) Second, as I pointed out earlier, if imidacloprid is causing immune breakdown, then an irradiated box, like a sterile hospital room, will be less likely to sicken patients.

The most damning evidence against imidacloprid is circumstantial: Whatever is killing bees is using its MO. For instance, Florida's Jerry Hayes said that when he first saw colonies with CCD, "My first thought was imidacloprid because we have that here in Florida for termite control. It makes them forget how to get back to the nest and causes their immune system to fall apart. Those are classic symptoms of imidacloprid. *Classic.*"

Dave Mendes runs seven thousand hives of bees up and down the East Coast, from blueberries in Maine to cranberries in Massachusetts and citrus in Florida. He's collaborated with the CCD Working Group, but he doesn't buy their IAPV theory. "In my own hives that aren't collapsing, we've identified IAPV, we've identified deformed wing virus, we've identified *Nosema ceranae*. All the problems that are out there I have in my bees, but they're not dead yet." He thinks the culprit is more subtle. "I believe that systemic pesticides are a significant factor in this whole thing." Low levels of imidacloprid and aldicarb have been found in bee bread in Mendes's hives. "It's fed to the brood in the developmental stages when their nervous system is developing. We don't seem to understand a lot about the nervous system of the bee. Something is happening in the developmental stages. I explained this to somebody and they said, 'Oh, your bees have birth defects.' Yep, I think that's what it is. It starts in one generation where you're exposed and the bees that hatch out look normal. There's nothing visible. But there's something wrong with them. It takes several generations. You have to remember that the bees that hatch out become the nurse bees that take care of the next generation."

Here's how Dave Hackenberg described his sick bees to me: "They act different. They just sit there. Won't cluster, won't go anywhere, won't eat, won't build up. And the queen will be off in some corner of the hive where she should never be. If you look at the labels on neonicotinoid products, they tell you that they cause memory loss, appetite loss, disorientation, and immune-system collapse in insects. They cause nervous system disorders. You look in those hives, and man if you don't see nervous system disorders."

In termites, part of the immune-system collapse happens because the addled insects stop grooming themselves, allowing fungi and other pathogens to spread over their bodies—a pretty good description of CCD bees. Grooming is an important defense mechanism against disease and parasites in honey bees, too. Just as AIDS doesn't kill its human victims—it simply knocks their immune systems out so that pneumonia and other diseases can deliver the coup de grâce—it's possible that, as Bayer claims, imidacloprid isn't doing the killing; it lets fungi and starvation take care of that.

Even though lab and field studies imply that the amounts of

imidacloprid present in crop pollen and nectar are too low to be causing CCD, the similarities are too strong to let it go. If you are Joe Detective and you know Jack the Ripper likes to poison women and leave a red glove on the body, and a new body turns up with a red glove on it, and you know Jack was in the area, you're going to keep Jack on your suspects' list even if he has a few good alibis. For now, imidacloprid is being watched closely by the detectives, even if no one's ready to press charges.

For instance, we know how much imidacloprid it takes to kill a bee outright, and we know how much imidacloprid it takes to turn a bee into a shuddering space cadet in an hour, but what happens if you give a bee a slow, steady drip of imidacloprid *for its whole life*? Studies have shown that as little as 0.1 to 1.0 nanograms of imidacloprid can modify a bee's learning and orientation abilities. It's possible for a foraging bee to be exposed to that much imidacloprid every single day. No one knows what effect that might have. Consider the case of cigarettes. Their lethal dose for humans would be extremely high. Somebody can puff away all day and still look fine. Only after chronic exposure do cigarettes' deadly effects become clear. Might that be the case with the neonicotinoids?

And what of larvae raised by bees foraging on imidacloprid-treated crops, which could consume 0.3 to 0.5 nanograms of imidacloprid during development? Clearly not enough to kill them, but what might it be doing to their neurons?

Dave Hackenberg, for one, believes this is why CCD showed up in November 2006 in the United States—a few months after bees had been foraging on imidacloprid-treated crops all summer. Pollen from those crops is stored in the hive and fed to the brood. The brood that pupates in late fall becomes the winter bees, the ones that are supposed to live six months instead of the usual six weeks. Was the behavior of the 2006 generation of winter bees changed in some fatal way by their food supply?

Nobody knows. "Nobody looks at effects of sublethal doses of single pesticides or exposure over time," says Maryann Frazier. "Sublethal effects may be such that we don't even recognize them." In 2008, Frazier dropped a bomb, announcing the results of her pesticide study. Her 196 pollen and wax samples came from CCD hives, control hives, and hives that had been pollinating Pennsylvania apple orchards. The orchards were chosen because they had a thoroughly documented history of their pesticide use, and because they were in a location where the bees had no other floral sources. Of the 196 samples, 193 had pesticide residues. Only 3 were clean. "We were surprised at the variety of chemicals we found in a single sample," she told me in her understated way. "Quantities were quite variable. A lot of these things were present at just a few parts per billion, but there were a few cases where we found pesticides at levels that would be a concern in human food."

Frazier found forty-three different pesticides in her samples, plus five more metabolites—the products pesticides break down into, which can be more toxic than the pesticides themselves. She found chemicals in every class, organophosphates, pyrethroids, you name it. She found fourteen systemics, including neonicotinoids, fourteen fungicides, and six herbicides. She found as many as seventeen pesticides in a single sample, five on average.

How would Frazier interpret these results? "It turns out bees are quite good at picking things up. We know that some pesticides that the bees picked up had not been sprayed for a long time. How they're getting those materials is . . . interesting."

How would I interpret her results? The land is more soaked in pesticides than we could have imagined. And they don't go away as completely as we thought they did.

What about imidacloprid? Surprise: Only 7 pollen samples contained it. The levels ranged from 6.2 ppb to 24 ppb, with an average of 14.9—much higher than Bayer claims manifests in pollen, and occasionally higher than that 20-ppb level Bayer believes could cause damage. Still, imidacloprid was way down the list of the forty-three pesticides, and the 7 positive samples did not correlate with the CCD hives.

Two other chemicals did: fluvalinate and coumaphos—the active chemicals in Apistan and CheckMite. Not surprisingly, they were the two most common pesticides, fluvalinate appearing in 160 and coumaphos in 146 samples. Every single wax sample was loaded with the stuff. Levels of the two miticides were three to five times higher in weak or dying colonies—no smoking gun, but certainly a red flag.

Coumaphos's association with dying hives makes sense, but fluvalinate has a reputation for being notably nontoxic. Even one beekeeper I know who favors wholly natural methods told me, "I used Apistan for five years until it didn't work anymore. It was a good product. It wasn't a dangerous chemical. You just put it in the hive for three or four weeks, then took it out, and that was it." How could fluvalinate be a problem?

Well. Fluvalinate's pussycat reputation was established back in 1983 when it was first registered by Zoëcon Corporation. Back then, its LD_{50} (the amount needed to kill half a study group) for honey bees was 65.85 micrograms per bee—relatively nontoxic. But fluvalinate has followed a winding road since then, changing hands twice—to Sandoz Agro in 1983 and to Wellmark International in 1997—and being reformulated along the way. The new version, known as tau-fluvalinate, has an LD_{50} of 0.2 micrograms per bee, meaning it's 329 times more toxic than we thought. It's now rated *highly toxic* to honey bees. Frazier found concentrations of fluvalinate (and coumaphos, for that matter) at nearly toxic levels in every brood she checked.

I was at the conference where Frazier announced her findings to most of the commercial beekeepers in the country. The room was surprisingly quiet, considering she'd just informed them they'd been poisoning their bees with a deadly neurotoxin for fifteen years. Frazier summed up the situation with characteristic bluntness: "We have to get these chemicals out of the hive."

Clearly, the question is not as simple as what imidacloprid, fluvalinate, or any other single pesticide does to honey bees or other animals. Since farmers, homeowners, golf courses, and fish and wildlife agencies are free to use any legal pesticide on the market, and certainly aren't checking with their neighbors to see what they are using, we can assume that multiple pesticides are mixing freely in the environment. Farmers will even "stack" chemicals, mixing them together so that they can be applied in one sweep through the fields. What have EPA studies found about the possible effects of this mixing?

Well, the EPA has never actually studied the effects of mixing pesticides. In fact, the EPA rarely tests pesticides at all. It relies on the companies to do their own safety testing and provide reports. The EPA reviews the reports, but only does additional tests when something suspicious occurs.

The chemical conglomerates, then—Bayer, BASF, Dow, Monsanto, DuPont, and Syngenta dominate the world market—must be responsible for testing how their new products are likely to interact with the other poisons already in the environment, right?

Actually, they don't test for interactions at all.

No one does.

That's what worries Jerry Hayes. "The testing of these chemicals on honey bees is pretty superficial and rudimentary. They're all tested, but they're tested individually. They basically test if it'll kill, but they don't look at sublethal doses and they certainly don't look at the mix—what happens when you mix ten different pesticides and have it appear in the honey bees' food and they eat it? When you're exposed to something sublethal twenty-four/seven, and you're exposed to fifteen other things like that, what does that ultimately do? Does it kill the workers? Does it kill the larvae? Does it do something funky to the queen? Does it kill all the sperm in the drones, which we already know some pesticides can do? We have no scientific data. We here in the West have this awkward history of waiting until we have a crisis to fix something."

The crisis seems to be at hand. For example, a recent study found that the fungicide Procure, used to control powdery mildew on cucurbits (cucumbers, melons, squash, pumpkins, and zucchini), apples, pears, strawberries, and cherries—all crops pollinated by honey bees—has a synergistic effect when combined with a neonicotinoid, increasing the toxicity to honey bees more than a thousand times. And one of the common formulations of fluvalinate includes a "nonactive" ingredient called piperonyl butoxide (PBO), 100 micrograms of which make the formulation twenty times more toxic to honey bees. Since these are two of the few combinations that have been studied, we can assume hundreds more toxic cocktails are being mixed every day in the world's fields and streams.

Chapter 6

FLORIDA, NOVEMBER 2007

STATE ROAD 44 cuts through Florida's Lake County, straight as only a road in laser-flat Florida can be, past cattle ranches, pine scrub, all-you-can-eat catfish joints, bass boats for sale, and always, pinwheeling vultures on the horizon. You won't see any palm-fringed beaches or giant grinning mice in Lake County. Though Daytona Beach is just an hour to the east and the Magic Kingdom an hour south, Lake County is a world apart. It has plenty of lakes, as you'd expect, all thick with gators, and husky shirtless kids fishing from docks. It's what great swathes of the state were like before Florida became Florida.

The citrus industry took off in Lake County in the twentieth century, because land was cheap, and beekeepers followed the blooms. The town of Umatilla, nestled against Ocala National Forest, became one of the beekeeping capitals of the state. Today, Bill Rhodes is one of the only beekeepers left in Umatilla. With somewhere around 4,500 hives, Rhodes has the largest apiary in the state, mostly by attrition. When CCD first asserted itself in 2005, he had 10,000.

I wanted to visit Bill Rhodes because he's at the center of the

CCD mayhem. Not only is he the biggest beekeeper in Florida, but he's also a great businessman. He's got a great location and plenty of resources. If he can't make it, no beekeeper can. Yet his bees were dying by the millions. "If you wanna see some dying damn bees," he told me over the phone, "you better get down here right away. Otherwise all you'll see are empty hives."

Rhodes, who is about sixty, has the build, salt-and-pepper mustache, accent, and hard-driving manner of a Southern football coach, which he might have been. After a star career as an offensive guard at Florida State University in the sixties, he was offered a three-year contract by the St. Louis Cardinals. Ever the businessman, Rhodes signed a Canadian Football League contract for slightly more money and spent the next two years in Montreal, living in the crazy-cube Habitat 67 apartment building, constructed for the 1967 World's Fair, and, he said, "chasing women every night. Oh my God. That was in the miniskirt era; they didn't wear any clothes. It was a great time to be in Montreal." That is, until a fall down the treacherous Habitat 67 stairs blew out his knee. He showed up the next day for a game and could barely walk. A trainer injected his knee with painkillers so he could play. "I went out and had a great game. I felt great. Then I partied that night. Well, I didn't party long. That sucker started throbbing. Oh, shit. I spent the night in the hospital. I thought to myself, 'You know, it isn't worth it. I've got a mother, a brother, I enjoy working on the farm. I'm gonna go back. It ain't much money, but at least I can be around my friends.' I walked in one day and told the owner I was retiring. He said, 'You're *what*?' I said, 'I'm going home.' "

Rhodes's family had a thousand-acre farm in Lake County, with dairy, corn, and other good Florida crops. He helped out his older brother on the farm for a few years, then decided to do his own thing. He'd seen how well bees did in the area. He bought his first 50 hives in 1973, then bought 350 more. He hasn't had to buy many since.

One of the great attractions of honey bees is their exponential reproduction. Variations abound on how to split a hive, but the basic idea goes like this: Take a hive bursting at the seams with bees, eight full frames of them, and take an empty hive box. Swap four empty frames from the hive box for four frames full of bees and brood. Place a new queen in the new hive. Presto, you have two half-strength hives instead of one full-strength. If conditions are right, they won't stay half-strength for long. The queens will quickly fill the empty frames with eggs, which soon turn into bees. Presto, two full-strength hives. Or you can "double up" a hive by adding an empty box on top of a full-strength hive, letting the queen expand egg-laying into that one, and once it's full, separating it and introducing a new queen—in a queen cage, of course.

Rhodes would split his hives right before the oranges began blooming in early spring, then often would have to split them again two weeks later, halfway through the nectar flow. Four hundred hives in February could become sixteen hundred hives in April, heavy with bees and orange blossom honey. "You can make a pile of splits off of four hundred hives—if you've got good hives. If not, you got a damn nightmare. That's what's happened lately."

In retrospect, the seventies and early eighties were the golden age of American beekeeping. No CCD, no mites, no price competition from third world countries. Florida honey was some of the best in the world—not as light-colored as the clover honey made up north, but better flavored. What didn't sell domestically got snapped up in Europe. Lake County was the citrus capital of the state, of the country, even, and all you had to do was get out of the way and let each hive make hundreds of pounds of delicate, floral, ultra-desirable orange blossom honey every spring.[1] Gallberry and palmetto followed the citrus. In summer, when nothing much blooms in Florida, Rhodes sent his bees to the Dakotas for clover. In the fall, they headed back to Florida for Brazilian pepper. In the winter, enough maple, willow, and wild cherry would bloom to keep the bees going until the citrus returned. "I had years in the eighties when I made two hundred pounds of honey per hive. That's average. Some of 'em must have made three hundred pounds." He'd pull all the supers of honey after each crop, leave a little honey for the bees, and keep dividing his hives so they could make more bees. The bees and Mother Nature took care of everything else. "We didn't *feed* bees back then. No one had ever heard of *feeding* bees."

Soon Rhodes had thousands of hives. He was making money

---

1. Citrus is an interesting pollination case. Because it makes extraordinary honey, beekeepers have always climbed all over each other to get into the orange groves. But most citrus is self-pollinating—the male and female parts on each flower will combine to grow fruit—so growers always assumed they were giving away nectar without getting anything in return. Now research shows that more plentiful and robust fruit occurs when bees pollinate citrus. Without bees, oranges would be twice as rare and far more expensive. The situation is different, however, with clementines (also known as mandarins). A decade ago, clementines from Spain became a huge hit, the Unofficial Snack of America's Children, because they were seedless and easy to peel. California jumped on the bandwagon, ripping out thousands of acres of oranges and planting clementines. Growers didn't know that if a clementine gets cross-pollinated with another citrus variety, it produces seeds. And no one wants a seedy clementine. So clementine growers are at war with California beekeepers, attempting to establish no-fly zones for miles around their citrus groves during bloom.

hand over fist. And he developed a real appreciation for his bees, the only things in Lake County that worked as hard as he did.

That appreciation was still in his voice as he walked me through his beeyards, only now it took the form of a kind of stoic heartbreak. It was November 14, 2007, and in the past month he'd watched four thousand hives die. "So many of 'em we had to nurse along, and then they'd finally die. It's just sickening."

A month ago, when the bees arrived from South Dakota, he said, "you couldn't even see the damned hives there were so many bees on them." Rhodes had split the hives, just as he's been doing for thirty-five years, moving half the full frames into an empty box and introducing a new queen. "We came back a week later and we knew something was going on. A lot of the queens were still in their cages. The bees were dying so fast that they couldn't even chew the queens out. The guys had to go through and manually open the queen cages."

At that point, Rhodes had his foreman, Felipe, put a jar of corn syrup on every hive to feed the bees so they'd pull through. "Felipe said he thought they were gonna make it. I haven't seen 'em for two weeks. I don't have any idea. Let's take a look."

We walked between rows of hives. "I don't see a lot of bees flying. That doesn't mean a lot, though," Rhodes said. He lifted the cover on the first hive and cursed softly. "Maybe a dozen bees. But it's full of honey. Pick this up. At least twenty-five pounds. But no bees, and nobody's trying to rob 'em." He shook his head. "Should be bees all over that dad-gum hive."

We lifted the lid on the next hive. "One frame of bees. That means they're dying."

Surveying the rows of hives laid on palettes, I felt as though we were wandering through a MASH unit, doing triage on the wounded. And our side was losing. "This one's dead . . . That one's gonna die . . . Dead . . . Dead . . . These here might make it, but they're not very big. Two or three frames of bees. The key is what they're doing for pollen. There's a little Spanish needles and goldenrod around."

Rhodes needed only an instantaneous glance under the cover to gauge the health of each hive. "That one's lopsided. That ain't right . . . This one's down to a frame and a half, but at least they're organized-looking." He was moving fast down the row, as if he couldn't bear to look at each hive any longer than he had to. "Dead . . . Dead . . . That one ain't gonna make it. A full super of honey and not a damn bee in there . . . This one's dead." He sighed. "They're all gonna die. Felipe's a good man. He's trying to say something that will make me feel good. But I know the reality."

The next hive had a few bees crawling over the top. "This one's history."

I pointed out the bees, trying to sound hopeful. So Rhodes stopped, pulled the cover all the way off, knelt down, and tried to condense thirty-five years of bee-watching into a few words. "See how they're walking around all crazy-looking? They're not organized. Not clustered. No wad of bees anywhere. Just walking all over the damn hive. They don't know what to do. Unorganized."

I wasn't sure I could see it. What did organized bees look like? But later Rhodes showed me some healthy hives. The difference was obvious. What at first glance seemed like the purposeless crawling of thousands of insects quickly coalesced into waves of intention. All the bees were working together, guided by those invisible directives of feedback loops, instincts, and simple communications. The hive mind. In a healthy colony, intelligence flashes between individual bees like electrical signals between neurons. Every bee is on task. The impression is not of thousands of individuals but of one fluid intelligence—an impression made all the stronger when the intelligence efficiently flicked out a tendril and stung my ear. But the collapsing colonies I witnessed gave no sense of intelligence. There were usually a few bees, yes, but they were wandering without purpose like survivors of an apocalypse, which they were. With their organization in tatters, they drifted across the frames searching for direction. Great lobes of the hive mind had died, and what bits remained had lost any organizing principle. If this was a mind, it was one with advanced Alzheimer's disease.

Rhodes has zero doubt about what is causing it. And he also knows that he saw it before it had a name. "Now that I know what it is, I realize I've seen it before, but never to the extent of this year. The first time I really noticed it was four years ago. The last load of bees from South Dakota just didn't act right. They just went downhill. Started shrinking down and dying. I kept thinking, 'What the hell's with these bees? They got into something somewhere.' "

In fall 2004, Rhodes shipped 5,500 hives of bees from South Dakota to California for almond pollination for the first time. He'd always run a straight honey business, but with rental fees approaching eighty dollars per hive, he decided it was time to try almonds. He shipped them to holding yards in California to stay warm until the February pollination. One day his foreman called to report that the bees were dwindling. Rhodes told him to throw another gallon of corn syrup on each hive.

A "hive" can mean anything from a few frames of bees to a full-strength, eight-frame colony. Almond growers pay full price only for full-strength hives. Rhodes got paid for 1,100 of his 5,500 hives. The rest were rejected. "We got 'em back here as quickly as possible, but they were just shrinking down. We couldn't figure it out. I knew it wasn't mites. I've never had a major mite load in my life—always been clean as anyone there is. That same year we had three truckloads of bees come back from South Dakota completely dead. Not a bee in 'em. I thought, there's something in South Dakota that's killing these bees, but that didn't make any sense, because everybody takes their bees to South Dakota."

In 2006, Rhodes lost another 2,000 hives in South Dakota. Trying to make up his losses, he sprayed the frames with apple cider vinegar, as he'd been instructed, placed the deadouts on top of good hives, and fed the hell out of the colony so that the queens would expand their laying into the deadouts. "After about four feedings, I went to check on them, and they were dead. I said, 'Holy shit, these damn dead hives have killed the damn good bees! There weren't any dead bees around. That's when Hackenberg started talking and they started calling it 'colony collapse disorder.' They came and looked at my bees and said, 'You've got the same damn thing.' "

Rhodes started doing some research and asking questions. He learned that imidacloprid had been banned in France. That clicked. "South Dakota used to be a lot of prairie, alfalfa and hayfields. But now, with ethanol, it's all corn and soybeans and sunflower. All that seed's dipped in Gaucho and planted. Anything that eats it dies. You ain't gotta be a rocket scientist to figure it out."

Rhodes doesn't send all his bees to South Dakota for the summer. He always keeps some to split. By doing so, he unintentionally created a control group for a scientific experiment. If CCD is caused by a virus that was picked up by his South Dakota bees, those bees should transmit it to his Florida bees upon their return. If CCD is caused by an insecticide that gets into nectar and pollen, then the South Dakota bees wouldn't transmit it to the Florida bees—unless the Florida bees had access to tainted South Dakota food, as when Rhodes placed the South Dakota deadouts on top of the Florida hives.

In the past, when all Rhodes's bees were reunited in the fall, the South Dakota bees, who had been feasting on clover and sunflowers all summer, were way ahead of the Florida bees, who had been getting by on corn syrup. Since the coming of CCD, it's been reversed. Rhodes happened to have a yard in South Florida that was half South Dakota bees and half Florida bees. The bees were on a huge pepper flow. His son, who didn't know the origin of the bees, was checking on them to see if they needed new supers. He called Rhodes. "Dad, there's something strange with these bees. They're up in the supers a little bit, but they're not making any honey." Rhodes asked him how the bees in back (the Florida bees) were doing. "Hell," his son said, "they're making the shit out of it."

Rhodes doesn't believe CCD is an automatic death sentence. After the call from his son, Rhodes went to see his bees. "The first yard I went into, I saw it. They were in a major honey flow, but they didn't have enough beepower to move the honey coming in the hive entrance up into the supers." The house bees were so weak, and few in number, that their assembly lines had broken down. They were all stuck in the bottom of the hive with every cell full of honey. "We had queen excluders[2] on the hives, which made it worse. The queen couldn't find a place to lay. I said get the damn queen excluders off, hoping to turn it around, which it did. But what the hell? All these hives that usually make eighty to a hundred pounds of honey can't even get out of the brood nest?"

But they didn't die, either. "The only thing that saved us was the new pollen and nectar coming in. They shrunk, shrunk, shrunk, didn't quite die; now they're trying to come back. Maybe they quit dying and they're not gonna die anymore. I'm counting

2. Gates that allow workers, but not the larger queen, to access the supers.

on them pulling through. If they die, too, holy shit. But they made no honey at all. I bet we didn't make a drum of honey from those four thousand hives, and they should have five hundred drums on 'em."

Rhodes believes that the bees are sickened by pesticides in the Dakotas, but that if the bees get moved to a fresh source of untainted, high-quality food, they can sometimes clear their systems. He believes this is why, for the past few years, his first semi loads of bees to arrive from South Dakota, which were sent directly to the Brazilian pepper nectar flow in South Florida, did okay, while the last arrivals from South Dakota, too late to catch the pepper nectar, died. But even that changed in 2007. "This year it affected the first load of bees [from the Dakotas], all the way through."

A common assumption among the public is that beekeepers suffering from CCD are all involved in the pollination business, stressing their bees by moving them every two weeks and exposing them to numerous pathogens in the fields. Not Rhodes. His bees have never resided anywhere except Florida and South Dakota, and they are moved only a handful of times a year. Other than his one almond disaster, he's never done any pollination work. His apiary's earnings come entirely from honey, which makes him a dying breed. He's not sure how long he can hold on.

"We had a good year about five years ago. Made twelve hundred drums of honey in South Dakota alone. I made 900 drums on the orange, 400 on gallberry. That was a hell of a year. But ever since then, I've hardly made any honey. On the citrus last year, I made 300 drums. The year before that it was 200. This year, I'll be lucky to make 150. This may be my last year on the citrus."

The citrus industry's decline in Florida has been swift and steady. The first blow came as a series of ruinous freezes in the 1980s. I remember as a kid in Florida seeing citrus growers in my area desperately misting their groves as temperatures fell through the afternoon, hoping that the ice would shield the leaves from the killer frost.

It didn't. The Central Florida citrus industry was dead by the 1990s, and it brought down some beekeepers with it. The rest had to truck their bees hours to the south, where citrus endured, and try to find available beeyards. Now a new disease called "citrus greening"—another little present from China that turned up in Florida in 2005, kills trees in a few years, and has no known cure—is wiping out the remaining groves. To fight the psyllid insect that carries citrus greening, growers use—yes—systemic insecticides. Beekeepers must either stay away or risk losing their flocks or contaminating their honey. When the state of Florida released its new suggested spray schedule for citrus, March was the only month without spraying.[3]

But even without citrus greening, the writing is on the wall, thanks to development and foreign citrus competition. No one I spoke with expects the Florida citrus industry to exist in fifteen years. And along with that will go the sublime orange blossom honey.

What about other floral sources? Well, gallberry and palmetto are abundant in the pine forests that stretch from Central Florida up through Georgia. Palmetto dominates in the southern part of the range, gallberry in the north. But in case you haven't heard, a lot of people are moving to Florida. Driving the flatbed between beeyards, Rhodes and I passed a place called the Villages. A retirement community sprawling across miles of old pasture and defunct citrus groves, the Villages boasts twenty-eight golf courses,

3. Tests of hives that had been in groves treated for citrus greening revealed disturbing levels of aldicarb, a pesticide highly toxic to human beings.

forty recreation centers, a polo club, and a population of seventy thousand. Even its supermarkets, shopping centers, and hospitals are linked by golf cart trails.

The Villages goes a long way toward explaining why land is no longer cheap in Lake County. Not only is the citrus gone, but there is also less and less palmetto and gallberry every year. Ironically, the great saviors of Florida beekeepers have been the invasive plants melaleuca and Brazilian pepper. Melaleuca, a small Australian tree with papery bark, was planted as an ornamental in Florida in the 1800s. People noticed that it thrived in wet areas, and in 1941 the U.S. Army Corp of Engineers began planting it along the Lake Okeechobee dikes to stabilize them. That worked so well that they began planting the tree in the Everglades to dry up wet areas and make them more developable. The tree didn't actually drink up more water than native plants, but with its abundant flowering and seed production, it sure outcompeted them. By the 1990s melaleuca had annexed hundreds of thousands of acres of the Everglades, turning the native saw grass prairie into swampland, which wasn't an improvement for anybody except beekeepers, who suddenly had a nectar bonanza on their hands.

In the 1990s the state of Florida began an aggressive program to wipe out melaleuca, using physical removal and herbicides. They started with the outlying areas—the exact ones utilized by beekeepers, who were not pleased. Today, melaleuca still infests great swathes of the Everglades, but little is accessible to bees.[4]

So far no one has managed to turn the tide on Brazilian pepper,

4. One of Rhodes's truck drivers once decided to take a shortcut through the swamp on a dirt access road. The road gave way and the semi and all 240 hives tipped into the swamp. They managed to save about 50 hives that were sitting on top of the drowned ones.

a baylike shrub that colonizes roadside ditches and other disturbed areas and bears red berries along its length, earning it the nickname Florida holly.[5] Pepper also arrived in the 1800s as an ornamental, but it didn't really take off until the 1950s. Today it dominates seven hundred thousand acres in Florida, mostly along roads and fields. The only significant nectar plant in Florida in the fall, "pepper" is now Florida's number-one honey plant. In total production, anyway. Its honey is considered inferior in flavor and is sold as bakery grade, earning around sixty cents a pound on the wholesale market, versus eighty cents for table grade.

As we drove the flatbed through the Okeechobee area to pick up 240 hives, Rhodes pointed out the pepper to me. It was everywhere, a lush curtain lining the ubiquitous roadside canals. But then we passed a section that looked like someone had taken a flamethrower to it. Spraying, Rhodes explained. The state is enlisting Roundup and its kin in the pepper wars.

Rhodes is still bitter about losing the melaleuca; if he loses the pepper, too, he's out of business. "There used to be areas thick with it, but shit, not anymore." When the state initiated its spraying programs, he actually drove up to Tallahassee and gave them hell. "I said, you people have all your signs, Save the Manatee, Save the Panther, Save the Bear. You better find one that says Save the Goddamn Beekeeper. Because you're gonna put us out of business. You don't think you need us now, but it's gonna come back and bite you big-time." The state people explained that the invasive plants weren't indigenous. "Neither is the orange tree!" Rhodes responded. "Who are you guys to say what's what? Who are you to draw the line in the sand and say what goes and what stays?"

5. Gourmet "pink peppercorns" are actually dried Brazilian pepper berries.

Citrus groves don't spread unchecked, but he had a point. I could see the irony in one exotic species (us) debating which other exotic species to kill with chemicals (melaleuca, Brazilian pepper, Asian citrus psyllid), which to protect (citrus, dairy cows), and which to ignore (honey bees), while every day one exotic (us) took over hundreds more acres. The thirsty city of Miami sucks up more Everglades water than all the melaleucas in existence.

And Florida has no monopoly on runaway development. "My headquarters is near Houston," Mark Brady, president of the American Honey Producers Association, told me. "Every place in Texas we used to make honey is concrete now. Bees can't do much with concrete." California, with its unique mix of wildflowers, including some extraordinary honey plants like sage, was once a beekeeping paradise, but now many of its wildlands have succumbed to development, climate change, or forest fires. A drought-stricken tinder box from June until November, California has become one of the more challenging bee habitats. The Midwest, with its barren corn desert, is even worse.

Yet if you asked Bill Rhodes or Mark Brady to list the biggest challenges they face, development wouldn't even make the top three. CCD wouldn't necessarily be number one, either. That honor would go to China and its deluge of honey—real and otherwise.

I rode with Rhodes and his crew to Groeb Farms, the largest industrial honey packer in the country and one of the largest in the world. We were there to pick up a few hundred empty metal drums Rhodes owned, but while there I got to see the Great Wall of Honey—perhaps a thousand bright-green, 650-pound drums of Chinese honey, stacked fifteen feet high. Another twenty-foot-high wall held giant plastic vats of corn syrup. Groeb Farms packs 250,000 pounds of honey *a day*, and it ain't coming from your local beekeeper. About 70 percent of the honey consumed in the United States is imported, with China the top source.

As in so many other product areas, China dwarfs the rest of the world in honey production. And Chinese honey producers sell cheap. So cheap, in fact, that the United States levied tariffs against Chinese honey in 2002, following a lawsuit by U.S. honey producers. At that time, the price of honey was around fifty cents a pound—unchanged from 1979. Since the cost to produce honey in the United States is somewhere around a dollar a pound, American beekeepers were going under fast. The tariffs were a way to level the playing field.

But shippers quickly mastered the "honey laundering" game. Overnight, new companies in other Asian nations, where the tariffs don't apply, began approaching honey packers, offering mountains of honey for sale at bargain-basement prices. On the international records, you can see months where Chinese exports plummeted and exports from places like Malaysia, Thailand, and Vietnam, which had never had significant honey industries, went sky-high. The original source of the honey was undeterminable. Some Chinese honey was shipped to Canada, then sold into the United States as Canadian honey. If you look at the official records, China supplies just 27 percent or so of U.S. honey imports. Many people believe the true number is closer to 80 percent.

U.S. Customs quickly caught on to this game and seized some of the shipments from these third-party countries. As part of the routine, the honey was tested. Another surprise: It was contaminated with the antibiotic chloramphenicol. A powerful drug used to treat anthrax and other severe infections, chloramphenicol is banned for agricultural use in the United States, Canada, and Europe to prevent bacteria from developing resistance to it. It also can cause deadly aplastic anemia—bone marrow failure—in people. Enter the U.S. Food and Drug Administration. Between August 2002 and February 2003, FDA agents seized massive amounts of chloramphenicol-contaminated Chinese honey from several importers in Louisiana and Texas. A temporary ban was imposed on Chinese honey.

A February 2003 raid is particularly distressing. Back on August 19, 2002, the FDA had informed the packer that its honey might be contaminated with antibiotics. But the packer continued to sell the honey, including 155,000 pounds to Sara Lee, which put that honey into five hundred thousand loaves of bread that were sold to consumers before Sara Lee finally stopped using the honey ten days later. On September 18, 2002, the FDA informed the packer that its honey was indeed contaminated with antibiotics. Why it then took the FDA five months to seize the honey, and how much was used in the meantime, is unclear.

Following the ban on Chinese honey and the FDA seizures, the wholesale price of honey spiked to 88¢ a pound and kept rising, briefly hitting $1.50 a pound. American honey producers were ecstatic—they could actually make a living again. Honey packers were not so thrilled. The biggest buyers of honey are major industrial players like Sara Lee, and they were not about to triple the price they were paying for honey. The packers were caught in the middle.

But not for long. The ban on Chinese honey was lifted after China outlawed the use of chloramphenicol in its agricultural products. Meanwhile, Chinese companies found a loophole in the tariffs law. A provision in the law allowed new companies, which had no record of price dumping, to post a bond instead of paying their tariffs when they shipped their honey. The U.S.

Commerce Department would then take a year or more to assess the price situation and determine appropriate duties. So the Chinese companies posted bonds to cover their tariffs and shipped honey at the same rock-bottom prices. When the time came for the United States to collect, the companies had mysteriously disappeared or gone out of business. But there was always a new start-up ready to ship its ample honey supplies into the United States and post more bonds. So far, fourteen million dollars in honey duties has been collected, while another sixty-four million dollars remains unpaid. And the price of honey has plunged back to its previous levels.

Stung once by soaring prices, the honey packers, the middlemen, resolved that they would never again be caught short. Honey, you'll recall, can stay good for decades. So now we have walls of Chinese honey in Florida and warehouse after warehouse of clover honey in the Dakotas, ensuring that whatever happens on the world market, industrial honey in the United States will remain cheap.[6]

You might not want to eat it, however. As I write this, I have on my desk a lab report from ADPEN Laboratories, a leading food safety lab in Jacksonville, Florida. In January 2006, ADPEN analyzed a random sample of Chinese honey, taken from a Florida honey packer, and found 48 parts per billion ciprofloxacin in it. Yes, Cipro, the last-defense, über-antibiotic used to treat the anthrax attacks in 2001. Applica, the top German food safety lab, has found

6. In 2008, beekeepers again managed to close the loopholes on Chinese honey. That, coupled with the collapse of the Argentine beekeeping industry due to both drought and Argentine farmers' switch from clover and alfalfa crops to soybeans for the ethanol market, along with yet another record-low honey crop in the United States, caused a worldwide shortage of honey. World honey prices again spiked. For how long, no one knows.

Cipro in numerous batches of Chinese honey.[7] Apparently Chinese beekeepers are tossing it into their hives to deal with the raging bacterial chaos simmering in a country with rampant pollution, spotty sewage treatment, and few agricultural standards.

And not just their hives. Cipro is one of a class of antibiotics known as fluoroquinolones, which made the news in 2005 when they were found in Vietnamese catfish in supermarkets throughout the Southeast. Then, in 2007, fluoroquinolones and other antibiotics, some linked to cancer, were found in catfish, shrimp, and other farmed seafood from China. A full 15 percent of the samples tested (and the FDA tests only one of every twenty shipments) was positive for antibiotics, leading to a complete (though, again, temporary) ban on Chinese seafood by the FDA.

When it comes to food supplies, the United States has zero tolerance for fluoroquinolones, our best remaining antibiotics, because of the danger of resistance. That's no distant threat, either. Antibiotic-resistant strains of *Staphylococcus aureus* ("staph" infections) are spreading rapidly, killing at least twenty thousand people a year more than AIDS. These killer strains used to turn up only in hospitals, which was bad enough, but recently new strains have been tearing through the general population. Because they can't be treated with antibiotics, they are often fatal.

Where did these new bugs come from? As Michael Pollan reported in the *New York Times Magazine*, experts believe they evolved on factory farms, where cattle, pigs, or chickens are housed in concentration-camp environments and dosed with antibiotics to combat the inevitable germs. Most of the germs die, but the survivors, which have the drug-resistant genes, then get to

7. The honey was rejected by the European Union, so it made its way to the United States, where inspection standards are less stringent.

breed a race of überbugs. That's happening right now. Sixty percent of the pig farms in the Netherlands have drug-resistant staph. Twenty percent of the pig *farmers* in Ontario are infected with it.[8]

No data exists for the state of drug-resistant bacteria on Chinese farms, but the numbers must be terrifying. The scale of both China's aquaculture industry and its water pollution is hard to fathom. There are 4.5 million fish farmers in China, many working in waters that are designated unsafe for human contact. Heavy metals, mercury, flame retardants, sewage, and pesticides like DDT turn up regularly in Chinese waters. To keep their fish alive in these toxic, overcrowded conditions, they need to steadily dose them with antibiotics and other chemicals—chemicals which then wash downstream. The Chinese claim this is changing. "Before 2005, we did use drugs blindly," said one aquaculture association's chairman in the *New York Times*. "They were very effective in fighting disease. But now we don't dare because of the regulations."

The presence of the same antibiotics in Chinese honey must mean Chinese beekeepers are treating diseases caused by the same problems—overcrowding and pollution. The *Los Angeles Times* published a particularly chilling report in 2007 on the state of the Chinese honey industry. It profiled a beekeeper in rural Shaanxi province who bought vials of penicillin for ten cents a piece at his local drugstore and treated his bees with it. The bees were sick, he believed, from drinking water contaminated with runoff from a nearby chemical plant. An estimated 70 percent of Chi-

---

8. Doctors desperate for a weapon to fight antibiotic-resistant staph have turned to an ancient remedy showing amazing clinical promise and now recognized as one of the premier antimicrobial substances on the planet. It's honey, and I'll tell you all about it in Appendix 4.

nese beekeepers use antibiotics. One entrepreneur leased a nature reserve of acacia trees from the Chinese government and recruited forty-five beekeepers who agreed to make honey in the reserve without antibiotics and without metal storage containers, which can contaminate honey with iron and lead. For his troubles, he was ambushed by fifteen other local beekeepers who didn't like the competition, beaten, and left with a concussion.

Most Chinese beekeepers are probably perfectly upstanding. (To be fair, most American beekeepers use antibiotics, too, just not illegal ones.) And China has some extraordinary floral resources, such as an acacia forest twenty-five miles long and five miles wide producing vast quantities of fragrant, light honey that is as slow to crystallize as tupelo. Still, I wouldn't put any Chinese seafood in my mouth, and I'd ask a lot of questions before I'd put any Chinese honey in there.[9] In general, I try to buy honey straight out of the hand of a beekeeper, which is now possible at farmer's markets and roadside stands across the country. Honey shouldn't have to arrive by container ship.

Of course, on an ingredients label for honey-mustard dressing or honey-baked ham, you have no way of knowing who made the honey. Thanks to the international shell games, neither do the food manufacturers. It sure as hell isn't from sacred acacia forests. But here's where things get weird, because it may not even be honey.

Honey is expensive to produce, while corn syrup is cheaper than dirt. (Nutritionally, you get what you pay for.) Honey producers in the 1970s got rich cutting honey with corn syrup—honey cost fifty-six cents a pound while corn syrup cost six cents a pound—but methods for detecting it soon developed. Then the adulterators got better. In 1998 major honey buyers in North

9. What's more, I try to keep Chinese toys out of everybody's mouth.

America received a fax from a company in India offering to supply "honey analog" by the ton. This analog, made from corn or rice syrup, was "enzymatically processed" to resemble honey, physically and chemically. The company assured buyers that the syrup would pass any test for natural honey and could be used to cut their real honey. Such "honey analogs" are what U.S., Canadian, and European beekeepers are up against. And they're what we may be eating in our honey-roasted peanuts. A new copy of an international food product buyer's guide lists eight suppliers of honey and fourteen suppliers of "honey replacers."

Sometimes the fraud is chemical, as when rice syrup is doctored to resemble honey, and sometimes it's ontological. For instance, what is honey? If you answered something like "a syrup made entirely out of nectar by bees," then consider yourself hopelessly out-of-date. Let me introduce you to "Packer's Blend," the latest offering from China. It appeared on the market in 2006, shortly after the bond-posting loophole was closed by Congress. Chinese *honey* may be subject to tariffs, but if a product is less than 50 percent honey, it isn't covered by the law. This "funny honey," as beekeepers call it, is between 40 and 49 percent honey. The rest is syrup: corn syrup, but also rice syrup, lactose syrup—whatever's on hand and cheap. The importers who bring in these blends may sell them to manufacturers as blends or as pure honey, adding some nice American or Canadian clover honey to give the blend a semblance of the real thing and get it past the manufacturers.

Packer's Blend sells for forty cents a pound and may be in more foods than any of us realize. You won't see "Packer's Blend" on an ingredients label. You may see "rice syrup" and "honey," listed separately, or you may just see "honey." Do food manufacturers understand what they're getting when they buy Packer's Blend? Are they being told it's honey? Do they know they're using Chinese honey that may be contaminated?

We can't say for sure. But what we can say is that American beekeepers can't compete, no matter what their economies of scale. Not too long ago the Horace Bell Honey Company in Deland, Florida, about twenty miles from Rhodes's apiary, was the largest in the United States. Bell, who started the company with his wife, Luella, in 1964, had forty thousand hives, employed a staff of fifty, and made a million pounds of honey a year. But faced with forty-cent honey from China and Argentina in 2000, he sold all his bees and said good-bye to his staff. It wasn't just honey prices, Luella told me. It was also the arrival of varroa mites and the rising use of agricultural pesticides. They didn't like having to treat the bees with miticides and antibiotics, didn't like the risk of pesticides getting in the honey. So they got out of the business.

Today, wandering the remains of the Horace Bell Honey Company is spooky. Two giant warehouses, one fifteen thousand square feet, the other half that, sit virtually empty. Grass pushes through the cracked pavement around the warehouses. The sign advertising honey for sale is still up, and if you make enough noise, someone will come and sell you one of the remaining bottles of darkening honey from years ago. But the sound of hammering echoes from one corner of the big warehouse, where a handful of day laborers are building new hives. A ten-acre field nearby is newly plowed and lined with hives topped with jars of corn syrup. After thirty-six years of keeping bees, Bell couldn't keep away. And he's again seen the writing on the wall. The honey industry in the United States and Canada is as good as dead. Bell's no romantic, and he has no intention of making honey with these bees. No, he's feeding them hard on the syrup, building them up through the warm fall, and offering them for sale in *American Bee Journal.* Many will become kamikazes on a one-way mission, heading west to the last place in America that has lots of money to throw at bees—and is desperate enough to do it.

Chapter 7

THE ALMOND ORGY

EVERY FEBRUARY, A three-hundred-mile-long slice of central California turns snow-white. Although the season seems right, it isn't snow. Not here in the Central Valley, where daytime temperatures are already pushing into the 60s. The whiteness is almond petals. You can drive for hours and that is what you see quilting the hillsides and valley floors in neat stripes, twelve hundred square miles in all, a massive mono-forest. Practically the only species living in this artificial landscape are the almond trees, the grass that runs in perfect strips between each row, the humans who tend the groves, and for a few weeks each year, the bees that service the almonds in a half-million-acre orgy of buzzing tree sex.

California almonds are big business. I associate almonds with Spain, with bar snacks and glasses of sherry in tapas bars, and Spain is indeed the second-largest producer of almonds, with a whopping 5 percent of the world market. California has 82 percent of the market. It *is* the world almond industry.

A perfect storm of factors helped make this so. It all starts with the almond tree itself. Almonds are closely related to peaches; their common ancestor evolved in central Asia, with the peach moving east into China and adapting to the humid lowlands and the almond moving west and adapting to the dry hills. The two trees have a similar appearance: maybe twenty feet high, with a basic trunk opening into four or five main stems. Almond flowers resemble peach flowers, but instead of a fleshy fruit and inedible seed, almonds grow a leathery hull surrounding an edible pit.

The tree is native to central Asia and was first cultivated more than six thousand years ago in the Levant, the crescent of land along the eastern Mediterranean, from Turkey through Jordan, Syria, Israel, and out to Iraq and Iran. King Tut had almonds in his tomb, and they are mentioned throughout the Bible. Almond trees are quite finicky when it comes to climate and will thrive only in Near East conditions: hot and dry summers, cool and moist winters. They flower very early, around Valentine's Day, but any freezes after that can kill the growing fruit. These exacting requirements mean few places on earth can successfully grow almonds: Spain, Greece, Turkey, Iran, some small parts of China. In the United States, California's Sacramento and San Joaquin valleys are the only candidates. As early as the 1840s, people tried to grow almonds in the Southeast and even New England, but spring frosts and humid summers scuttled those attempts.

Yet a perfect climate alone won't grow almonds. Insects must pollinate the flowers—*a lot* of the flowers. With peaches or apples, which require thinning to yield large, attractive fruits, only a 10 percent set is necessary to make a full crop. But with almonds we eat the pits. Crowding isn't an issue, and smaller nuts are actually preferred by consumers. Nearly 100 percent pollination is necessary to ensure a bumper crop of small, uniform nuts. That requires a lot of pollinators in the almond orchard.

But not many insects are out and about in Sacramento in February. Maybe there were more back in the original forests of the Levant. In the pesticidal wasteland of Big Agriculture, however, with every acre in production and nary a weed for miles, there are few beneficial wild insects at any time of year. It's up to the honey bee, and has been for a long time. The standard reference on the subject, *Insect Pollination of Cultivated Crop Plants,* written in 1970, says, "The honey bee is practically the only pollinating insect of economic importance on almonds, and growers throughout the world have been urged to use it. The importance of a heavy honey bee population cannot be overemphasized."

It gets harder still. Almonds, like many fruit and nut crops, are self-incompatible. The pollen from one flower won't set fruit on another flower on that tree, or even on any other tree that shares the same genes. Nature avoids incest. Members of any particular variety of fruit tree, however, are grafted clones. To make each almond, an insect must take pollen from one almond flower to another almond flower of a different variety. This means almond growers need to grow at least two varieties of trees. Traditionally growers planted three rows of Nonpareil, their almond of choice, followed by one row of a variety that could cross-pollinate Nonpareil.

Now, once again, think like a bee. You shoot out of the hive in late morning, as soon as the sun has taken the chill off, and zoom over to the nearest blooming almond tree. You visit the first flower you see, pushing the sticky anthers out of the way and sucking up nectar. It takes the nectar of multiple flowers to fill up your honey sac, so where do you look for your next target? The flower right next to you, or the one across the orchard that happens to be a different variety? Right, save time and energy and head next door. Ideally, fill up entirely from this one tree and then head straight back to the hive to unload.

What does it take to make a bee visit more than one tree on the same foraging flight? Well, if she can't find enough nectar or pollen on one tree (because her sisters have already emptied the flowers), or if every flower is already stuffed with suitors, she'll be forced to look elsewhere. This means that in addition to growing more than one variety of almond, growers need to saturate their orchards with bees. Intense competition for every flower pushes bees to visit numerous trees and hopefully mix varieties. Cross-pollination of every single flower on every single tree demands supersaturation.[1]

The catch is the early bloom. Honey bees are union workers, grounded during cold or rain. The almond industry actually keeps track of "bee hours": the time during each year's almond bloom that the temperature is over 55 degrees Fahrenheit, winds are under 15 miles per hour, and there is no rain. (Bee hours have ranged from a dismal ninety-two in 2004 to two hundred in sunny 2002.) Worse, almond blooms are only maximally fertile on the day they open. Within three days or so, they're done. It can be 75 degrees in the Central Valley in February, but it can also be a bleak 50. So almond growers need enough shock and awe in their air force that, should the weather be lousy, intense flower bombardment can occur during whatever windows appear.

We're talking a lot of bees. The going rule is 2 hives per acre; 2.3 is considered ideal. The experts say 1 hive per acre is enough under normal conditions, but most growers prefer the insurance

1. If you're wondering how almond trees ever got by before mankind figured this out, remember that, in their homeland, wild almonds didn't evolve to grow in great stands of clones. There was plenty of genetic diversity in the forest. They also didn't need to produce banner crops of almonds every year; a few new seedlings was enough. Only in the weirdness of hyperproductive clonal forests do you need weird pollination strategies.

of 2-plus. By the time you read this, there may be seven hundred thousand acres of almond trees on line. That means, yes, around 1.5 million full-strength hives. Which is just about every remaining functional hive in the country. Come January, pretty much any beekeeper who wants to can rent his hives to an almond grower.

Yet why would he? With the crowds and competition, finding nectar in an almond grove by late February is like trying to find a Furby doll in Manhattan on Christmas Eve. By the time a bee locates a flower that still has nectar in stock, she's flown her little wings off.

It's also not in a beehive's nature to be at full strength in February. The European honey bee would normally spend December and January in semi-hibernation, shivering in a cluster, not making much brood, and waiting for the spring bloom. To have a full, eight-frame hive of bees by the beginning of February, beekeepers need to trick their bees into believing that spring has come in December and that food is abundant. They need to park the bees somewhere relatively warm for November, December, and January, and feed, feed, feed. Only then will the queens start laying so that a full phalanx of foragers will be ready for the February almonds. This "feedlot beekeeping" can be done—and is, more and more—but it's a significant expense for the beekeeper and a risk for the bees.

There are other disincentives for beekeepers: the soaring price of diesel, the threat of theft. Most professional beekeepers experience occasional theft or vandalism of their hives. Sometimes it's kids on a dare, but as hive rental fees soar, so does theft by other pros using forklifts and trucks. Sitting unguarded in vast almond groves, hives are easy pickings. Some beekeepers have taken to branding their hives like cattle or even installing traceable microchips in them. But the thieves simply dump the bees into their own hives and abandon the stolen equipment. During 2007 and 2008, California beekeepers suffered at least $330,000 in losses.

Then there's the "brothel effect": With so many of the country's bees visiting the same flowers during this three-week orgy, it's easy to pick up whatever hot new disease or parasite is making its way through the population. The prospect of weak, starving, sickly hives straggling out of the almonds in March means that almond growers have to make the deal very, very sweet for beekeepers: cash—more cash than a beekeeper can imagine earning any other way.

So why bother? If it's so tricky and expensive to make a good almond crop, why not grow something more flexible? Answer: "Because there's gold in them-thar ammens!"[2]

Almonds are the greatest agricultural success story of the new millennium. You may have heard about the California wine industry? Well, almond exports, at more than a billion dollars a year, are twice as big as wine exports. Almonds are the most financially successful crop in all California. They were just another nut for much of the twentieth century, until some recent events conspired to turn them into a California gold mine.

A lot of that success has to do with pollination. The almond guys have always known that bees and cross-pollination were necessary, but lately they've realized just how much—and that if they have enough bees, they can plant their trees closer together and get much higher yields per acre. Growers noticed that in the traditional 3:1 layout of interspersed varieties, the middle row of the three, which wasn't adjacent to a "pollinating" variety, had

2. In almond country, they pronounce the word so it rhymes with "jammin'."

lower nut yields. So they switched to a 2:1 layout. They also brought in more bees; at $10 per hive in the 1970s, it was cheap fertility. Yields more than doubled. But even with a 2:1 layout, the side of trees facing their own variety yielded 30 percent less than the side facing the pollinating variety. So farmers switched to a 1:1 ratio. Yields exploded again. In the 1960s, growers hoped for 1,000 pounds per acre. By 2002, they were averaging over 2,000 pounds per acre. Today, many of the newer varieties and dense layouts yield 3,000 pounds per acre.

Marketing fueled the rest of the almond boom. The Almond Board promoted almonds as the new health food, capitalizing on studies showing that their vitamin E and antioxidant contents could help prevent cancer and heart disease. World almond consumption went through the roof, from 600 million pounds in 1995 to more than 1.6 billion pounds today.

Even the stupendous yields of recent years couldn't keep up with this kind of demand. Prices skyrocketed: $1 per pound in 2001, $1.50 in 2002, $2 in 2003. In 2005, hailstorms caused the crop to fall 150 million pounds short of predictions. Brief insanity followed, with prices reaching $3 and then $4 per pound and almond buyers panicking. Since then, each year has produced a record crop and prices have stabilized around $2 per pound.

Put all these numbers together and you get what's being called the "almond rush": from 400,000 bearing acres in the 1990s, to 500,000 in 2000, 550,000 in 2005, then 670,000 in 2008.[3] A

3. For comparison, Maine's wild blueberry fields, one of the other top pollination crops, cover just 60,000 acres. In 2007 they produced 77 million pounds of blueberries that sold for 94 cents per pound (up from 65 cents in 2005—a jump partially due to increased hive rental fees). At $72 million, the crop is worth just 3 percent of the almond crop.

grower getting yields of 1,000 pounds per acre and prices of $1 per pound a decade ago, for a total earnings of $1,000 per acre, might suddenly be making 3,000 pounds per acre in 2005 with his new plantings and selling them for $3 per pound, for a total of $9,000 per acre.

Now everyone in the Central Valley wants to grow almonds. Cotton is the other big crop in the Central Valley, but cotton prices have been in the cellar for years. By 2008, in fact, cotton farmers could make more money selling their "water rights" to water-desperate almond growers than they could by raising cotton. Others tore out their cotton and planted almonds during the rush. And all those orchards are starting to bear fruit.

Without bees, however, those trees are worthless. With only perhaps 350,000 colonies left in California and demand pushing 1.5 million, beekeepers are in a major seller's market. Those $10 hive rentals of the 1970s are long gone. Each recent year has seen stomach-dropping increases. Almond growers paid $50 per hive in 2004, $70 to $90 in 2005, $120 in 2006, then $150 and up in the CCD frenzy of 2007. Contracts between beekeepers and almond growers in 2008 started at $160 to $180 per hive, with some last-minute contracts paying $200 per hive.

It's eerie how almonds' rise of the past ten years has paralleled honey bees' fall. It's miraculous; had almond growers not suddenly had lots of money to pay beekeepers, at exactly the time they did, the U.S. beekeeping industry would already be a corpse. The almond cash infusion has been life support—and not just for beekeepers. As the pollination broker Joe Traynor has pointed out, by being willing to pay so much for hive rentals, the almond industry is indirectly subsidizing all the other agricultural enterprises that need honey bees but can't afford to pay full costs—apples, blueberries, cranberries, watermelons, pumpkins, and all the rest. The almond industry also donates quite a bit of money to pollination research—more than the beekeeping industry does.

Yet there is also tension between the industries. As hive rental prices spiraled upward and more beekeepers, having lost all other ways to turn a profit, scrambled to get in on the game, some people took advantage. Almond growers were paying by the hive, right? Well, there are hives, and then there are hives. If you weren't into bees, you might not appreciate—from the outside—the difference between a hive with eight full frames of eager bees and a half-dead hive with a few frames of sickly ones. But you'd sure appreciate it when your nut set was poor.

After a few years of unscrupulous beekeepers carting their deadouts into almond groves and cashing checks for it, some growers got wise to hive strength and began inspecting hives before accepting them. Many prefer to find bees through a broker like Joe Traynor, who guarantees eight frames of bees per hive. A lot of hives are rejected, adding to the misery of beekeepers who spent good money trucking their hives to California and then have to decide what to do with the half-dead colonies stuck on somebody else's land.

Most experts believe the problem of rejected hives is going to get much worse. Ryan Cosyns, a California beekeeper and pollination broker who lost 50 percent of his hives to CCD, says, "In the past two years, I'm not sure the beekeeping industry really has covered the need. There were plenty of boxes, but what was in those boxes? You'd have a major catastrophe if a lot of those hives got inspected." Perfect weather during the bloom in 2008 allowed weak hives to squeak by, but sooner or later a rainy spring and weak hives will combine to ruin an almond crop.

A few beekeepers may be knowingly using subpar hives, but

many more, like Bill Rhodes in 2005, probably had full-strength hives when last checked, but either en route or while waiting in holding yards in California, colony collapse set in. Others had colonies that seemed to be doing well when they were idling, but the stress of almond pollination caused them to collapse in the first week of bloom. The risks of rejection and of running their bees to death are two more variables beekeepers have to figure into their calculations.

At first, you'd think the beekeepers have the upper hand in these negotiations. The almond growers *must have* bees. No bees, no almonds. And they have the cash to pay for them. So far their wallets have proved pretty elastic. They pay $180 per hive and still make a profit. But those prices may have gone about as far north as they possibly can. With a hundred thousand extra acres coming on line, and each year's yield busting the previous year's record, prices should stay low, barring some weather catastrophe.[4] Future competition from Australia and China, which has shanghaied 100,000 Uyghur peasants into a massive almond-planting offensive, may add to the challenge.

Not long ago, hive rentals accounted for about 8 percent of an almond grower's production costs. Now that number is around 20 percent. It costs around $2,000 to grow an acre of almonds, and every line item in that budget—fuel, irrigation, labor, equipment, pollination—is rising sharply. Growers need to cut costs, and hive rentals are target number one.

As much as almonds must have bees, beekeepers need almonds. When the annual cost of maintaining a hive is around $100—if nothing goes wrong—and a hive can produce perhaps

4. A "storm of the century" in the Sacramento Valley in January 2008 wiped out thousands of acres of almonds.

$50 to $80 worth of honey, a $160 check from an almond grower is the difference between a business and a money sink. The almond industry is the only thing keeping beekeepers west of the Mississippi in business. If it goes, they go. Joe Traynor jokes that the American Beekeeping Federation should change its name to the "Almond Pollination Association."

Eric Olson is a good example. He runs one of the largest apiaries in Washington state, based in Yakima. "Last year our bees were fantastic," he says. "I heard about all the problems everyone was having and I assumed it was PPB"—piss-poor beekeeping. "This year we're not doing so good and suddenly PPB has a whole different look." Olson had thirteen thousand colonies over the summer of 2007, but was down to nine thousand by almond-pollination season in 2008. "If the almond price was eighty dollars per hive, I wouldn't be here."

Even on the East Coast, more beekeepers are following Horace Bell's path: starting to think of beehives as disposable almond pollination boxes. Some older beekeepers, tired of the struggle, just want to send their bees to the almonds, cash one last check, and be done with it.

More almond trees, fewer bees. These two trends grind together like the tectonic plates under California. The next few years will torque that pressure to intense levels. Total bearing acreage will be 670,000 in 2008, 720,000 in 2009, and 760,000 in 2010.

Who the hell is going to pollinate all those blossoms? There won't be enough American bees. Canadian beekeepers are leery of mixing with the Americans, preferring to stay in places like Alberta, where the clover is endless and exotic pathogens are scarce.[5]

---

5. Hives in Alberta and Saskatchewan have been known to make four hundred pounds of honey during the four-week bloom.

Those package bees from Australia, the ones that may or may not be spreading IAPV, are shouldering more of the load. Perhaps one hundred thousand packages will be imported this year, each holding thousands of famished bees. The timing is nice. Since Australia's summer is our winter, bees coming from Australia in January have been feasting on nectar flows Down Under and are bursting with vitality. Yet, at $115 per package, the Aussie bees are little more than a stopgap. The trip by 747 to San Francisco takes something out of them, and they need a home when they arrive. A lot of the foragers are old at that point. Tests of the pollinating power of a four-pound package of Australian bees versus an over-wintered, full-strength American colony found that the package bees had only half the pollinating strength. They're good insurance to bolster weak hives, but can't do the job alone.

The economics of migratory pollination just may have reached their limit. Whether falling almond prices or peak oil finishes off the system hardly matters. What does matter is that California can no longer support the pollinators it needs. The state has gone from a bee heaven to a place where bees are lucky if they get out alive after their three-week tour of duty.

Twenty years ago, before the coming of CCD or even varroa, Andy Nachbaur, a well-known beekeeper in California, was already warning beekeepers about their dangerous path:

> Almond pollen by itself is not a good food for bees . . . Bees require a balanced diet and to get this almost always require more than one kind of pollen. In pollinating almonds (and other crops), so many bees are concentrated in a relatively small area that many hives will not have a chance to collect pollen from more than the orchard or orchard floor. And leave no doubt that bee viruses have a better opportunity to spread

from hive to hive when near a million hives are concentrated in a limited area for almond pollination.

Nachbaur had watched many of his own hives collapse and had come up with his own terms for the syndrome: stress accelerated decline (SAD) and bee autoimmune deficiency (BAD). He liked the acronyms, he said, because that was how it made him feel when his bees died. "SAD or BAD bees do show symptoms prior to their collapse. These hives appear to be strong productive hives after a honey flow or extended broodrearing period. In the fall or early winter . . . they can change in a very short time, leaving boxes full of honey and empty of bees." The fact that they are most vulnerable after a honey flow or broodrearing period may seem counterintuitive at first, but not if you've ever raised a large family or worked overtime for months on end.

Nachbaur was bewildered by the state of the industry and predicted a dire future:

> I started keeping bees as an apprentice beekeeper [in 1954] to a generation of beekeepers now past. Their average production per hive was three times today's average. A family could make a good middle class living from five hundred hives including a new car every three years or so and college educations for the kids. Annual losses of bees in excess of ten per cent was above normal and indicated a poor beekeeper. The normal replacement of bees today in California is thirty percent approaching fifty . . . It is my opinion based on thirty-five years of observations and lots of library research that this dramatic loss of bees will continue, and at times we may even have more frequent episodes of epic, unexplained losses of bees.

He hit that one on the head. And though he may have chosen his term "stress accelerated decline" for the acronym, it just happens to capture what most experts have come to believe as they watch honey bees fail. Maybe we've pushed the bees too hard, and they just can't take it anymore?

Chapter 8

BEES ON THE VERGE OF A NERVOUS BREAKDOWN

TODAY'S HONEY BEES face pressures their ancestors never saw. The rogue's gallery includes varroa and tracheal mites, small hive beetles, Africanized "killer" bees, American foulbrood bacteria, fungi, and viruses of all kinds. Then there are pesticides, antibiotics, malnutrition, urbanization, globalization, and global warming. Jerry Hayes, Florida's soft-spoken state apiarist, put it best: "I'm surprised honey bees are alive at all."

When the CCD Working Group did its genetic survey of honey bees, it discovered a lot more than just Israeli acute paralysis virus. As Edward Holmes, the virologist in the group, explained it, "We found a remarkably high viral burden in bee populations, both those that have CCD and those that don't have CCD . . . One is strongly associated with CCD, but the bigger question is how these viruses interact in the population. That we really don't know." Even the bees that weren't exhibiting CCD symptoms were rife with viruses—sacbrood virus, deformed wing virus, black queen cell virus, Kashmir bee virus, and more. Something is deeply wrong in the bee universe. When one virus shows up in a dying population, the virus is probably responsible.

When fourteen show up, it's a case of immune collapse. And the classic cause of immune deficiency is chronic stress.

What causes stress in bees? Pretty much the same things that cause stress in people.

Picture an ideal workday. You wake up from a deep night's sleep and eat a healthy breakfast that provides plenty of good muscle food as well as brain food, so you operate at peak efficiency. All day you work in a comfortable environment with few distractions and an optimal temperature so you don't have to waste energy shivering or sweating to maintain your temperature. Your exposure to toxins is minimal. The support of your friends and family is strong. You remain alert and relaxed throughout the day, and you are incredibly productive.

Now, picture a different scenario. You stagger off a coast-to-coast red-eye flight and chug a Pepsi for breakfast to revive. You hop in your rental car and head for your business meeting, but wouldn't you know it, the GPS is malfunctioning in the car and you get lost. You show up for the meeting late, edgy, and shaking. You have to excuse yourself to hit the bathroom because you've got a stomach bug and the antibiotics just aren't helping. Not to mention the fleas that seem to be leaping from the carpet into your socks. Halfway through the meeting a pest-control guy steps in and sprays the room with a white fog that makes you retch. You are useless throughout the meeting and don't make the sale you'd hoped to make. But you can't dwell on that because you have to head directly to another meeting. In fact, you have meetings all day, until late at night, and then you have to hop another red-eye home. No time to sit down and eat, so you wolf down a box of doughnuts as you drive.

You're in bad shape. Not only are you constantly irritable because of the impossible schedule, but lack of sleep, a sugary diet, and chemical contamination are taxing your immune system. You'll probably get more illnesses, and your work performance will continue to suffer. When you finally make it home to your mate, you won't be terribly interested in romance, because you've got too much on your mind—such as the fact that your kids seem to have some sort of learning disabilities.

We all have limited energy reserves, and anything that saps those reserves counts as a stressor. Fighting illness, uncomfortable travel, detoxifying dangerous chemicals, worrying about threats, or just forcing yourself through a day when you're sleep- and food-deprived all take extra energy that would otherwise be channeled into long-term health projects like the immune system, reproductive system, and the body's ability to repair cellular damage.

A honey bee is designed to lead a life of slow, controlled progression from brood to house bee to forager. Viruses and other pathogens have accompanied honey bees throughout their two-million-year history, but they normally play a quiet, background role. A bumper crop of flowers can't be counted on every year, but there are usually enough varieties out there, and enough food stores in the hive, that something has always been available. Life should be slow, predictable, and low-stress.

Unfortunately, in 2008, most honey bees aren't leading that kind of life. Trucked to new sites every few weeks, jacked up on high-fructose corn syrup, dosed with pesticides and antibiotics, invaded by parasites, and exposed to exotic pathogens, they are worn thinner and thinner. Like us, honey bees could shrug off one or two of these stressors—a mite here, a bad eating day there—and perform normally, but the combined effect of all these stressors, the steady drum beat day after day, takes its toll: suppressed immune systems, inhibited reproduction, shortened life expectancy, failure to thrive.[1] Eventually it takes just one more push to send them off the edge of a cliff.

Technology has done a lot of the pushing. The massive migrations, the Faustian bargain with Apistan and CheckMite, the steady shelling of far-flung diseases and parasites. As the honey bee geneticist Tom Rinderer puts it, "What has happened to our bees? Jet planes have happened."

No species is built for the light-speed diaspora of life-forms spurred by fossil fuel, but honey bees have fared worse than most. When the honey bee genome was decoded in 2006, we learned that honey bees have only half as many genes devoted to detoxification and immunity as do most insects. They don't deal well with new invaders. But that's exactly what they've had: varroa mites, tracheal mites, nosema, IAPV. Citrus greening came from China and turned one of honey bees' favorite types of forage into a killing field of aldicarb. The small hive beetle, which is attracted to the honey bee alarm pheromone, stowed away on a shipment of African fruit and arrived in 1997 in Florida, where it quickly decimated twenty thousand hives, eating its way through honey, eggs, and comb. Africanized bees were shipped from Africa to Brazil in the 1950s. They wrecked the South and Central American beekeeping industry and headed north, arriving in Texas in 1990.

1. A stress anecdote: A New York state beekeeper overwintered his apiary in four buildings to keep the hives warmer. One of the buildings also had a sawmill going all winter: the kind of off-on screech that stands your hair on end. In the spring, the hives in the sawmill building had died, while the hives in the other three buildings were fine.

No one knows when the next uninvited guest will drop in on the European honey bee. All we know is that more gate-crashers will come, and the honey bee will face another challenge. Place your bets: The conopid fly, a parasite whose larvae are currently eating honey bees from the inside out in Borneo? The Asian hornet, a China native that arrived in France in 2004—after stowing away in a shipment of Chinese pottery—and likes to dismember bees and feed them to its young? Or something we can't even anticipate?

There had been real hope among beekeepers, fruit growers, and the general public that CCD would be a one-year blip, like some of the dwindling diseases of years ago. That hope was gone by 2008. Dave Hackenberg's irradiated hives, which had looked so good while feasting on clover in the Dakotas over the summer, began going downhill around Thanksgiving 2007. They were the best remaining bees he had, but by January, 80 percent were dead.

The word was no better from Florida. "You know those bees that I was hoping were gonna make it?" Bill Rhodes asked me. "Well, they ain't gonna make it."

South Dakota's Adee Honey Farms, the largest beekeeping operation in the United States, sent seventy thousand hives into the almonds in 2008. They lost twenty-eight thousand, a full 40 percent. "It's off the charts this year," said Brett Adee. "It's not a sustainable thing, what's happening now."

Jerry Bromenshenk summed up the situation in early 2008. "In the last two months we've sampled operations in Arizona, Idaho, eastern Washington, Minnesota, North Dakota. We've got reports of it from the Dakotas, Florida, Texas, Colorado, California. It's at about the same level and same type of distribution as it was a year ago at this time. I'd like to say it went away, but unfortunately I don't think it has."

Suburbia Disease

By 2008, the research community had virtually given up on finding one smoking gun for CCD. Most beekeepers believe imidacloprid is the main culprit, yet almost no scientists do. The evidence is too mixed. They've chased every tantalizing lead, piled up promising bits of evidence that A, B, and C are very bad for bees . . . and failed to make a slam-dunk case against anything.

Part of the problem is the interactions between potential causes, triggering all sorts of sinister synergies. Pesticides can interact with fungicides to become far more lethal. They can even exacerbate viruses. And viruses almost certainly interact with each other, though no one yet knows how. Viruses also interact with varroa mites. The mites cause immunosuppression in the bees by secreting a substance that prevents the bees from producing the enzymes and antimicrobial peptides they normally use to kill microscopic invaders.[2] Lowering the host's immune defenses can trigger a viral outbreak,[3] as can the mites themselves, which carry the virus between hosts and drill handy entry holes for it. This seems to be what happened with deformed wing virus (DWV), which has become a much greater problem since varroa appeared. One study found that DWV rapidly proliferated in bees with high mite loads that were exposed to *E. coli* bacteria, but not in bees without mites. It took the combination of all three—DWV, mites, and bacteria—to cause a rapid collapse of the colony in two weeks.

---

2. Ticks, mites' relatives, also do this, possibly to prevent an immune response at the point of feeding.
3. Herpes is a classic example.

The small hive beetle also interacts with varroa. Once the beetle infests a hive, it takes only half as many varroa mites as usual to kill the colony.

And the roundabout continues. Dumping Apistan and Check-Mite into hives kills varroa, but also weakens bees and makes them more vulnerable to everything else. But which evil do you choose, the chemicals or the mites?

Then there's antibiotics, which most commercial beekeepers feed to their bees to combat bacterial diseases like American foulbrood. The antibiotics do control foulbrood, but what else do they do to the bees?

One of the CCD researchers' most interesting and underreported discoveries was of a cadre of beneficial lactic acid bacteria (LABs) lurking in the bee digestive system. Nancy Moran, a bacteria specialist, explained the finding:

> It turns out that all bee colonies everywhere in the world have the same set of bacterial associates in their bodies, probably mainly inside their guts and intestines. These bacteria have not been found in any other environment or any other host. They don't appear to play a direct role in CCD because they were all present in CCD bees and healthy bees. Instead these bacteria probably perform essential functions in the bees. In other insects, it's known that bacteria can provide essential nutrients that the insect requires for nutrition, or that they can contribute defenses against pathogens and natural enemies. At this point we don't know what these bacteria are doing in bees, but we know they're present in all bees sampled and that they're a very distinctive set. There's about eight such bacteria, and these fall into a variety of major bacterial groups, but they're all unnamed species about which we know very little.

In 2008 the Swedish researchers Tobias Olofsson and Alejandra Vásquez discovered ten previously unknown species of LABs in bees' stomachs. All were lactobacillus and bifidus organisms, like those that inhabit our gut and keep us healthy.[4] When first checked during the summer, the bees were feeding on raspberry blossoms and had flourishing microflora. But over the winter, the bees lived on sucrose solutions. The good bacteria disappeared and the bacteria responsible for foulbrood disease proliferated. Then, when linden bloomed the following spring, the foulbrood died out and the good bacteria reappeared. Could these natural communities be a first line of defense against bee pathogens?

That's how it works in us. Harold McGee sums up the benefits of LABs in *On Food and Cooking*: "Particular strains of these bacteria variously adhere to and shield the intestinal wall, secrete antibacterial compounds, boost the body's immune response to particular disease microbes, dismantle cholesterol and cholesterol-consuming bile acids, and reduce the production of potential carcinogens." They act as freelance immune systems.

When we take antibiotics, they wipe out our LABs along with the bad guys, which is why we're told to eat yogurt to replenish the community. Natural yogurts advertise their LABs right on the label. And the bee equivalent of yogurt, as discussed in chapter 2, is bee bread, which turns out to be not just a way of making pollen digestible but also a way of fueling bees' otherwise rudimentary immune systems. But it's anyone's guess how many LABs, whether in bees or bee bread, can survive a steady diet of Tylosin or other antibiotics.

---

4. The lowly appendix, it turns out, is a bacteria garden, incubating a backup supply in case a person ever runs low.

Interestingly, Tylosin gets fed to cattle, too. I used to wonder how a cow, which is basically a huge chunk of protein, could build that body on a diet of low-protein grass. Now I know that the rumen, the first compartment of a cow's stomach, is the key. The rumen is basically a fermentation tank filled with bacteria.[5] The bacteria take all that indigestible cellulose in the grass, break it down with special enzymes, eat it, and reproduce like rabbits. Some of the bacteria then get passed to the next stomach and digested by the cow. At 60 percent protein, they are micro-steaks. In a sense, cows farm bacteria, just as we farm cows.

But when feedlot cattle are forced to eat corn, instead of grass, the environment of the rumen changes in ways that destroy the bacterial communities. The result is a host of diseases, which Tylosin treats. In *The Omnivore's Dilemma*, Michael Pollan asks a feedlot veterinarian what would happen if they stopped the antibiotics. He replies, "We'd have a high death rate and poorer performing cattle. We just couldn't feed them as hard. Hell, if you gave them lots of grass and space, I wouldn't have a job." It's more cost-effective to keep sick cattle in one place, feeding them corn and Tylosin and keeping a vet on staff, than it is to let them range and eat grass, so that's how most beef production happens.

The same goes for bees. Pasture is expensive; corn syrup is cheap—and so are the antibiotics needed to treat the diseases that occur with feedlot beekeeping. But if the drugs are also making the bees sick in unexpected ways, maybe they aren't a bargain after all.

Any way you look at it, the big-picture problem is, simply, sick bees. Bees are sick and have been getting sicker for decades. The

5. There are more bacteria in one rumen than there are humans on earth.

energy-draining stresses of illness and overwork reach a certain point, and "dwindling disease" appears.

Human beings have a powerful desire to know the cause of something; we like straightforward answers. But we are coming to understand that, when health is the issue, often the only answers that make sense are holistic ones. If CCD is a disease of industrial civilization, like cancer and diabetes, maybe the best approach is not high-tech treatments but preventative medicine. Having failed to turn up a bogeyman for CCD, the beekeeping community is starting to get practical, focusing on what can make bees stronger. In a way, that was the advice of the CCD researchers all along. "Maintain healthy colonies. Keep varroa levels low. Keep nosema levels low. Supply supplemental nutrition when need be."

Much as vegans combine corn and beans to make complementary proteins, honey bees require an assortment of pollens to create the complete proteins necessary for complex life processes like making babies, brains, and immune systems. Under normal circumstances, nature takes care of this by providing a changing palette of flowers. Colonies have a built-in taste for variety; they'll go out of their way to mix their pollens.

But it's a rare and fortunate colony that still gets to spend its life grazing natural areas. More often, bees are trucked to pollination jobs where they have exactly one type of flower to visit for weeks at a time. Maybe that flower offers high-quality protein, maybe it doesn't.

Like other foods, pollen's quality depends on its growing conditions. A 2007 study by Thomas Ferrari of Pollen Bank found that the majority of almond, plum, kiwi, and cherry pollen was dead due to lack of soil nutrients. Weather can greatly affect pollen. As UC Davis bee expert Eric Mussen explained it on Salon.com,

> If we are having a typical year, and the rains come, there aren't too many places in the United States where the bees cannot find their mix of pollens to meet their dietary needs and get them through a normal life cycle. The question is, What happens when things don't go like that? Well, you get this blast of hot temperature, which is about the time the flower buds are forming and the pollen grains are beginning to form. What does that do? You get sterile pollen. A beekeeper could look into the hive and say, "I've got all kinds of pollen in there and the bees disappeared." Well, right, you've got pollen grains, but do they have any nutrition in them? . . . I think something happened at the end of [2006] in many places in the temperate climate around the world, not just here, and fouled up the bees' food supply.

No matter how a colony gets short on protein, the results are the same. The nurse bees eat through the limited pollen stores, parceling out the protein in the royal jelly they feed members of the colony. As the protein runs out, the level of vitellogenin in the nurses' bodies falls. Since vitellogenin isn't just protein but also the key to immune defense and stress reduction, those malnourished nurses soon become stressed, weakened, short-lived foragers. Low vitellogenin levels may even stimulate winter bees to try foraging when they shouldn't. The colony begins to dwindle because the foragers are dying faster than new bees are being born.

Those new bees aren't doing so hot either. The quality of a bee's diet during its first four days profoundly affects its behavior. If it doesn't get a normal supply of vitellogenin, it tends to begin foraging earlier, is more likely to prefer nectar over pollen, and lives a shortened life span. It's like a kid who grows up on

Pop-Tarts, has a rough childhood, matures too early, leaves home at sixteen, never gets over the sugar habit, and is dead of diabetes at age fifty.

This protein dearth can snowball. First the foragers die early, then the nurses abandon their posts to begin foraging and die young as well. Pretty soon nobody's home to take care of the kids. If those neglected, malnourished brood hatch at all, they'll be underdeveloped and diseased.

That's a pretty good description of colony collapse disorder.

At the USDA's Bee Research Center in Tucson, Gloria DeGrandi-Hoffman, a specialist in modeling population dynamics, ran some colony simulations to see if poor nutrition could cause CCD. She took a standard model of the yearly cycle of a colony, with a steady supply of clustering winter bees, a dip in March as the winter bees begin to die off, then a strong rise through spring and summer as new brood are reared. Then she merely shortened the life span of the worker bees by four days. This could reflect a shortage of pollen, or it could even be caused by warm winter temperatures that encourage the bees to fly and waste their energy reserves when no food is available. Lacking those four extra days, the colony still went into winter strong, with thirty thousand bees, but this time, when it hit that late-winter swoon, it couldn't pull out in time. The colony crashed and died in February.

Under normal bee circumstances, a pollen deficit isn't severe enough to cause this kind of dramatic collapse. The protein level gets low, but the bees conserve resources the best they can, eventually a fresh pollen source comes along, and the colony slowly restocks pollen and fattens up the nurses. This is what Bill Rhodes saw in his sickened bees that recovered once new pollen came in.

But for most bees, circumstances are far from normal. It's now standard practice to feed bees high-fructose corn syrup whenever they seem weak. If the colony is starved, this can indeed buck them up. If you're famished, a few jelly beans is better than nothing.

Beekeepers hoping to score lucrative almond-pollination contracts commonly feed their bees lots of corn syrup during the winter. The syrup makes the bees start building up, laying eggs and raising brood. The goal is eight frames crawling with bees by the beginning of February. But the reason bees start building up is because they think it's spring. Until very recently in the honey bee's existence, nobody was placing jars of sugar syrup on its hive; if nectar was coming in, it meant flowers were blooming and offering pollen. Bees fed syrup will make brood, but if no new protein is coming into the hive, then suddenly the same amount of protein that was filling twenty thousand bees is being spread out among forty thousand. Instead of some strong bees with bristling immune systems, there are a whole lot of bees with sugar-stoked disabilities.

What happens next? The bees must do the hardest job of their lives almond pollination. Few experts, much less anyone else, can tell a protein-rich bee from a malnourished one, so these hives, which are indeed crawling with bees, get top dollar. The beekeeper turns them loose on the almonds, cashes his check, buys himself a fancy dinner, and pats himself on the back for being foresighted enough to feed his bees.

A week later, he gets a call. All the hives have collapsed. The almond guy is furious, and the beekeeper is perplexed. What happened? There were bees everywhere.

What happened is there were lots of bees, but they had nothing inside. Trucked across the country, plunked down in the same valley as a million other hives, and forced to compete for limited resources, they quickly came to the end of their foreshortened life spans. Not only that, but with their vitellogenin gauges on empty, they had no immune systems to fight off the multiple pathogens they were encountering in all those other hives.

Thanks in part to the great deal of attention paid to bee nutrition in the wake of CCD, beekeepers are coming to understand the importance of keeping bees nutritionally fortified. Corn syrup isn't going to cut it. The era of protein shakes for bees is here. Some are made by beekeepers themselves from secret recipes of eggs, brewer's yeast, pollen, sugar, and all manner of mystery ingredients. Some are sold commercially. The leading protein supplement on the market is a product called MegaBee, a bouillabaisse of protein, fat, sugar, minerals, and vitamins that comes as a patty that resembles a cornmeal flapjack or as a liquid, which is more like a cornmeal smoothie. MegaBee is the centerpiece of a bee health regimen known as the Tucson Bee Diet, designed by Gloria DeGrandi-Hoffman and her colleagues at the Bee Research Center in Tucson.

From November 15, 2006, to February 7, 2007, the Bee Research Center tested 260 bee colonies in a remote lot near Bakersfield, California. There wasn't a scrap of natural forage to be had, which was the point. The bees had to rely on whatever they were fed. Groups of colonies received different protein supplements, while one control group received high-fructose corn syrup. Some of the groups died within twenty days; they couldn't utilize the protein in the formulas. Bees given corn syrup survived the winter but produced no brood. Without protein coming into the colony, the nurse bees were undoubtedly eating most every egg the queen laid—if she was even laying—in an effort to keep their protein levels up. These bees would have gone into almond groves and collapsed. The MegaBee colonies, on the other hand, had three times as many brood as they'd had in November. Those healthy kids were on their way to becoming high-functioning adults. These colonies were ready to tear up the almond trees.

Treating bees through nutrition, rather than chemicals, is a step in the right direction. Bees are living things, and when beekeepers think holistically about them, good things happen. Yet what kind of world is it where we have to feed bees? Bees managed to get through millions of years just fine before we began serving up flapjacks and soda. There's no substitute for a balanced diet of natural foods. Like any livestock, healthy bees require good pasture. And that's what fewer and fewer bees can find. You might say that, like us, they're suffering from "suburbia disease": more roads, big-box stores, and developments, fewer wildflowers. Whether it's clover in the Great Plains or gallberry in Georgia, it's disappearing, and beekeepers are forced to travel farther to find it. Even the famed tupelo forests along Florida's Apalachicola River, source of Van Morrison's favorite honey, are fading under the pressure of development, river dredging, and upstream water diversion. If drought-parched Atlanta gets the water it wants from the Apalachicola, you can kiss tupelo honey good-bye.

Sometimes the culprit is suburbia, sometimes it's monocrops, but the result is the same: less and less of the pastoral landscape where bees—and humans—thrive. It's important to reiterate that beekeepers didn't ask for this life for their flocks or themselves. They didn't leave the small farms; the farms left them. Faced with a choice between bankruptcy and a migratory business, beekeepers opted to stay in business. And they've kept adding one more thing into the mix—forklifts, bigger trucks, antibiotics, miticides, fungicides, Australian bees, MegaBee patties—in an effort to keep going. They've been amazingly resourceful. They've managed to keep juggling two million hives, even as we pull pieces of ground from under their feet. But they have their limit, and CCD may be the crash of those hives hitting the ground.

A beekeeper named Kirk Webster, whom we'll meet more thoroughly in the next chapter, published an essay in the September 2006 issue of the *American Bee Journal* that addressed just such concerns and now seems prescient in its anticipation of CCD:

> All of American agriculture is suffering terribly now from trying to force a process based on the workings of Nature into an industrial and business model . . . We remaining beekeepers are on the front lines of the struggle to prop up a system of agriculture that wants to produce food without people . . . Commercial beekeepers are moving their colonies further and further every year in an attempt to make ends meet; at a time when fuel prices could, at any moment, go into an upward spiral that would make all migratory beekeeping unprofitable. And we can't tell if the final blow will come from mites, the chemicals we formerly used to control the mites, or from a moronic government that would rather buy all food overseas than produce it here. From whatever angle you look at our industry now, the last word you would use to describe the scene is healthy.

When anything we've relied on starts to fail, our instincts are to fix it, to prop it up and keep it going. So it is with agriculture and pollination. More fertilizer. More chemicals to fight the parasites and diseases. More intensive diets to keep the bees flying and breeding in January. When breakfast is at stake, it's hard to consider anything else. But maybe the time has come to stop the inputs. It's pretty cool that smart and well-meaning scientists can develop a flapjack that keeps bees alive. Yet it's also a little insane. Is it a solution, or a Band-Aid on a system that is coming apart at the seams? Perhaps the time has come to ask ourselves the very hard question of whether the system itself is what needs to go.

Chapter 9

RESILIENCE AND THE RUSSIANS

A HUNDRED FEET above the verdant forest of Vermont's Green Mountains, a cluster of dark bees thrums the air. Their huge eyes and stout bodies mark them as drones, and they cut slow circles through the mountain air. Experts call these aerial gathering places "drone congregation areas." You and I might call them pubs. The males congregate, hang out, swap information. No one knows how they choose their spots, though it has something to do with landmarks and air currents. Somehow they all know how to get there.

Suddenly, a svelte bee with a long abdomen—a virgin queen—shoots by, trailing an olfactory invitation that says, "Come and get me, boys!" Instantly they drop their beers and the chase is on. Zipping over the mountains, staying high in the air, they form a morphing cloud known as a "drone comet," racing to outdistance their rivals and catch the fleet queen. One finally gains on her, and it's love at first flight. He grasps her midsection with his front legs and snuggles his abdomen close, sliding his phallus into her as they fly. For an instant they sail over the mountains, locked in love. Then the relationship sours.

In what is quite literally the climax of his life, tremendous air pressure builds inside the base of the drone's abdomen until it explodes, driving several million sperm, as well as the severed phallus, into the queen like a torpedo. He plummets to the ground, his last minutes of life leaking out. Like body snatchers, his genes have moved on to a new host, leaving the useless husk behind.[1]

The queen, however, is just getting warmed up. The other drones race after her, and she takes the fastest few, one at a time, uncoupling from each to let it death-spiral. She won't stop until she has received the contributions of ten to thirty-six suitors over several mating flights.

Don't blame her for her exuberance. The flights are her only trips outside the hive. They're college and dating and a year abroad rolled into a few mornings. After that, it's back to the hive and a lifetime of making babies.

The bees certainly don't penalize her. For them, promiscuity is a plus. The queen's pheromone changes in composition depending on how many drones she mates with, as does the number of her retinue of workers, who can smell it. They revere her (as measured by "licking and rubbing behavior") and extend her reign as monarch based on how many times she has mated. The more diverse the colony, the more genetic tools it will have for dealing with the world.

The queen keeps the sperm from all those guys in a special sac near her oviduct, dripping it onto her eggs as they roll down the production line. She labors on, being fed royal jelly by attendants

1. Here's how one source describes it: "Termination of mating is audible, recognized by a snapping sound caused by compressed air in the drone genitals."

until, two or three years down the road, her ovaries give out and she is murdered by her unsentimental daughters.

The honey bee mating flight is a scene played out in aeries all over the world every spring and summer. Yet this one, high above the jagged spruce of the Green Mountains, is a little different. For these dark bees are like few others.

From Russia, with Hope

In 1994, as the varroa mite continued its blitzkrieg across North America, punching through the Maginot Line of miticides, a man named Tom Rinderer visited the isolated and rugged Primorsky region of Russia's Pacific coast. Rinderer, the head researcher at the USDA's Honey Bee Breeding, Genetics and Physiology Laboratory in Baton Rouge, Louisiana, was searching for bees that had hit upon their own ways of combating varroa, and he had reason to believe that Primorsky harbored them. There, he knew, honey bees had lived with the mites for at least forty years, possibly much longer. That remote part of Asia was where, people believed, the mites had first jumped from *Apis cerana* to *Apis mellifera* before traveling west in honey bee shipments. That fact, along with the region's geographical isolation, made it unique.

Rinderer traveled the Primorsky countryside, making contacts and observing hives. What he saw gave him hope that these Russian bees had developed partial resistance to varroa. The mites were endemic, but colonies weren't dying at an elevated rate. The next year Rinderer returned and took a road trip, collecting fifty Primorsky queens and beginning a five-year test of their varroa resistance, while running the same test on U.S. hives back in Baton Rouge. Sure enough, the Russian bees kept mite loads down to a fraction of their U.S. counterparts. How? Part of it seemed to be "autogrooming"—they removed the little suckers from their bodies and tossed them out of the hive. Somehow Italian bees have never figured this out. The Russians could even tell when varroa were munching on a pupa in a wax-capped cell. They'd uncap the cell and chuck the baby and bathwater altogether.

In 1997 Rinderer received permission to bring one hundred fertile Russian queens from sixteen different Primorsky beekeepers back to Louisiana. He quarantined them on steamy Grande Terre Island, Louisiana, where they wouldn't be visited by any randy U.S. drones, and began one of the most vital breeding programs in recent history, letting the daughters and drones of those Russian queens start interbreeding. Every year he selected the best of the best to interbreed, building up multiple lines of resistant stock and infusing the gene pool with fresh bees from Russia, all characteristically dark, more tan and black than yellow and black.

In 2000 he released the first mite-resistant Russians to beekeepers. One hint of the Russians' hardiness came when a Mississippi beekeeper who was partnering with the project was hit by a record cold winter. Thirteen hundred of his 1,500 Italian colonies died, while only 2 of his 2,000 Russian colonies did. Rinderer released new lines of Russian bees every year until in 2008 the final lines were released and development was turned over to the industry. Today some breeders specialize in Russian bees. But it was Kirk Webster who took the Russian bees and went Darwinian with a vengeance.

The Bee Mystic

The Russian bees bombed with most beekeepers. The beekeepers appreciated the varroa resistance, sure, but that was about the only thing they liked about these bees. When Russian bees bred with

Italian stock, it tended to bring out the worst traits of both races; they didn't make honey like an Italian or survive like a Russian. But even purebred Russians simply didn't act like the Italian bees that beekeepers were used to. For one thing, they didn't quickly build up their colonies in early spring. They wouldn't rear brood until plenty of pollen was available. And they would shut down brood production anytime pollen became scarce. This was a big departure from Italian bees, which ramp up brood production first thing in the spring and keep cranking out bees, regardless of the environmental conditions, until winter is upon them. This suits the many beekeepers who make their living by rapidly dividing colonies and selling nucs.[2] Beekeepers who tried to do this with the Russian hives found themselves without enough nucs to fill customers' orders. Southern operations modeled on the runaway reproduction of Italian bees, and especially beekeepers needing a full air force in February for almond pollination, didn't like the Russians' conservative habits.

Even worse was the Russian bees' propensity to swarm in the spring. Each swarm means losing half a colony to God knows where, so beekeepers do everything they can to prevent it. Even the remaining bees will be out of production for a few weeks until a new queen has rebuilt the population. A colony that swarms is physically healthy but economically disastrous.

With Italian bees, you can usually spot a swarm in the offing. The population of the hive is bursting at the seams. Their honey

---

2. A nuc (pronounced "nuke") is the nucleus of a colony: a queen, some workers and brood, and a few frames of comb. Hobbyists buy nucs in the spring, add a super or two, let the colony build up, and harvest honey in the fall. Theoretically, the colony makes it through the winter and sustains itself indefinitely. If not, there are always new nucs to buy in the spring.

cups runneth over. New queen cells suddenly appear. A beekeeper who sees these signs will quickly pinch off the queen cells, divide the colony into two hives and, hopefully, with plenty of room for everyone, the urge to swarm will pass.

Russian bees, however, will throw off a swarm at the drop of a hat, even when their numbers are small and no Italian colony would think of swarming. They always seem to have queen cells in the works, which freaks out beekeepers used to interpreting this as step one toward swarming, or at least supersedure—killing the old queen and replacing her with a younger, faster model. Supersedure, while not quite the setback swarming is, still means no new bees for a few weeks. Beekeepers who took the time to become familiar with the Russian hives learned that the presence of queen cells didn't mean supersedure or swarming was imminent; Russian bees just like to keep backups on hand.

But having these virgin queens on the shelf means that the Russians *can* swarm at any time, without warning, and they do—especially in spring, when things are just getting started. This drives beekeepers straight out of their minds.

It drove Kirk Webster nuts, too—at first. Webster, a beekeeper in Vermont's Champlain Valley, purchased some of the first bees available from the Baton Rouge lab in 2000. He lost some bees to unexpected swarms, panicked when he saw all those queen cells being readied, and fretted over the lack of buildup in the spring. But Webster is not like most people. A practicing Buddhist in his fifties, with a shaggy salt-and-pepper beard, thick glasses, and an infinite calm, he's been called a "bee mystic." Living a monklike existence in a simple wooden house, he had already devoted several years of his life to breeding resilience back into bees when the Russians came along. He eagerly introduced their stock to his apiary.

Some years before, Webster had been extremely ill with mercury poisoning from bad dental fillings. He nearly died. During that time he discovered meditation. More important, he became comfortable with the idea of impermanence. Webster doesn't cling to things—money, possessions, caustic emotions, old ideas. That was the key with the Russians.

"These Russian bees require a completely different mind-set," he told me. "But I really like them. I've been won over. They've helped me to overcome the varroa problem, so I'm forever grateful to them. It's just a matter of changing the way you think and letting them show you the right way, instead of trying to make them be like some other bees you had in the past. I think they're very nice bees with lots of great qualities. They are very good winter bees, very good at providing their own food."

Webster realized that all the Russian traits that annoyed beekeepers actually contributed to the bees' survival. Swarming in the springtime helped control varroa because the mites reproduce only in the brood chambers. A swarm carries no brood and few mites. Swarming also interrupts the brood cycle in the old colony, which will have a brood gap until the new queen starts laying. The Russian penchant for supersedure was an even simpler way to interrupt the brood cycle and keep varroa reproduction down to a dull roar.

The Russian bees' habit of overwintering in small clusters, and not building up in the spring until pollen supplies were plentiful, was another excellent survival strategy. Italian bees tend to convert their food stores into more bees, no matter the season. They evolved in Italy, land of floral riches, and they've been bred for fecundity ever since. This is great if you want to make as many bees as you possibly can, but it means that Italian bees in a northern apiary often set themselves up to starve in winter, with more bees than honey. They must be fed. Russians, coming from a harsh climate and a low-tech beekeeping culture, evolved to keep their population closely aligned with what the land can support, and to survive winter with the bare minimum of bodies necessary to maintain heat in the hive.

It's tempting to call these dark Russian bees as fatalistic as their human namesakes. Living in an unforgiving environment with a troubled history, they seem to have a sense that bad things can happen in life, so you'd better be ready. Winters will be rough, queens will die, sickness and invaders will come, food won't always be available. So don't put all your eggs in one basket, don't live beyond your means, and keep a few princesses on reserve, just in case.

The golden Italians, on the other hand, seem to trust in a state of perpetual Mediterranean ease. Why swarm when things are so good right here at home? Why stop having kids? Why groom yourself today when you could be out probing the flowers instead? For the Italians, life is one long summer of love.[3]

Until it isn't. When the going gets tough, the tough Russians get going, while the Italians die.

I was won over by the Russians, too, as I spent a long August day helping Webster harvest fifty-pound supers of honey that revved like race cars. The bees seemed industrious. I watched thousands of bees rise from the hive, get their bearings, and shoot straight for some flower possibly miles away. A wall of black thunderheads advanced from the Adirondacks and lightning tessellated the western sky. I suggested we head for cover

3. That love extends even to small hive beetles, which Italian nurse bees have been known to *feed*. Russian bees, however, toss small hive beetles out on their ass.

but Webster was unhurried. "See the bees," he said. "They're still going out. They know when it's about to rain." When you see a funnel cloud of dark bees coalescing across the fields and making for the hive with purpose, you know it's time to batten the hatches.

Conforming his practices to nature, rather than the other way around, has been the guiding principle of Webster's life. When he graduated from high school in 1972 he took a job with Champlain Valley Apiaries, Vermont's largest. He worked for the legendary Charles Mraz, the man who pioneered the use of bee stings to treat arthritis. Already Webster was learning about bees' potential to heal, both individuals and ecosystems. After college he settled in Concord, Massachusetts, and began keeping his own hives. They did well. It was that golden age; honey prices were good and pests and diseases were few. He found queen breeding particularly interesting. It made him alert to personalities and traits and the way they could carry through generations. He was becoming less a controller of bees and more a steward to young monarchs—a perspective that would serve him well when varroa hit.

In the 1980s, Concord became too expensive and crowded for the simple lifestyle Webster wished to lead, so he moved his apiary to the Champlain Valley, a flat land of dairy farms, cornfields, and leaning barns that resembles Wisconsin more than the Vermont of tourism brochures. He tended his bees during the spring and summer and worked as a carpenter during the winter to pay the bills. When recession hit Vermont in 1991, the carpentry jobs dried up. Webster turned to bees full-time.

Because queen breeding was the heart of his apiary, Webster was already a strong believer in the need for holistic solutions to any problems that arose, rather than quick fixes. He needed to keep his stock healthy. He said as much in a series of articles he wrote about his varroa experiences for *American Bee Journal*:

> In my own search for a healthy beekeeping future, I have found the World of Nature herself, the old beekeeping books and journals, and the original accounts of the pioneers of modern organic farming to be far more helpful and inspiring than most of what has been published, talked about and done by the beekeeping community during the last 8 or 10 years. Here were people who worked hard to solve their own problems in a creative way, often with very few resources. They looked deeply into the world of Nature searching for examples of balance and stability, and always gave their crops and livestock the last word.

Central to Webster's worldview was the work of Sir Albert Howard, the father of the organic farming movement. Howard, Britain's imperial economic botanist in India in the early 1900s, studied the farming practices of India's peasants and wrote two books based on his observations: *An Agricultural Testament* and *The Soil and Health*. He was knighted for his work in 1935.

For Howard, successful farming and food production—healthy plants, animals, and people—required balance. Any agricultural enterprise must achieve a state of equilibrium that mimics nature if it is to survive and prosper. Everything rested on a foundation of healthy soil that contained all the microorganisms necessary to break down humus, all the micronutrients necessary to build healthy plants, all the structure necessary to retain water, and so on. Growth and decay must be in balance, and the mix of plants and animals must be such that whatever fertility is removed from the soil is returned to it. A healthy farm would produce crops and livestock that could maintain their health with little intervention, and would in turn produce healthy people capable of the same.

When an *imbalance* took hold, Howard believed, nature let you know. The heralds of this imbalance were often pests and disease, which could get a foothold only if something was out of whack in the system. In this way, pests and disease are not the enemies of the farmer; they are actually allies, helping to illuminate weaknesses in the system before irrevocable damage—exhausted soil, genetically weak crops or animals—is introduced.

With this key observation, Kirk Webster was able to turn the conventional view of the mites, and of how an apiary should be run, on its head. For most beekeepers, mites are the minions of evil, destroying colonies and livelihoods with their disgusting fangs. Suddenly, Webster was in the pages of *American Bee Journal* saying that the mites were his friends.

Naming the imbalances in the system that the mites were laying bare was easy. Too much transportation. Too much tenement living in "cities" of a hundred million or more. Too much overwork, leaving bees weak and immunosuppressed. Webster could avoid these imbalances by simply not engaging in any of them. But the overriding problem was not so easily solved: Until recently in their two-million-year existence, European honey bees had never been exposed to varroa and had no natural defenses to it.

Parasites and their hosts tend to coevolve into states of endurable equilibrium. Aggressive strains of parasites that kill all their hosts die out, while less aggressive strains maintain a population of hosts to live on. The varroa mite and the Asian honey bee had worked out just such a truce over the eons. With the Asian honey bee, varroa can reproduce only in drone cells, which are available for a short time each year and naturally limit the mite population. But the unnatural collision of varroa and the European honey bee—accelerated by planes, trains, and automobiles—produced a tremendous imbalance. The larger brood cells and longer pupation periods of European honey bees let the mites reproduce year-round. Multiplying exponentially, they quickly overwhelm the hive. Over decades, this imbalance would get worked out, but it could cripple commercial beekeeping and industrial agriculture in the process. Pesticides slow down varroa, but, as Sir Albert Howard might have warned, they also sicken the bees, exacerbate the imbalance, and make the eventual "correction" that much more traumatic when it comes.

Kirk Webster thought there was another way. In 1998 he decided to stop fighting the mites and instead see what he could learn from them. By his own admission, he might not have done it if an easier solution had presented itself. Like everyone else, he used Apistan until it stopped working. Then along came Check-Mite, a powerful hormone disruptor. "That's when I got off the bandwagon," Webster said. "Since queens were the whole basis of my business, I knew I didn't want to do that. I decided this whole thing was a freight train heading for a wreck, and that I was going to go through the wreck early. And hopefully recover early."

It turned out to be a bad time to jump. The weather that year was disastrous. Purposefully not treating his bees, Webster had to sit there and watch hundreds of colonies die. Only a few survived. It was financially and emotionally devastating, but Webster's new perspective was in place. The mites were not his enemies. They were helping him fix a problem. And that problem was weak bees.

If your ancestors came from Europe, as mine did, they probably survived the black death. Smallpox, too. We know our ancestors were some of the lucky ones, because we're still here. No one would argue that the plague was anything other than a calamity, but you also can't deny that it left a population with more genetic resilience. Today, with antibiotics and disinfectants taking over the front lines that used to be manned by our immune systems, we are probably more vulnerable to an epidemic than we have been in centuries.

For decades, Italian honey bees have been selected for traits that had little to do with resilience. Maximum honey production tops the charts, with maximum bee production closely linked to that. Gentleness is essential. Qualities that contribute to self-reliance—resistance to pests and disease, overwintering ability, frugality—are less valued because it's more efficient to rely on petrochemicals to solve such problems. Who needs bees that can overwinter when it's cheap to truck them down to Florida for the cold months? Who needs to worry about self-reliant bees when it's more cost-effective to buy new queens and nucs from Southern breeders or Australia in the early spring?[4] Why find forage for bees when high-fructose corn syrup is cheap and plentiful? Why spend years breeding mite- and disease-resistant bees when the chemical conglomerates have all these miticides, fungicides, and antibiotics available right now?

It's a slippery slope. As beekeepers kept pushing their bees to

4. Some Northern beekeepers even took to treating their bees like an annual crop, killing them in the fall, so all the honey could be harvested and no feeding would be required, and buying new bees every spring.

do things like survive a cross-country trip[5] or produce a bustling winter hive for almond pollination, they were squeezing them into unnatural forms, undoubtedly losing other traits along the way—traits they wouldn't even realize were gone until they needed them. You can manipulate a natural system into doing things it wasn't designed for, but you're always running the risk of collapse.

Characteristically, Webster pulled no punches in calling the industry on this:

> Beekeeping now has the dubious honor of becoming the first part of our system of industrial agriculture to actually fall apart. Let's stop pretending that something else is going on. We no longer have enough bees to pollinate our crops. Each time the bees go through a downturn, we respond by making things *more* stressful for them, rather than less—we move them around more often, expose them to still more toxic substances, or fill the equipment up again with more untested and poorly adapted stock. We blame the weather, the mites, the markets, new diseases, consumers, the Chinese, the Germans, the (fill in your favorite scapegoat), other beekeepers, the packers, the scientific community, the price of gas, global warming—anything rather than face up to what's happening. We are losing the ability to take care of living things. Why?

I can't imagine such diatribes made Webster terribly popular with his fellow beekeepers. I also doubt he cared. Somehow Kirk Webster had managed to make a complete paradigm flip in his mind. The suggestion that bees be treated with deadly

5. Dave Hackenberg likes to say, "We've really bred a bee that can ride."

organophosphates helped him see that the increasing domestication, industrialization, and chemicalization of bees (indeed, of all agriculture) was the problem, and the mites were part of the solution.

That's quite a leap. It's like a rancher viewing wolves and coyotes as partners in his enterprise. It takes a man more invested in natural systems than economic ones.

It takes a man willing to live in poverty, and that's what Webster did for years. He brought together the few survivors of the varroa massacre and bred them. Not all of these bees had varroa resistance; some just had dumb luck. But each generation of survivors had a bit more resistance than their ancestors. Each rediscovered a little more resilience hiding in its genetic bag of tricks. Webster was making progress. The trouble was, varroa was so virulent, and so few bees were surviving, that his apiary risked becoming inbred.

Then the Russian bees came to the rescue in 2000. Webster introduced them to his apiary, eventually purchasing three distinct lines. Within a few generations, his old bees' genes had disappeared. The Russians were better survivors.

By letting nature take its course, Webster was breeding more robust bees. And he was also breeding less virulent mites. By killing the weak mites and removing them from the gene pool, Apistan, CheckMite, and other chemicals select for supermites. Webster didn't want supermites, but as his bees got stronger, he realized that he didn't want no mites, either. "Now that I've gotten to the point where I have seventy percent overwinter survival rate, the mites are more valuable to me alive than dead. They're constantly weeding out the weak thirty percent and showcasing the best colonies in a much easier and cheaper way than all the things the scientists are doing: counting mites with sticky boards, spending countless hours peering at them. That's my message now: Let the mites do that!"

Instead of using high-tech gadgets to do genetic sequencing, looking at mites with microscopes, or attempting to develop new medications, Webster opted to solve his problems the way nature has solved them since life first formed. It's an approach that requires a lot of patience.

We tend to view population crashes as disasters, but sometimes they're nature's way of fixing a problem. In my neck of the woods, a particularly vicious strain of rabies in the past decade killed 80 percent of the fox population. That crash eliminated all the sick and susceptible animals, and now a more resistant fox population has rebounded to its previous numbers. These boom-and-bust cycles can be the norm for insects and other creatures that reproduce quickly.

It's almost as if, with varroa, bees *wanted* to crash. It's their way of purging the sickness, just as a body's way of purging sickness is to clean out the gastrointestinal tract and start afresh. Feral bees did crash. Varroa eliminated virtually all of them. Now mite-resistant colonies are reappearing in American forests. Domestic honey bees wanted to crash, too, wanted to go through the train wreck and get it over with, but we wouldn't let them. By propping them up with chemicals and supplements, we drew out their crash into torturous slow-motion.

But we had to. Bees may be part of a natural system built on strong fluctuations, but they are also part of an economic one that doesn't thrive on boom-and-bust cycles. How many consumers are willing to forgo fruits and nuts for a few years? How many commercial beekeepers can go without income while their livestock shuffles its genes?

Not many. But Kirk Webster could. And after seven years with the Russian bees, Webster has a self-reliant apiary, while others have made little progress against varroa.[6] When I worked with Webster, the dark bees crawling all over me bristled with health, despite a drought, and their honey was superb. As we drove home, shellacked in honey and propolis, Webster said matter-of-factly, "What you just saw is not supposed to be possible. People think I must be cheating somehow. They say bees could never live for five years without being treated."

Key to Webster's success was finding the right form for his apiary. It was another example of letting the bees choose. They like to swarm early and frequently to reduce their mite load, so Webster would help them out by splitting them early. He eventually settled on a three-branch system. One branch (about 225 hives) is a traditional honey-producing apiary. The hives are scattered on farms in the Champlain Valley where they have good access to clover, alfalfa, and other important nectar plants. To make lots of honey, these hives need to build their numbers throughout the spring and summer. They can't be divided and they have lots of brood, so they're the most susceptible to varroa. They manage to produce excellent honey crops in fall, but many still don't survive the winter.

Webster's other 700 hives are devoted to nucs and queen-breeding. Most beekeepers who sell bees try to build their colonies quickly in the spring (it helps to be in the South, where spring comes in winter, as Yogi Berra might say), then split them into nucs and sell them right away. Webster, in his quest to breed hardy

6. Webster isn't the only beekeeper trying to breed better bees. Marla Spivek at the University of Minnesota has bred excellent mite-resistant lines of Italian bees, although those traits can get watered down in an apiary of nonresistant bees.

bees, revamped the system. He makes his nucleus colonies in midsummer, then lets them prove themselves. He wants his queens to face the acid test of a Vermont winter. When you buy bees from Webster on Mother's Day, you know you're getting survivors.

The queens are the real jewels.

When most commercial beekeepers split hives, they buy fertile queens from breeders in the South and drop them into the queenless hives so laying can begin immediately. They don't let hives make their own queens because it takes too long. Likewise, letting an old queen slowly fail and die, then waiting for a new queen to hatch, kill her rivals, mate, and start laying, means losing weeks of prime brood-rearing, meaning fewer bees for pollination and honey making, and less income. Instead they requeen.

An emerging problem in the industry is the survival of these queens. They aren't holding out as long or laying as robustly. Supersedure is on the rise. The workers keep pulling down the faltering queens, looking for a fruitful one, but that kind of queen is getting hard to find.

What's wrong with the queens? I have a few guesses. Queens raised in hives treated with coumaphos (CheckMite) almost always fail. They show physical abnormalities and are accepted by the hive only 5 percent of the time, versus 95 percent acceptance for coumaphos-free queens. Even when exposed to coumaphos as adults, they show reduced weight and reduced longevity. In one 2007 study, the number of queens still functioning after six months was 75 percent lower in hives treated with coumaphos.

Then there's the other half of the fertility equation. Coumaphos cuts drones' sperm production in half, and the sperm that are produced have this nasty habit of dying after six weeks. (Honey bee sperm must survive up to several years inside the queen.) Even fluvalinate (Apistan) reduced sperm production and drone survival.[7] Any time a queen runs out of live sperm and stops producing workers, supersedure isn't far off.

Even beekeepers who stop using fluvalinate and coumaphos aren't in the clear. Beeswax is a sponge for chemicals. The miticides accumulate in the wax. A 2007 study found that worker bees exposed to coumaphos-contaminated comb had significantly reduced life spans. No one knows what synergistic effects coumaphos and fluvalinate may have, but Maryann Frazier's pesticide data isn't encouraging. In my mind, I keep going back to a scene I witnessed of a goggle-eyed Midwestern beekeeper, clearly at the end of his rope, almost shouting to his fellow beekeepers, "We're doing things I can't even tell you about! They may be illegal, but at least my bees are alive!" If that doesn't send you running into the arms of your local organic beekeeper for your next jar of honey, I don't know what will.

I also wonder about the impact of artificially inseminated queens. That's the new trend among breeders, because you can select sperm from a drone that possesses useful traits, but if the queen hasn't mated with multiple drones, she won't last—and shouldn't. In a study of a colony created by a queen who had mated with fifteen drones, versus a queen who had mated with one, the genetically diverse colony constructed 30 percent more comb, stored 39 percent more food, performed more waggle dances, and better resisted disease.

---

7. The new "soft" treatment for mites is formic acid, which has been used for many years in Europe. Bees can tolerate more than ten times the amount of formic acid that mites can (or humans, for that matter), so it's quite effective—when used properly. Beekeepers, who never met an instruction manual they liked, have been burning off their fingertips with formic acid and searing their lungs, as well as killing hives. There's also some evidence that even formic acid reduces drones' production and longevity.

Webster and some other beekeepers who practice natural methods won't buy queens. If your goal is to get bees well adapted to your local environment, then continuously populating your hives with little Texans isn't going to help. You need to pick your queens and your drones from the survivors, those that thrived under whatever conditions your corner of the globe offers. It's exciting, because you know every generation is going to have skills and attributes its parents didn't. You keep getting better bees.

As long as you know what you're getting. At drone congregation areas, drones come from miles around for their chance to tango with a queen. There's no telling where the drones in an area have come from, or what lurks under their hoods.

That's why, to develop your own race of bees, you need miles of isolation from other colonies. Grande Terre Island if you're Tom Rinderer, or the Green Mountains if you're Kirk Webster. The Champlain Valley is the bee's knees—lots of farms and tree huggers, few pesticides—so it's chock-full of bees. But the Green Mountains aren't. Above three thousand feet, conifers dominate and the snow lingers into May, so there's not much forage for bees. No other beekeepers bring their bees up here. On the unlikely chance that a colony of feral bees somehow survived in the mountains, Webster would welcome their rugged genes into his apiary. All his queens get raised in the highlands, then brought back to the valley to populate his hives. Aside from the Africanized bees, they are some of the only bees in North America that have been solving their own problems—establishing their own culture—without the help of scientists, chemicals, and emergency intervention.

Webster has nothing against technology itself. He's aware that the scientific method has brought much progress. But he also sees that it isn't always the best approach. Controlled studies can handle only one or two variables at a time. So science breaks down a problem into the smallest units possible, then studies them one at a time to see what manipulating that one variable will do. It establishes tiny blocks of knowledge.

But when dealing with complex systems, with countless variables and feedback loops, science must throw up its hands. Look at the amount of attention paid to human nutrition, with rudimentary progress. Or our continuing inability to predict weather. Science's goal is to understand *why* something works so that it can manipulate and control that system. We have an obsession with knowing and controlling, and disdain more intuitive relationships with the world. But sometimes it isn't necessary to master a system in order to work harmoniously with it.

Webster, steeped in non-Western wisdom traditions, knew what his goal was: to establish an apiary that wasn't reliant on heroic human intervention and technology. If all the problems he and his beekeeping colleagues were having stemmed from human technology, then he was happy to let go of the reins and let the bees guide the development of their own apiary. He would be the caretaker, taking cues from the bees.

In his essays, he explained, "I tried to design a system where all the components of health (stability, resilience, diversity, and productivity) could function and grow—whether the mechanisms were known or unknown. Nature is much bigger than we are, and just allowing her methods to work could be the key to the future—both for the bees and for us." Later he added, "We'll never understand everything about Nature, but we can learn to live and work under her benevolent care and protection. Many have done this in the past, and there's no overriding reason why we can't do the same now and in the future. Working this way not only allows us to move away from the predatory and destructive economic and social system we live in now—it creates a real alternative. Making a living this way allows Nature to heal because of our work, rather than be continually degraded."

Of course, it also meant years of poverty. But what is poverty? "The state of one who lacks a usual or socially acceptable amount of money or material possessions," according to *Merriam-Webster's*. It exists only in the context of an economic system. If you can't afford the same sneakers or minivans or steak as your neighbors and you feel humiliated or inferior or just plain sad as a result, then poverty can cause real mental and physical duress. But if your goal is "to have a nice life in the country, centered around farming, gardening, and especially—keeping bees" (that's Kirk Webster), then poverty starts to look an awful lot like a traditional, healthy existence.

The problem, as Webster might see it, is that farms have been co-opted into the modern economy, and farmers are forced to start acting and thinking like other businessmen. There's nothing wrong with a farmer having a good head for business, but farms—at least, environmentally conscious ones—can't be run like other businesses. Businesses are predicated on the assumption of endless growth. When starting a business, you write your five-year business plan, then borrow a big wad of money and hope that your growth stays ahead of your interest payments. It's a Ponzi scheme based on new waves of consumers funneling money into your business. And it depends on the assumption that you can always make more product. No matter how mature your company gets, you are expected to keep making more product. If Coca-Cola or Exxon has a flat year, shareholders savage the company.

But in the world of biological systems, nothing grows unstoppably except a cancer. A healthy farm is immersed in the cycles of nature: steady growth, steady decay, a well-maintained balance. To grow economically, it has to either eat up more land or produce more on the same land. Those have been the basic farming trends for half a century or more. But neither can go on indefinitely. Land is finite, and many technological innovations that have allowed farmers to wring more product from their land have come by sacrificing the long-term health of the soil. In other words, the innovations weren't really offering something for nothing. Like fossil fuel, they were taking a resource built up over millennia (fertility) and liquidating it in a one-time spree.

There are good reasons why we shouldn't measure farms with the same yardstick we use for other businesses, but how do we do that in a culture where the economy has become the default measure of value? Weekly grosses of movies are printed in more newspapers than movie reviews are. When any disaster befalls the country, from September 11 to Hurricane Katrina, we look to the Dow Jones to gauge the nation's trauma.

For many years beekeepers have felt the tension of trying to work within a growth-based economic system while shepherding animals who don't thrive under that pressure. Why are there so few young beekeepers? Children watched their parents struggle to make a living in an inflationary world and decided they wanted no part of that life. Beekeepers wanting to stay in business have followed "economies of scale" principles, borrowing lots of money, buying out other apiaries, getting larger and larger, and expanding their pollination coverage to stay afloat.

Kirk Webster had other ideas. He understood that all the trends in the industry—indeed, in the country—would only lead him and his bees to greater misery, so he decided to step off the train and follow a different path. He counseled his colleagues wanting to opt out of the industrial model to cultivate self-sufficiency.

> Beekeepers must become experts at producing honey, pollen, queens or other bee products; and enjoying a simple, low-cost lifestyle in a rural place. By investing some of your time and money in the self-sufficiency aspects—raising your own queens, building your own equipment and buildings, welding, gardening, etc.—you become partially removed from the instability of the overall economic system. It takes really good management to make all these jobs fit together right, and some income is sacrificed in the boom years; but over the long run the apiary is more stable, resilient, and enjoyable to work with.

The Art of Survival

The word "resilience" turns up a lot when Webster talks about his apiary. Lately it turns up a lot everywhere. Resilience is a new ecological science that focuses on a system's ability to recover from a disturbance. Webster told me he'd never heard of the science of resilience, but his writings read like a manual for it. A resilient apiary can take a blow—whether a virus, parasite, or drought—bounce back, and keep going. An apiary that lacks resilience will fall apart from the same blow.

My favorite way to think of resilience is to picture a sailboat. As the wind blows harder, it pushes the sailboat over more and more. But underneath the boat is a keel. The farther the boat heels, the higher the keel is lifted and the more gravity tends to pull it back down. No matter how much the boat oscillates, it always comes back to a stable point—straight up and down.

Or, almost always. If a gale blows hard enough, suddenly the boat's rail dips under the surface, water swamps the hull, and the system flips to a whole new state—capsized. Even if the gale should cease entirely, the boat will no longer return to its old state.

Resilience is the science of managing systems to keep them from flipping to undesirable states. Step one is having the humility to acknowledge that such states are possible and often closer at hand than we think. We're seeing them all around us. The collapse of the cod fishery is a classic example. People believed that the lower the population got, the more likely it was to bounce back, like the heeling sailboat. It turned out that if a fish population gets low enough, it collapses instead. Capsizes. And then no moratorium will bring it back.

In March 2008, Anthony Ives published a paper in *Nature* that used a single simple equation to explain the resilience of a seemingly erratic population fluctuation—and its breakdown. Iceland's Lake Myvatn had a robust population of midges, which, as larvae, live in the lake sediment and feed on diatoms. Generally, a growing midge population feasts on the diatoms until there are virtually no diatoms left, at which point the midge population starves and crashes. Once the midges have collapsed, diatoms that survived in rocky areas where midge larvae can't live are responsible for repopulating the lake. Then the surviving midges gorge on diatoms and have a new population explosion. Meanwhile, fish in the lake depend on the midge larvae as their main food source. In this way, the lake population of diatoms, midges, and fish rocks back and forth, like a sailboat. For millennia it existed within a certain steady state and the fish supported the people of the area. Then, in 1967, a mining operation began dredging the lake bottom. The fish population, for the first time in memory, collapsed. Ives shows how, once the diatoms began populating the dredged area, they no longer expanded to the sediment. The midges starved, and with them the fish. Although the dredging stopped in 2004, the fish have not recovered. A new steady state was reached—a fishless one.

Once you start looking for resilience, you see a world littered with systems that have flipped to undesirable states. Deforestation and soil erosion. The Arctic: Sea ice reflects most light (and heat) that hits it, but water absorbs almost all of it. Once the water gets a foothold, it tends to send the system in the opposite direction. Even democracy seems to be a system that reinforces itself, but once toppled is very difficult to restore.

Most systems involve complex relationships and feedback loops, making it difficult for us to predict how hard they can be pushed before suddenly shifting. Yet we tend to think of systems in overly simplistic terms. In our minds, a flooding river will eventually return to its old banks once the rain subsides. And usually it does. But if the flooding gets bad enough, the river can jump its banks entirely, carve a new channel, and never return. We picture the sailboat or the pendulum: The farther something swings in one direction, the farther it will swing back. But systems are more like roller coasters: if they get pushed far enough, they hit a new downward slope and zip away.

Managing systems for resilience, instead of efficiency, means making them bottom-heavy so they are highly unlikely to reach an unexpected tipping point. This involves maintaining backup systems, fire walls, and "expecting the unexpected"—often at the cost of short-term gain. For instance, our sailboat captain could make her boat more resilient by having a small sail and a heavy keel. Both will help keep the boat upright—but at the cost of speed. The boat will make less efficient use of the wind. It will lose races to a lighter boat that carries more sail—until the day that the race hits a storm, when it will be rescuing the crew of the lighter boat.

That's anathema to most businesses, which would never "sacrifice income in the boom years"; their shareholders wouldn't allow it. The Gospel of Efficiency guides our culture. Corporations merge and downsize to eliminate every redundancy. They outsource everything possible in the name of efficiency. But sometimes when you outsource, you eliminate invisible support systems you didn't even know were there.

For decades, we've been wringing every last drop of efficiency from our agricultural system, not noticing that we were sacrificing resilience to get it. Animals (including bees) are kept in regimented feedlots where thousands can be fed by machine. It's supremely efficient and cost-effective—until a new antibiotic-resistant staph infection rips through the population. Then, suddenly, the cows on the isolated organic farm look a lot more valuable.

We may be entering an era where interconnectedness has lost its shine. Since the first heady days of the World Wide Web, we've believed that success was somehow tied to being linked to the rest of the world. But the more complicated and interlinked the system, the more one small problem can bring the whole thing down. We've seen this with the Northeast power grid, with the global movement of pathogens, and with the financial system. As the business writer James Surowiecki describes it, "When you have systems with lots of moving parts . . . some of them are bound to fail. And if they are tightly linked to one another—as in our current financial system—then the failure of just a few parts cascades through the system. In essence, the more complicated and intertwined the system is, the smaller the margin of safety."

In California, 750,000 acres of almond trees in neat rows, with quadruple yields, is a miracle of efficiency. To make it work, we laid off all the local pollinators, because they were taking up valuable space. Now that efficiency is built on a crumbly pillar of 1.5 million hives of freelancers. There are no backup bugs, no other options, no alternative suppliers. If any number of things goes wrong—disease, drought, ten-dollar-a-gallon diesel—then the whole enterprise collapses.

And it isn't just almonds. All monocrops—which means virtually all our food—are part of a system of industrial agriculture whose astounding yields are predicated on the continued supply of a number of resources—groundwater, honey bees, functioning pesticides, migrant workers, and cheap oil, to name but a few. As Kirk Webster wrote in *American Bee Journal*, beekeeping has the honor of being the first part of the system to fall apart. But none of the other parts are looking too spiffy right now, either.

Which is why, to me, trying too hard to find a single cause of CCD misses the point. CCD, like varroa, is a symptom of a larger disease—a disease of fossil fuels and chemical shortcuts, of billion-bee slums and the speed of the modern world. An imbalance in the system. Maybe IAPV or imidacloprid or fluvalinate is the latest manifestation of the disease, but until local agriculture replaces global agriculture, there will always be another parasite, another virus, another mysterious collapse. "You keep digging to the bottom," said Webster, "that's what you'll always find. It's not a problem with the bees; it's a degradation of the whole environment."

Are there other options? What would it take to reintroduce resilience to our agriculture and ensure that our children's breakfasts still have cranberries and almonds and cherries? Maybe it's time we started thinking about what makes a resilient community, whether that community is a bee colony, a town, or a countryside. Diversity is needed: diverse habitats, diverse livelihoods, diverse creatures, and diverse genes.

Kirk Webster is lucky enough to live in an area where resilience and diversity still exist at all scales. He can cultivate a resilient bee and design a resilient apiary, but he also needs a diverse landscape for those bees. And he gets it in the patchwork farms and fallow fields of Vermont.

Vermont is now home to an astounding number of organic farms, which help provide resilience to the area's honey bees but also find support from diverse pollinators both domestic and wild. A recent study by Claire Kremen of Princeton University found that organic watermelon farms near natural habitat received all the pollination they needed from native bee species, but that others didn't. A watermelon flower needs about 1,000 pollen grains per day to produce a full-sized watermelon, and those on the organic farms near wild areas averaged 1,800. Organic farms far from natural habitat received just 600 pollen grains per day, while conventional watermelon farms close to natural areas received only 300, presumably because of pesticide use. Conventional watermelon crops that were distant from wild areas received no pollination from native species.

Clearly, a patchwork of settled areas, organic farms, and wilderness works. (In fact, it sounds an awful lot like what existed through most of the past ten thousand years.) Some have argued that the collapse of the honey bee is really just step one of a return to such a system. No less a luminary than Barry Lopez called the disappearance of honey bees "not that big a deal. From an ecological standpoint, it is opening up the possibility for local pollinators like the mason bee to come back."

A tempting idea. Honey bees are an exotic species anyway, so let's get rid of 'em and let the mason bees and bumble bees handle all the pollination. In fact, governments are beginning emergency programs to cultivate other wild pollinators, including bumble bees and blue orchard bees. Call it a last-minute attempt to introduce redundancy and resilience to the system.

But are there enough wild pollinators left? Amazingly, no one knows. Only in the past few years have scientists turned their magnifying glasses from the apple orchards to the forests to see what the native pollinators are up to. Too often, they're having trouble finding many.

As I'm sure you can appreciate, that may be the first sign of a silent catastrophe so far-reaching that it will make you forget all about the diminishment of your granola.

Chapter 10

THE BIRTH OF BEAUTY

IF YOU WANT to find the Garden of Eden, look no further than the garden cultivated by bees and flowers 100 million years ago. We've always lived amid its rainbow colors and succulent fruits, its dazzling diversity and perfumes, so we think it's always been like this. *It hasn't.* It's still, in geological terms, a new idea. Land plants had been around for 300 million years before the first flower showed up. These ferns, conifers, and cycads relied on wind pollination to reproduce, sometimes soaring to great heights to catch the breeze. They tended to grow in pure stands, which is the nature of wind pollination. It's a one-in-a-million chance that the pollen one pine launches will just happen to find the cone of a friend, and those odds go down sharply with distance but are improved if the pine is firing into a crowd.

Facing little competition in the Carboniferous period, these wind-pollinated forests marched across the globe.[1] With little need to innovate, they kept things simple. Three hundred million years

1. And laid down the fossil fuels in your gas tank. They don't call it "carboniferous" for nothing.

ago, there were only about five hundred species of land plants on the entire earth.

Along with those plants came the animals. From the very beginning, insects and amphibians had accompanied the land plants, feasting on them, and reptiles joined the scene around 320 million years ago. Both dinosaurs and mammals got started in the Triassic period, 248 million years ago,[2] and birds appeared in the Jurassic, 208 million years ago. But no flowers. Dinosaurs and mammals wandered the earth for 100 million years before seeing their first fruit. Flying insects buzzed the air for 200 million years before confronting a flower. The forest was a monotone.

At the beginning of the third and final dinosaur period, the Cretaceous, 144 million years ago, there still were only three thousand species of plants on earth. How could a new species get a foothold with these conifers crowding everyone else out?

Enter the Next Big Idea. Angiosperms—flowering plants—began doing revolutionary things with color, form, scent, cleverness, and subterfuge. Their design was so different from anything that had come before that Charles Darwin later called their evolution "an abominable mystery." Insects, primarily beetles and flies, had already developed a taste for protein-rich pollen and ovules, the most nutritious parts of a plant. This was nothing but a nuisance to the conifers, but somehow, somewhere,[3] some plants decided to turn this negative into a positive. If the bugs were going to take the pollen anyway, why not have *them* deliver it to the next stop? Resources could go into fewer, more complex grains of

2. Mammals are as ancient as dinosaurs. Tell *that* to your fifth-grade teacher.

3. Probably on an island, where plants and insects could take a few million years to evolve and work the kinks out of the system before facing "real-world" competition.

pollen, since the chances of a beetle taking any one pollen grain straight to another plant of the same kind were exponentially better than the wind doing it. It was like using a smart bomb.

A smart-bomb beetle doesn't need a direct path to its target. Just dust it with pollen while it feeds, then let it fly over hill and dale until it finds some more tasty pollen of the same species. Individuals can be miles apart, with a whole forest of conifers between them, and that little winged smart bomb will slip right through.

Some modifications were necessary. For hundreds of millions of years, plants had been discouraging insects from eating them. Now, all of a sudden, these new plants were staking their whole future on being noticed. To do that, they employed the Cinnabon technique: pump out an unmistakable aroma that draws the world to your door. You need a good sign, too—something to catch the eye amid that great curtain of green chaos. A different color, perhaps, or a symmetrical shape.

And so the flower was born.

And the market went mad for it.

Probably some of the first bugs enlisted in pollen transportation were carrion eaters accustomed to feasting on stinky dinosaur carcasses. If a flower mimicked the scent of dung or rotten flesh, flies and beetles would be drawn right in. Approximating the look of rotten flesh would help sell the lie. And by the time the beetle nosed around and discovered that it had been duped—too late; it was already covered in pollen. Plenty of plants, such as red trillium and skunk cabbage, still use the stinky strategy.

Of course, most carrion mimics have nothing to offer insects. They don't make nectar, and their unwitting couriers don't always eat pollen. It's a bad deal for the bugs, which have wasted valuable time and energy on a wild-goose chase.

The really successful plants gave the insects what they needed. Eat a little pollen, take a little pollen, keep coming back. Lots of willing buyers and sellers. A market emerged unlike any the world had seen. Before the angiosperms, birds and lizards and other animals were undoubtedly signaling their fitness, sexual readiness, and anger to their own kind via feathers, throat pouches, mating displays, and so on, but very little interspecies communication was going on. Few plants had ever attempted to attract animals.

But it worked. And the race was on to become the most beguiling object around. The "angiosperm explosion," as botanists call it, took the number of plant species from 3,000 in the early Cretaceous to 22,000 by its end. Today there are 250,000 to 400,000 species of plants, virtually all angiosperms.[4] Creativity flourished. The wind isn't going to change its behavior based on anything a plant does, but for angiosperms, like entrepreneurs, risk-taking is rewarded. All those flowers are attempting to be irresistible to somebody, and they're doing a pretty good job. Through trial and error, they've hit upon the right combinations of pattern, color, and scent that drive bugs—not to mention us—wild.

The first flowers were pretty simple affairs, just a stigma and some stamens bunched together so bugs couldn't get to one without bumping the other, plus some colorful petals to act like road signs, luring diners off the Cretaceous superhighway. Some of these diners even began to specialize in pollen. Wasps are meat-eaters, but many, such as yellowjackets, will nip a little plant protein when the opportunity presents itself. About 80 to 100 million

4. Some angiosperms such as birches, aspens, and grasses have gone back to wind pollination.

years ago, in the mid-Cretaceous, some of these wasps turned vegetarian. These were the first bees. They got hairy, which meant that, like flying dust mops, they were just great at getting pollen stuck all over themselves. They even developed panniers lined with hair on the rear legs for packing pollen. They evolved superb compound eyes and antennae for finding flowers. Most important, they became loyal customers, the kind every business dreams about. They stopped by and made multiple purchases every day.

But things soon got complicated. As the flowering plants conquered the world and the conifers retreated, the market matured. Competition intensified. Bees and other insects were faced with more varieties of flowers offering perfectly decent protein than they knew what to do with.

When everybody is flooding the airwaves with alluring ads, to get noticed you have to offer customers something extra: the freebie. Millions of years before Florida restaurants came up with the same concept, flowers began featuring free dessert with the early-bird special. They placed this nectar at the base of their flowers, behind the stamens and stigma—kind of the way supermarkets funnel you through aisles of stuff they hope will lodge in your cart before you get to the item you came for in the first place. In truth, nectar is more than dessert. With many vitamins and amino acids, it's more like the original sports drink.

Once you start a giveaway, it's hard to stop. Today, most flowers offer nectar, and nectar is the main draw for most pollinators. It's a good deal for the flowers, because carbohydrates are cheap to manufacture, while protein is expensive. Stuff your diners with unlimited bread rolls, then skimp on the steak.

But with so many different pollinators looking for the same stuff, and so many flowers offering it, problems arose. The whole point had been to mail a package directly from one individual to another of the same species. But if everybody is using the same postal service, and packages are unloaded at random at each stop, then very few packages are being delivered to the right address.

What would you do in such a situation? Well, you'd get a private courier service. That drives the stunning diversity of flowers we see in today's forests and meadows. Specialization is the name of the game; the fewer courier services you use, and the fewer the competitors who also use your service, the less likely a package is to get delivered to the wrong address.[5] It's a partnership between plants and animals, sometimes carried to extremes, that are among the most unlikely and breathtakingly beautiful creations in nature.

How to Read a Flower

Once you become fluent in the language of flower, a world of poetry awaits. Wander a garden or meadow and what had been colorful gibberish suddenly bursts with meaning. It's like hearing an aria in Italian. You can appreciate the emotion and the melody without knowing the language, but how much deeper the engagement when you know why everyone's so worked up.

Times Square has nothing on the average garden. The intensity, the Technicolor advertising, the hustle for business—a dazzling variety of goods and services are changing hands. But just as one customer is hankering for a slice of pizza, one wants sushi, and one is just looking for a friend and a hotel room for an hour, so different things are being offered in the garden.

---

5. Of course, if you use only one courier service and it goes out of business, you're screwed; more on that later.

Not all flowers like to specialize. Sometimes it pays to be McDonald's: reliable hours, open to everyone, affordable, no wait. It might not have the most exciting food, but it has stuff that most everyone likes. There you have the dandelion, a very general flower. Dandelions open at nine A.M., just as most pollinators are starting their work day, and close in the evening. They are one of many flowers that close shop on rainy days, when few customers are around and when their wares could be

How to Read a Flower

POLLINATOR	COLOR	SHAPE	NECTAR	POLLEN
Flies	White, yellow	Small	Limited	Limited
Gnats	Brown	Enclosed	Limited	Limited
Carrion feeders	Meat, mottled	Varies	No	Limited
Beetles	White	Large, cupped	Limited or none	Plentiful
Bees	Blue and purple; also white, yellow, pink	Small tubes, bilateral symmetry	Ample, often hidden	Limited
Butterflies	Red, lavender	Long, thin tubes	Ample	Limited
Moths	White	Tubes, no landing pads	Ample	Limited
Hummingbirds	Red, orange	Deep tubes	Plentiful	Limited
Bats	White; ultraviolet	Vase; often no petals	Plentiful; high in protein	Plentiful
Wind	No	Tiny	No	Very plentiful; powdery fine

diluted. Their ubiquitous yellow disk is the floral equivalent of the Golden Arches. That color puts them smack in the middle of the spectrum, for broad appeal, and their short flowers offer easily accessible nectar to all comers, from tiny flies to bumble bees. On the other hand, there isn't too much nectar in a dandelion, so diners with the means to get something better probably will.

Not surprisingly, dandelions are visited by hundreds of different

AROMA	SPECIAL FEATURES	EXAMPLES
Varies	Often traps, sometimes in understory	Cacao, sundew
Mushroomy	Often low to ground	Wild ginger, Dutchman's pipe
Fetid	Sometimes heat-generating	Red trillium, skunk cabbage
Spicy, fruity, stinky	Lots of room for orgies; often traps	Magnolia, arum lily
Bright, perfumed	Nectar guides, lipped landing pads	Clover, monkshood, lupine, lobelia, apple, almond, goldenrod
Fresh, fragrant	Nectar spurs and guides, broad landing pads	Sedum, milkweed
Thick, sweet	Nocturnal	Evening primrose, night-blooming cereus, yucca
No	Reinforced	Bee balm, fuchsia, cardinal flower, columbine
Intense, mousy, musky	Nocturnal; large and reinforced	Saguaro, century plant
No	Male and female flowers separate	Corn, birch, pine

insects. Bees, flies, and butterflies of all kinds frequent dandelions, as do beetles. None of these pollinators is terribly loyal to dandelions, so a lot of dandelion pollen probably gets rubbed off on a lot of wrong flowers. If dandelions were rare, or didn't tend to grow en masse, that might be a problem. But look at a lawn and you'll appreciate saturation strategy: any bugs working that patch of ground can't help but visit another dandelion sooner or later. The plan works, as you can tell from the seedy white heads of pollinated dandelions.

Now, say a plant wants to cater to a little more exclusive clientele. How to do it? The easiest way is to come up with an odor, appearance, or flavor that appeals only to certain types. As an example, consider . . . me. I'm forever sniffing daylilies. Something about the orange color and the elusive alpine scent, not to mention the fact that they're large enough to accept my nose, means that I can't pass a nice one without leaning in for a snootful. I'm not even terribly aware that I'm doing it, except that later my wife will glance at me and say, "Have you been sniffing the lilies again?" It takes me a moment to realize that the powdery, yellow-orange smudges on the tip of my schnoz have given me away.

On the other hand, I hate the sickly sweet smell of phlox. When it comes to pollination, I'm a fairly good daylily specialist. Were I the only pollinator in my garden, over the years the phlox would disappear and more and more daylilies would spring up. Not only that, but each generation of daylily would better reflect my personal tastes as I unwittingly cross-pollinated the ones that drew me. The lilies would evolve to please their pollinator. It's a supremely elegant system, constantly refining itself.

Another flower trick is to limit access. Putting the nectar at the end of a narrow tube will keep out most flies and beetles, whose mouthparts aren't long enough. That's a good way of targeting bees, who are highly sought clientele because (A) they work hard, pollinating more flowers per day than almost any other pollinator; (B) they have furry bodies, perfectly adapted to picking up pollen; and (C) they are loyal to a particular species of flower on any one foraging flight, meaning they don't deliver packages to the wrong address.

Bees' vision is shifted one notch to the right of ours; they can see ultraviolet but not red. They favor shades of blue and violet.[6] In general, they are better pollinators than flies and beetles, which can't see color and tend to go for the brighter white and yellow flowers. So blue and violet flowers are targeting a more exclusive bee clientele and providing the superior nectar it expects.

The many members of the mint family (mint, sage, wild bergamot, self-heal, bee balm) fall all over themselves to attract bees through color, aromatics, and shape. Not only do the tubes match bees' long tongues, but take a look at the floral lip. Mints have an underbite that makes an ideal landing pad for bees. Like little helicopters, bees can hover while feeding, but they have to burn fuel to do so. A helipad is much appreciated.

Bee balm, you may point out, is sometimes red, which bees can't see. And indeed, its floral tubes are the longest in the mint family—too long for honey bees but perfect for hummingbirds, who favor bee balm above almost anything except those drug-dispensing

6. However they will quickly learn to abandon their favorites if offered something better. That's why the nectar-rich white and pink flowers of fruit trees become mobbed with bees, even though those colors aren't at the top of their list.

hummingbird feeders. Birds love the color red, which is why hummingbird feeders incorporate it.[7] A classic hummingbird flower will feature extremely deep tubes, no scent (birds are weak smellers), copious nectar, and a strident red color. Such a quintessential flower exists: the cardinal flower, denizen of Northeast wetlands, which relies on ruby-throated hummingbirds for almost all its pollination. If you want a hummingbird feeder, skip the department store and buy yourself a cardinal flower.

The pollinators drive this evolution of flower tubes toward increasing length. Having a long tongue means you can access any nectar, shallow or deep. A look through the fossil record shows that the evolution of a longer-tongued pollinator is invariably followed by flowers lengthening their tubes to cater to it. The columbines, which evolved in North America quite recently, are an ideal example. They arrived as short-tubed flowers in a world already filled with long-tongued bumble bees and hummingbirds, and wasted no time in transforming into the extreme long-tubed ones we know today—so long, and difficult to access because of their pendant position, that only hummingbirds can easily reach the obvious knobs of nectar in the tips of the flower tubes.[8]

But what about a red flower that is relatively flat-topped, with lots of tiny, long-tubed blossoms and limited nectar? It can't possibly be for hummingbirds, which need tons of food to support their amphetamine-amped lifestyle. Hummingbirds burn through food at an astounding rate; if they don't eat during all of their waking hours, they starve. A full night's sleep would be fatal, except most of them go into torpor every night, reducing

7. It's also why so many berries are red.

8. Bumble bees, however, ever innovative, have learned to nibble off the knobs and savor the nectar, and you can do the same for a woodsy treat.

their metabolisms to a semi-comatose state. During the day, they can't afford to waste their time on any but the best plants. Butterflies, however, also love red, and have much humbler needs. They're also built more like gliders than helicopters; they can soar a long ways but can't navigate much in tight quarters. They need flowers with fairly broad platforms. They aren't very fast or prolific pollinators, but their gliding means they are especially good at cross-pollinating over long distances, improving the resilience of plant populations.[9]

Now, what about a night-blooming cereus, legendary cactus of the Sonoran Desert? By blooming nocturnally, it rules out the usual couriers. Flies, bees, butterflies, and birds are all fast asleep. Moths, however, are on the wing. Hawk moths, with their unrolling garden-hose proboscises, are night-blooming cereus's natural partner. At night, there's no point wasting energy on fancy colors; the challenge is to be seen at all. Most nocturnal flowers are white. Aroma becomes all the more important; strong, penetrating scents are needed to draw suitors through the dark.

Some night visitors demand more rewards than others. Another Sonoran dweller, the saguaro cactus, also blooms at night, but its flowers are huge, vase-shaped, and absolutely gushing with nectar. The average saguaro blossom has 5 milliliters of nectar, which is fifty thousand times that of a typical flower. It's also a hundred times more than a honey bee can drink without exploding. Honey bees sometimes catch saguaro flowers just opening, but they're useless as pollinators because they simply drink their fill, slosh back to the hive, and tell their colleagues to go check it out. No

9. Butterflies also prefer "sports drink"–style nectars that are high in amino acids. In tests, butterflies given nectars rich in amino acids laid more eggs and produced more offspring.

cross-pollination occurs. The intended pollinator—the only one in the region that can drink such quantities of nectar and still want more—is the lesser long-nosed bat.

Honey bees have also been known to scramble the plans of alfalfa plants. Alfalfa, like other legumes, has an ingenious mechanism built into its flowers. Examine one and you won't see any stamens or pistils. They're hidden beneath a slanted landing pad known as a keel. When a bee lands on the keel, its weight trips the mechanism, and the spring-loaded stamens and pistil launch upward, clocking the bee in the chin. The beauty of this system is that a bee can visit lots of other flowers in between alfalfa visits, but the alfalfa pollen is likely to remain untouched under her chin until another alfalfa pistil connects with it.

This works great with big, tough bumble bees and alkali bees, the native, ground-nesting bees of Utah that are used commercially to pollinate alfalfa seed crops. Honey bees, on the other hand, have those union contracts, which stipulate no punching in the chin. They don't like it, and quickly learn to avoid it by landing on the side of alfalfa flowers, tiptoeing in to steal the nectar without tripping the mechanism.

Many flowers hide their nectar and pollen in one way or another, relying on bumble bees' intelligence to free the goods. Tomatoes, which have no nectar, keep their pollen grains hidden inside tiny pores in the anthers. Honey bees didn't evolve with tomatoes, a New World species, and are clueless as to what to do with them. They land, look around, and move on. Some native bees, however, including bumble bees, know the secret. They land on the flower, grab the filaments with legs and mouth, and vibrate their wing muscles. When they hit the right frequency—about three hundred vibrations per second—the pollen grains come dancing out of the pores.

Greenhouse tomato production has engendered an entire industry of mail-order bumble bees. They arrive in cardboard boxes, like Happy Meals, and are turned loose in the greenhouses to buzz the tomatoes. Thank a bumble bee for your next hydroponic love apple.

"Buzz pollination" is a surprisingly common strategy among plants for selecting their couriers. Not only do the nightshades—tomatoes, peppers, potatoes, eggplants—practice it, but also blueberries and cranberries. About 8 percent of the world's flowering plants require buzz pollination, many of them from Australia.

Such cooperation has driven the coevolution of flowers and their pollinators, and it doesn't end at conception. The last thing a flower wants, once fertilized, is for pollinators to continue poking around in it. They might damage something, and in any case they'll have better luck elsewhere. Plants have many ways of signaling that they want to be left alone. Some change color once pollinated. Our old friend the almond has nectar that fluoresces under ultraviolet light, forming neon signs that help honey bees know which flowers still have food. The vanilla orchid flower makes the matter very clear by folding up and withering within a half hour of pollination.

The naturalist Bernd Heinrich noticed that bumble bees would often approach and reject multiple white clover blossoms before finally settling on one. He wondered whether scent was the clue: "I decided to take seriously the aphorism about sniffing the flowers. I lay back in the clover with my eyes closed, and a student held blossoms to my nostrils. With almost no practice I could, with 88 percent accuracy, determine whether or not an individual flower had been previously visited by a bumblebee. Unvisited flowers had a strong, sweet clover scent; visited flowers had a very weak scent."

Boutique Flowers

In small towns and rural areas, stores mustn't be too specialized. With a limited clientele, they have to sell products that appeal to a broad spectrum. Cities, however, with their teeming, multicultured demographics, can support all kinds of weird shops: the kite store, the gourmet cheese shop, the cult video enterprise. In fact, to succeed in retail in a city, you almost have to come up with a gimmick. So it is with flowers. The real eccentrics usually turn up amid the largest and most diverse markets—in the tropics. To us, feet planted on the ground, a tropical rainforest looks like a bunch of tree trunks. But the real action is a hundred feet in the air, where an elevated meadow, a floral banquet, is on display.

I've always thought there was something mysterious and vaguely unnerving about orchids—that dangerously alluring femme fatale quality. And it turns out I was right. For insects, the relationship really does get a bit twisted.

Orchids are cheaters. Some creative con-artist gene is at work in them, like a brilliant art forger, and it's hard not to admire them for it. They survive by their canniness. They make all kinds of promises, luring bugs in, then rarely deliver. Why give away nectar or pollen, after all, if you can get visitors some other way?

Some orchids mimic other flowers that do offer nectar or pollen. By the time the poor insect has nosed around and discovered the cupboard is bare, the orchid has tagged it with a special pollen packet, sticking it somewhere difficult to remove, like right between the eyes. Often the insect doesn't even know it's there. It's up to the next orchid to casually pickpocket the same insect.

What's really impressive about orchids is the number of scams they've come up with. What else besides food can lure a bug?

Shelter, and some orchids offer that. Aroma, at which the orchids are masters. Then there's the ultimate lure, better even than food or drink.

Sex. A number of orchids in the genus *Ophrys* have perfected the art of impersonating a horny female bee or wasp. Their lower lip looks, smells, and even feels for all the world like a furry female in a come-hither position. A male swoops by, lands on top of the "female," and goes for it. Entomologists call this "pseudo-copulation." After failing to find a pulse in his partner, the bee moves on in frustration to another, and another, and by the time he's exhausted himself, he's quite effectively cross-pollinated the lot.

A slightly more honest sexual transaction occurs in Central America between the bucket orchid and the golden bee, a tiny tropical jewel of iridescent gold, blue, and green. Male golden bees have developed a weakness for a cologne produced by this yellow, speckled orchid. In fact, they can't get a mate without it. The orchid is indeed shaped like a bucket, its modified petals swept back into eye-catching dragon wings, its oily cologne produced by two scent glands that hang over the bucket. At dawn, the flower opens and drips scent into the bucket for a few hours. Male golden bees quickly gather in agitated swarms, battling each other to get to the scent. They land on the thin edge of the bucket, rub cologne into reservoir glands on their back legs, and take off on a hot date, using the cologne to manufacture their own sexual pheromones.

But sometimes, in the scramble to get the cologne, a golden bee slips and falls into the bucket. He doesn't drown—the liquid comes to head-height—but he also can't fly while soaked in the oily broth. After thrashing around, he discovers a natural step, built into the orchid, that leads to an escape tunnel. It's a tight

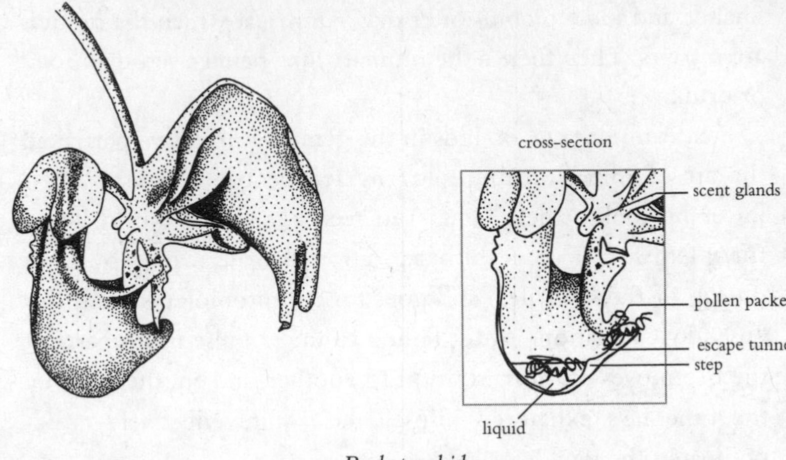

Bucket orchid

squeeze, but he manages to pull himself through the tunnel, brushing against a protuberance that, unbeknownst to him, hooks a pollen packet onto his back. Then, at last, the tunnel opens to freedom, and by then enough liquid has been squeegeed off that he can fly and still make his date. A few days later, he'll be back at another bucket orchid, which, if he falls in again, he will pollinate as he squeezes through the tunnel and leaves his pollen packet on a little hook in the tunnel designed for just that purpose.

I could go on, but you get the idea. A lot of the genius of our natural world owes its existence to the plant-pollinator partnership. Let's not take it for granted—not the 80 percent of our diet that depends on pollinators, the maple that makes our tables, the mangrove that stabilizes our southern coastlines, nor the rainforest that scrubs the carbon from our sweet air. We could go back to the drab, fruitless world of wind pollination that insects and land plants inhabited for 300 million years before flowers and bees arrived. I, for one, don't want to.

Chapter 11

FRUITLESS FALL

SOME VISIONS FROM a post-fertile world:

In Sichuan, China, thousands of laborers cling to the branches of blooming pear trees, pulling themselves carefully from limb to limb. They dip "pollination sticks"—bamboo twigs with chicken feathers and cigarette filters attached—into plastic bottles of pollen that hang in the trees, then touch the sticks to every blossom, hand-pollinating billions of flowers. The pollen comes from anthers that are plucked from flowers about to bloom, then dried in cardboard boxes under bare lightbulbs or on electric blankets until the pollen grains are released. Though it is spring and the hillsides are a lacework of white blossoms, no bees buzz through the orchards. The farmers say they haven't seen any insects in years, since pear orchards were planted on every hillside and massive spraying of insecticides began. Migratory beekeepers won't bring their bees anywhere near the area. So the "human bees" must go to work. Women—and children, when they're not at school—are best at reaching the thin upper branches.

On the Hawaiian island of Kauai, a botanist dangles off a cliff fifteen hundred feet over the sea, collecting pollen from male alula flowers and transferring it to female flowers. The six-foot succulent, which looks like "a bowling pin with a cabbage on top," grows only on sheer rock faces in Hawaii. Its only pollinator, a hawk moth, has vanished, and the plant hasn't reproduced in the wild in decades. It is extinct from Lanai and Maui and fewer than one hundred plants remain on Kauai.[1]

In the Himalayas, bankrupt peasants chop down their apple groves. Despite years of intensive irrigation, fertilization, and spraying, their trees have mysteriously stopped producing fruit. They don't know why, and believe there must be something wrong with the trees. Some locals have observed that the insects disappeared when the mountain forests were converted to apple orchards.

In Mexico, a vanilla farmer peels back the soft, greenish-white petals of a vanilla orchid, scraping pollen with a toothpick and transferring it to the stigma. The fertilized stem will grow into a vanilla pod. Each vanilla flower, which opens for one day only, has a flap protecting the pollen, and deforestation has wiped out the stingless melipona bees that knew how to manipulate the flap. No other pollinators have mastered the trick, and today all vanilla is hand-pollinated by humans, making it the most labor-intensive crop in the world.

These are not ominous visions of our near future. They are happening now. In fact, they've all been happening for years. The fertility crisis is under way. As with global warming, it sneaks up on you, and by then it may be too late.

If there is a silver lining in the cloud of colony collapse disorder,

---

1. Steve Perlman, the rappelling botanist, has been hand-pollinating alula for thirty years. The seeds he's collected have been used to propagate the plant in nurseries, so the species lives on, though the wild population is doomed.

it's that many people now understand that agriculture depends on honey bees. That's a big improvement over our naïveté of just a few years ago. But our enlightenment can't end at our dinner plate. Crops aren't the only plants that need pollinators. There are fruits and seeds of all kinds, most of them inedible and virtually unnoticeable to us. Yet, taken as a whole, they form the basis of our health and prosperity. They need their pollinators, and the pollinators need the plants just as much. They thrive together, and they fail together.

The exemplar of this mutualism is the strangler fig. Despite its menacing name, the strangler fig is a keystone species of the rainforest. Keystone species are the ecological equivalent of keystones in arches: Remove the keystone and the whole edifice falls. Understanding just how much depends on the fig and its bizarre pollination system will help us grasp the precariousness of even the largest, most intricate webs of life.

Figs are found in every rainforest, a thousand species in all. Considering their habits, they are unlikely candidates to support the whole forest. Fig seeds get their start not in the ground but in the treetops, deposited in the droppings of birds, monkeys, and other animals. From there, a shoot drops some hairlike roots toward the ground, wrapping other roots around its host tree for support. Spreading its own leaves among the host's, its roots grow thick as branches. Eventually they encircle the host's trunk and literally strangle it, cutting off the nutrient supply. With its own roots grown into huge columns drawing water from the ground, the fig can live for a century, long after the host trunk has decayed.

This all sounds a bit sinister, but by tackling the occasional giant, figs open up the canopy and help maintain the mix of species. The many crevices in fig trunks provide excellent habitat for small animals. Most important, figs are the best source of fruit in the forest. They bear fruit several times a year, and as you know if you've ever had to clean up after one in your backyard, they bear it prolifically. Different species of figs bear at different times, providing a nearly year-round high-energy food. Many animals depend on figs' productivity. Bats, monkeys, gibbons, parrots, hornbills, and toucans all eat the fruit off the trees. Small mammals and innumerable invertebrates eat the fallen fruit. Few of these creatures could survive without the figs, nor could the predators of these creatures. Take away the figs, and the rainforest breaks.

Yet all figs rely on a single, gnat-sized pollinator: the fig wasp. The entire life cycle of the fig wasp occurs inside figs. A fig is actually a composite flower folded in on itself; picture a petal-less sunflower closed into a ball, the thousands of tiny flowers opening into the middle of a hollow sphere. How on earth can a fig hope to get those concealed flowers pollinated?

One of the curious features of a fig is the eye, that pinprick hole in the fat end. It has but one purpose: to admit fig wasps. Inside the eye is a set of interlocked walls, like baffles in a water bed. The tiny fig wasps are the only ones with the diminutiveness and drive to navigate this labyrinth, and even they often lose their wings in the tight squeeze.

The interior of a fig is the only place on earth where a female fig wasp will lay her eggs. She makes it inside, already dusted with fig pollen for reasons that will soon be evident, and begins laying her eggs in the female flowers, which make perfect egg cups and even form a protective layer over the eggs. Half the female flowers have short styles and half have long styles, which are too long for her to lay eggs in because she can't reach to the bottom with her ovipositor—her egg-laying tube. But in the figgy darkness, she can't tell which is which until she drops her abdomen into them and pokes around. She lays eggs only in the short-styled flowers, but cross-pollinates the long-styled ones.

The long-styled flowers are fertile; each will produce a fig seed. The short-styled flowers are giveaways to the wasps. The pollen-sporting male flowers are bunched separately near the eye end.

Once the wasp has laid her eggs, she dies. A few weeks later, as the fig ripens, the eggs hatch, males emerging a day before females. The males are mole-cricket ugly. Smaller, wingless, almost blind, they have immense penises half the length of their body and strong, oversized jaws, which are good indicators of their only tasks in life. From the instant they hatch, they want to mate. They chew holes in the shells protecting the unhatched females and inseminate them. After that, they have just one more contribution. As the fig ripened, its eyehole closed, preventing further entry or exit. So the male wasps assemble at the eye end of the fig, where the male flowers happen to be, and chew quarter-inch escape tunnels through the wall. The males have neither means nor desire to leave the fig; they chew the tunnels purely as a service to the females. Once the tunnels are complete, the males withdraw inside the fig and die. The females then crawl to the tunnels, dragging their abdomens over

Fig

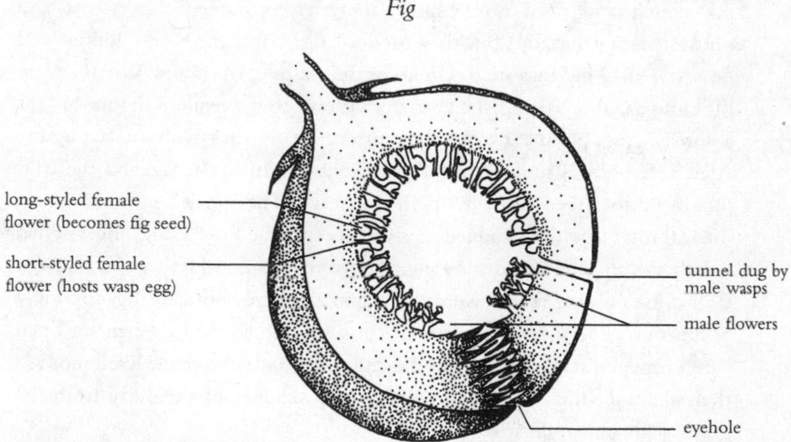

the male flowers in the process and picking up pollen. They squirm to freedom and fly off in search of a virgin fig for their eggs.[2]

This unbelievably esoteric pollination scheme helps explain why figs stagger their fruiting. It takes about a month from the time a female wasp lays her eggs to the time new females emerge from the ripe fig. If all figs ripened at the same time, there would be no virgin figs to take the next generation of eggs. Staggered fruiting suits the wasps, but it also provides the many frugivores of the rainforest a steady supply of food instead of a one-month bonanza.

Two halves of one metaspecies, figs and fig wasps starkly demonstrate the interrelations within an ecosystem, but they are an extreme. Rarely are a plant and pollinator so codependent, and rarely are so many other species reliant on the success of the relationship. Usually the relationships are looser, and the consequences of losing a partner less obvious. The disappearance of a

2. Right about now you may be thinking, "Are those crunchy things in my Fig Newtons mummified fig wasps?" Relax. Most cultivated figs are self-pollinating and need no wasps. Calimyrnas, however, the richest and nuttiest-tasting figs, do. But they produce figs containing only long-styled flowers—the kind that are too long for the wasps' ovipositors. When a wasp flies into a Calimyrna fig, she goes from flower to flower, looking in vain for a shorty, cross-pollinating the fig, and eventually dies without laying any eggs. Her body is soon dissolved by enzymes within the fig, and the fruit matures into a seed-filled, wasp-free delicacy. The "male" counterpart of the Calimyrna, which produces figs with both male flowers and short-styled female flowers and harbors the generations of wasps, is known as a caprifig. California's Calimyrna growers must maintain a grove of caprifigs to supply pollination. Every June, growers place wasp-riddled caprifig fruit in open paper bags and staple the bags to the limbs of Calimyrna trees. Even more so than almonds, this San Joaquin Valley crop dangles precariously from the grasp of its one pollinator.

single species of pollinator won't usually drive a plant into extinction; what's more likely is steady degradation—a continuous loss of resilience. As a pollinator's numbers dwindle, so do the populations of all the plants that rely on that pollinator for some of their pollination. Maybe other pollinators can pick up the slack, maybe they can't. Few of these plants or pollinators will be keystone species; most are just bricks in the arch. But if you take away enough bricks, the arch is sure to fall.

What is the health of these arches? How is the resilience of our wildlands? I'm afraid that for most of them, we simply have no idea. Science follows the funding. Who is going to fund studies of wild bugs so obscure they don't even have common names? May Berenbaum, chair of the National Research Council Committee on the Status of Pollinators in North America, spoke of "the pervasive absence of reliable data and the virtual nonexistence of efforts to acquire that data" when she testified before Congress in 2007 about the crisis. She put it this way: "Although data are insufficient to document population declines in flower-visiting flies in the U.S., there is a clear pattern of decline in the number of entomologists who can even identify these flies, much less monitor them." Even if we learn the current populations of certain pollinators, we have no previous baseline for comparison. We simply don't know how many bricks used to be in the arch. All we know is that bricks are crumbling every day.

Exhibit A: the bumble bee. Until recently, the most common bumble bee species in eastern North America was *Bombus affinis*, the rusty-patched bumble bee. If you were sitting in a meadow in Quebec or Virginia in 1990 and a large black-and-yellow-striped bee buzzed by, there's a good chance it was *B. affinis*. Not anymore. Sometime in the 1990s, something went wrong. Leif Richardson, a bumble bee researcher based in Vermont who spends a great deal of time collecting specimens in the field, hasn't seen one since 1999. At least four other bumble bee species have disappeared from Vermont in the past decade. The story is the same throughout the East.

The western bumble bee, *B. occidentalis*, was the most common bumble bee on the West Coast, from Alaska to California. It began disappearing from its range at the same time as *B. affinis* and is now completely gone from many parts of it.

Franklin's bumble bee, *B. franklini*, a bee limited to northern California and southern Oregon, is believed to have gone extinct over the same period.

Rarely can we pinpoint a direct cause for the decline of a wild insect. With these bumble bees, however, we have a pretty good guess. Remember those bumble bees being raised commercially for greenhouse tomato pollination? Europe pioneered the practice, and in 1992 and 1994 American tomato growers shipped bumble bee queens to Europe for breeding. Then the breeders sent bumble bee colonies back to the United States to work the greenhouses. Naturally, some escaped into the wild. Now it looks like those escapees carried a strain of nosema they'd picked up in Europe. The timing of the wild bees' decline coincides with the introduction of the greenhouse bumble bees. You could say that bumble bees have been suffering their own independent colony collapse, and we're only starting to notice.

While the nosema case has been dramatic, it's not the only threat facing bumble bees and other wild pollinators. By now, you can guess most of the causes. Habitat loss, pesticides, exotics. No doubt some surprising ones are yet to be discovered. For instance, University of Virginia researchers have learned that air pollution bonds with flowers' scent molecules and destroys them. Where pre-industrialization a flower's aroma might travel a mile, today, in areas downwind from cities, that range is reduced to a fifth of a mile, alerting far fewer pollinators to the presence of food.

In general, environmental threats are even more devastating for wild insects than for honey bees. Honey bees are temporarily exposed to agricultural pesticides while foraging, but wild insects, which often nest in the ground, are inundated. And they don't receive pollen patties when they look weak. When an introduced exotic ravages a wild population, who knows? When moths spend their evenings swirling around a light and never get around to eating or reproducing, who knows?

The only time we get an inkling that something is wrong is when the repercussions directly impact human interests. For instance, in 1970 the Canadian government sprayed the organophosphate fenitrothion over tens of thousands of acres of boreal forest in an attempt to control a catastrophic spruce-budworm outbreak. The spraying also killed most of the bumble bees in the blueberry-producing area of New Brunswick. Blueberry production fell to a shadow of what it had been and took many years to recover. Nova Scotia, which was not sprayed, suffered no dip in its blueberry output.

Ironically, the budworm outbreak was actually caused by the spraying of DDT years earlier. The spruce forest evolved to incorporate periodic budworm outbreaks every 40 to 120 years. Many trees would die, and this opened up the forest canopy, providing a feast for birds and other species that feed on budworms. The budworm would be decimated and the cycle would start again. It was an extremely resilient system.

But we wanted to save all that timber, so we sprayed yearly to control the budworms. This allowed unnaturally dense spruce growth to go on for years, forming a kind of protective mesh that prevented predators from reaching the budworms. The budworm population exploded beyond its natural limits, eventually triggering the intensive spraying that killed the bumble bees—which we never would have known were it not for New Brunswick's enraged blueberry farmers.

For a pollinator to get attention, it needs to be pretty or furry. Those are the only ones we know something about. In California, there's been a 40 percent decline in butterfly diversity in the past thirty years. Two of the three pollen-feeding bats in the United States are endangered. How are the less charismatic pollinators doing? We have no idea.

The National Research Council's 2007 report *The Status of Pollinators in North America* struggled with this lack of data: "Overall, whether there is a 'pollinator crisis' is difficult to ascertain inasmuch as there is no definition of 'crisis' that is universally accepted; however, if 'decline' is defined as a systematic decrease in population size over time, then there is evidence that some pollinators in North America representing a diversity of taxa are, in fact, in decline." Its list of failing pollinators ranged from honey bees and bumble bees to pollen wasps, the bay checkerspot butterfly, the rufous hummingbird, and many different bats.

The stingless bees of Mexico and Central America, the original pollinators of the vanilla orchid, are all but gone. A survey found that the number of managed hives in the Yucatán had fallen from more than 1,000 prior to 1981 to 389 in 1990, 96 in 2003, and a predicted 0 by 2008. Few wild colonies have been found. These bees were cultivated by the Maya for thousands of years; when they go, a millennial tradition dies with them.

In Brazil, the passion fruit industry relies entirely on hand pollination by day laborers due to the loss of the native carpenter bee.

In Europe, volunteer organizations have been monitoring pollinator populations for decades, so we can at least get some sense of the scope of the problem and extrapolate for the rest of the industrialized world. The group Butterfly Conservation found that the number of moths in Britain has dropped by a third in the past forty years. Two thirds of the species are in decline; a handful of opportunists are increasing their numbers. "There has been a definite increase in pollination rental fees in many parts of France," says Bernard Vaissiere, a pollination specialist with the French National Institute for Agricultural Research. "It is clear that insect-pollinated crops have a production price that is significantly higher than that of other crops."

The Survey of Wild Bees in Belgium and France and the E.U.'s Alarm Project have documented that most native pollinators seem to be faltering. In 2006, J. C. Biesmeijer of the University of Leeds looked at hundreds of sites in the U.K. and the Netherlands and found that, over twenty-five years, bee diversity had declined in 80 percent of them. Along with them went the insect-pollinated wildflowers: 70 percent of species have declined. "We were shocked by decline in plants as well as bees," Biesmeijer said. "If this pattern is replicated elsewhere, the 'pollinator services' we take for granted could be at risk. And with it the future for the plants we enjoy in our countryside. Whatever the cause, the study provides a worrying suggestion that declines in some species may trigger a cascade of local extinctions amongst other associated species."

Not all pollinators were in decline. Generalists, including many flies, were doing fine. As you might expect, it's the specialists—

along with their specialized flowers—that are disappearing. As these unique creations vanish, weed species move in. Dandelions will survive. Wind-pollinated and self-pollinated plants also have held steady over the same twenty-five-year period, which indicates that the pollinators are the weak link—and that the colorful angiosperm explosion may be fizzling at last.

There's some evidence that pollinators have always been the weak link. Of 258 species of wild insect-pollinated plants studied, 62 percent display "limited fruit set." In other words, they aren't producing an ideal number of seeds. They aren't getting all the pollinator visits they need. Has the state of the wild always been many plants competing for the services of a limited number of pollinators—and thus coming up with more and more creative ways to get them—or does this indicate a general malaise already settling into our ecosystems? Either way, it means we'd better start treating those pollinators like the precious commodity they are.

I could make the self-interest argument. I could say that wild pollinators contribute three billion dollars' worth of produce to U.S. agriculture each year. According to Rachel Winfree, a UC Davis researcher studying pollination on New Jersey farms, "I counted more native bees than honey bees on peppers and tomatoes, and similar numbers of honey bees and native bees on cantaloupes. At 91 percent of the farms I studied, native bees were fully pollinating the watermelons." Nothing can replace the honey bee as our pollination workhorse, but native bees count. Not only are they directly pollinating tomatoes, squash, blueberries, strawberries, alfalfa, watermelons, and other crops, but they also make honey bees better pollinators. When native bees and honey bees meet, the natives chase the honey bees, which hightail it to more welcoming rows, increasing the amount of outcrossing, which is essential to crops such as almonds, apples, and sunflowers. In this way, a few wild bees, acting like sheep dogs, can make honey bees up to *five times* more efficient at pollination. So I'm sympathetic to the self-interest argument. I don't want blueberries to become the new truffle. I don't want to splurge on them once a year.

I could also argue about "ecological services," which is really just the self-interest argument, one step removed. Bugs make berries. Bugs make willow trees, which stabilize our stream banks. Bugs make trout. Bugs make clean air and clean water. The rainforests of South America and Africa produce the water vapor that precipitates over crops in the Midwest, Texas, and Mexico, so even though American corn farmers grow a wind-pollinated crop, they can thank fig wasps in the Amazon for their rain.

Bird-watchers need bugs, too. Moths and butterflies may not be essential pollinators of many things that show up in our daily lives, but they do make caterpillars, which are nature's hot dogs—boneless, fatty, high-protein snacks, the perfect grab-and-go food. Not counting waterfowl, 96 percent of North American birds feed insects to their chicks. Frogs, toads, and other creatures also depend on them. Yet moths and butterflies are clearly in decline. When the chestnut forests of the eastern seaboard succumbed to the chestnut blight, five species of butterflies vanished with them. When the caterpillars go, so do the birds. In Delaware, for example, 40 percent of the native plant species are endangered, as are 41 percent of the forest birds. People want butterflies without caterpillars, but it doesn't work that way.

I could make the resilience argument. I could point out that we are far better equipped to bounce back from drought, plague, or pestilence if we have a variety of habitats and pollinators ready to pick up the slack, should the honey bee or any of our other main allies stumble.

Still, I don't want to end on any of these utilitarian arguments. They almost seem insulting. It's kind of like telling kids they need a mother because who else is going to make them toast and jam. It may be true, but it misses the point. They need a mother because a mother is a good thing to have.

So take your pick. We still have a choice about what kind of world we live and work in. Maybe we really can wipe out our pollinators, poison them and destroy their homes, and still get by. Maybe enough poor people will be so desperate that they'll willingly serve as human bees, sending their kids scrambling through the branches of orchards with cigarette filters in hand. Maybe a few of us will even be able to afford those fruits.

Or maybe we'll genetically modify all our resource plants to reproduce asexually. Maybe sex has run its course as a fruitful endeavor. Maybe we can trade the meadows, bogs, and rainforests for a land of well-regimented clones.

But why? Why choose the ugly world when we can still take the other one, the flirtatious one of fragrance and form? The one drenched in hope, possibility, and the ardent hum of new life being made.

Epilogue

FIRST FROST

IT'S FALL AGAIN, and there is urgency in the air. Goldenrod, the late-summer savior of so many bees, is gone, and the remaining pollinators work the last mallows and asters for whatever sustenance they can find. The crisp, cold nights have tipped them off; they know they are playing the endgame of another year. I wonder how many of the honey bees in the area will survive the winter, the heavy snows and 20-below nights. How many of these bumble bee queens will find comfortably appointed burrows before their bodies harden and desiccate?

This clear evening isn't cold yet. October sun is misleading. When it hits you straight in the face, it feels warm, but the heat doesn't linger. There will be a frost tonight. The fragile light and ice-blue skies give it away.

Having taken a bee's-eye view of the world for so long while working on this book, flowers will never seem frivolous to me again. I never liked cut flowers much. They seem like pornography—eroticism severed from context. Wildflowers, on the other hand, leave me breathless. The beauty and the genius of them. Now spotting a last pasture rose has something of the poignancy of finding a diner open at midnight, a light in the dark beckoning some hungry soul.

The sun's disk touches the western hills. Shadows reach toward infinity across my meadow. I let it go wild this year. In the past I brush-hogged it every summer, but now that I know how many bumble bees make their homes in the tussocks of thick grass, I couldn't bear to do it. If there's one thing I've learned by paying attention to bees for a while, it's that we need to get rid of this false dichotomy between productive land and unproductive land. There's no such thing as unproductive natural land. There's only a failure of human insight to recognize the ways it contributes, a failure of human imagination to recognize what we need.

I've ordered two nucs of honey bees from Kirk Webster. Russian bees. Survivors. They'll arrive in the spring and go in the northern edge of my meadow, facing south with a line of spruce trees behind them blocking the north wind, and if all goes well and bears don't get them and CCD doesn't find its way to my corner of the world, maybe they'll make a little honey. Maybe they'll even make a few extra zucchini and pumpkins on my neighbor's organic farm. I have no goals for their first year, other than to see them survive.

I could say much the same about the world's honey bees. I want to see them make it. And I think they will—but not without a lot of misery. CCD will continue to transform and appear in new guises, bees will continue to die, and our breakfasts will become either a lot more expensive or as monochromatic as the monocrops that provide them. It will undoubtedly get a lot worse than it is today. But out of that wreck, more resourceful and resilient bees will emerge.

I wonder if that's also true for beekeepers. I can't see how they're going to make it. Hobbyists, sure. But the economics of beekeeping simply don't work. In the next fifteen years, most of the commercial beekeepers in the United States will retire and won't be replaced. If CCD gets much worse, they'll give up sooner. "We can't stand another bug or virus or pest," Mark Brady, the president of the American Honey Producers Association, told me. "Right now this beekeeping industry is like crystal. It's that fragile. One slip and it will shatter."

If we are to avoid that, it will have to be a team effort—not just beekeepers, entomologists, and conservationists scrambling to find a miracle. We need to stop working the land quite so hard. We need to reenvision the place of beekeeping and farming in our culture. We need to let bugs into the club. If we don't, then not just our orchards, but all our efforts, will be fruitless.

At last, the sun dips behind the hillside and the wispy heat evaporates into space. The chill is instant. The gardens, abuzz with purpose only seconds ago, go silent.

Afterword

2009 UPDATE

PART OF THE pleasure of a traditional whodunit lies in the unmasking of the killer. The suspects are called into a drawing room. The brilliant detective works through their motives and alibis one by one, then dramatically turns, points, and the jig is up. A confession, an arrest, and the world goes back to working the way it used to.

If this book were a whodunit, it would be time to call the suspects into the room. But, of course, this is a work of nonfiction. Life doesn't work like a mystery story, and perhaps we should stop expecting tidy endings. Admitting our inability to control or predict complex systems may encourage us to design more resilient ones.

In 2009 the bee world made real progress in learning how to keep bees healthy, but we shouldn't expect a solution any time soon. "Some federal money did show up," Jerry Hayes told me. "There are several groups of really smart people with expensive equipment that will be working on this." But science is a slow, careful process, and Hayes is a realist: "This will take more time than most would like to admit."

The more researchers have looked, the more viruses they've found in honeybees. IAPV looks less like an evil genius and more like just another member of the rogue's gallery. On his beekeeper's blog on

The Daily Green, Kim Flottum, the editor of *Bee Culture*, called IAPV "a probable indicator, but not cause of CCD."

The jury is also out on the neonicotinoids. They still don't correlate strongly with colony collapse. That hasn't stopped Italy, Slovenia, and Germany from joining France in a ban on the pesticides. (Still, Europe suffered its worst losses yet in 2009, about 30 percent of all the bees on the continent.) In 2009 Britain's biggest farming cooperative also banned neonicotinoids as British beekeepers suffered their worst losses in memory and swarmed Parliament in protest. Does Europe know something the United States doesn't—or does the United States know more than it lets on? That's what the Natural Resources Defense Council wants to know: It has sued the EPA to force the release of studies done in 2003 on the impact of neonicotinoids on bees.

Bayer CropScience itself released a chilling internal study. The levels of Imidacloprid in fruit trees in its test plots, it turned out, were as high as four thousand ppb—enough to kill any bee almost instantly. These test plots had received a normal dose of Imidacloprid—the same as that used routinely on citrus and almond trees. Equally upsetting, other studies found that, in direct contrast to Bayer's earlier assurances, levels of Imidacloprid in crops did not dissipate with time, but sometimes actually increased a full year after application, to levels sufficient to obliterate any insect life that encountered these plants. Yet new neonicotinoids continue to be introduced to the market at the rate of about one per week.

But until we have more definitive evidence against the neonicotinoids, *Nosema ceranae* tops the Most Wanted list. It has turned up in many, but not all, collapsing colonies. Australia's beekeeping industry melted down in 2009 in the wake of a rip-roaring nosema outbreak. In response, Japan, which had relied on imports of Australian queen bees for much of its pollination industry, banned the Aussie queens, resulting in an immediate 50 percent spike in pollination fees and a countrywide crisis.

Fortunately, nosema is something that can be treated with the anti-fungal medicine fumagillin. The beekeeping community attacked nosema with vigor during the winter of 2008–09, tripling their use of fumagillin from the year before. Results looked promising. By January, beekeepers had lost around 20 percent of their hives—more than "normal," but far better than the 35 percent of the previous two winters.

In addition to treating nosema, many beekeepers finally got serious about bee nutrition. Out with the corn syrup, in with the protein patties. The result? The best bees in years.

These extra steps added to beekeepers' material and labor costs—at a time when their incomes were already severely stressed—but they were willing to take the gamble because of the record-high prices for almond pollination. Beekeepers took out all the stops and showed up in California with strong, expensive bees. And that's where things took a strange turn.

I'm not a mystery writer, but I am, it turns out, an ironist. Just as the beekeepers arrived, the almond market tanked. With the world economy collapsing, demand for almonds softened at last, and the record crop of 2008—1.7 billion pounds—left 300 million pounds of unsold nuts sitting in warehouses. The ineluctable laws of supply and demand again took hold, this time heading in the opposite direction. The wholesale price of almonds, instead of settling at $2 per pound as expected, plunged to $1.21 per pound, putting the value of the crop perilously close to the cost of production.

If that had been the almond growers' only challenge, they might have gone forward with their original plans, but an even bigger nightmare awaited. The state of California ran out of water. Growers had long relied on water allotments from state and federal irrigation projects to nourish their water-thirsty almond trees, and in February 2009 the announcement came that, due to the worst drought in decades, there would be none available for agriculture.

More than 200,000 acres of almonds in the San Joaquin Valley are flirting with fruitlessness unless they can find water sources.

Many growers canceled their orders for new almond trees. Many more abandoned thousands of acres of suddenly unprofitable groves, either ripping out the trees or simply not watering them. Bees? Who needs bees if you aren't making any nuts? In the words of Kim Flottum, California was "over-beed" and "under-treed."

Suddenly, almond pollination was a buyer's market. Those who still wanted bees were able to pick from a vast pool, and the price went down to as little as $100 per hive—not enough to support the beekeepers' new treatment-intensive regimens.

All bets are off as to where we go from here. The 2009 almond crop will be small, which should take care of the surplus. The total almond acreage is expected to settle in about 100,000 acres below the projections of a year ago—maybe more, if the drought doesn't ease. Either way, demand for honey bees will decrease. More beekeepers will go out of business or look for a different way to make money with their bees.

One thing they won't look to, unfortunately, is the industrial honey market. The price for industrial-grade honey remains depressed, and one reason, as Andrew Schneider documented in 2009 in an excellent series of articles for the *Seattle Post-Intelligencer*, is that honey laundering is out of control. Millions of pounds of illegal Chinese honey continue to enter the United States. The honey is first shipped to the Philippines, Thailand, Russia, India, Australia, and other countries, where papers are forged falsifying the country of origin. Then the honey is shipped to the United States. Some of the smugglers know it is contaminated with outlawed antibiotics. "There is definitely this problem," one Chinese shipper wrote to his U.S. importers. "I'm worried whether the FDA or USDA may get involved. Our future shipments will definitely have this fluoroquinolones, and it may take a couple of years to improve." The honey was sold to major

U.S. food companies. So far, the USDA has made a few arrests, but not enough to staunch the flow of illegal honey. Until they do more, two-thirds of the domestic market will remain unviable for the surviving U.S. beekeepers.

How many of those there will be remains to be seen. While west coast beekeepers were congregating in California, emerging from winter and daring to get a little hopeful that the worst was over, a shudder went through the ranks of their east coast compatriots. The ever thoughtful Kim Flottum captured the feeling on his blog:

"Colony Collapse Disorder strikes most often right about now, and up until right about now things were going just fine. Finer, in fact than in years. I, in my optimism, listened to all of the experts and all of the beekeepers and even saw all of the improvements . . . better nutrition, fewer mite-controlling chemicals, cleaner hives, less pesticide exposure. And it looked good. Really, it did. Or at least it did on the west coast."

In the southeast, however, CCD reared its head yet again. Many apiaries collapsed, showing moderate levels of nosema infection and numerous viral infections. There were no significant pesticide residues, and the bees had been well cared for. Flottum's conclusion? "If, indeed, Colony Collapse Disorder is a pathogen, this is the prime example of what it looks like. No cell phones. No pesticides. No bad food. A complex of viruses, bacteria and . . . and what?

"And just to cloud the picture, another east coast operation, with a history of having colony collapse disorder in the past, had it again right at the end of January . . . right on time. This time they were aware of what was going on and called in the scientists. Mites, *Nosema* off the scale, and a long, dwindling decline. An indistinct virus complex with no real other obvious causes . . . go figure. Maybe one of the viruses is in common with the rest. Maybe. Maybe not. Maybe something else. Like I said. It's not over till it's over. And it's not over yet."

Appendix 1

THE AFRICAN PARADOX

A honey bee exists that controls varroa mites, eliminates small hive beetles, forages for all its own food, makes tons of honey, reproduces prolifically, and thrives without treatments or intervention. Its traits don't get watered down by interbreeding with neighboring bees, because its queens hatch earlier than Italian queens and sting to death any rivals, meaning its genes quickly come to dominate the hive. In no time at all, this tough little bee can transform an apiary.

There's only one problem. It'll sting the bejesus out of everyone it can. Yes, it's the Africanized "killer" bee.

The killer bee is not the creation of some mad scientist's lab, though it did escape from a scientist in Brazil in the 1950s. Warwick Kerr had imported the bee from South Africa. It's a different race of *Apis mellifera*, and is probably a lot like what our honey bee was before it moved to Europe and went soft.

The European honey bee is adapted to a temperate lifestyle. Its survival strategies are built around a long, dormant winter and an intense nectar flow condensed into a few short months, requiring a steep buildup of foragers in the spring. It can adjust to a Floridian, subtropical lifestyle, but in the full tropics of Brazil, with much more sporadic nectar flows throughout the year, it struggles. Warwick Kerr figured the African strain of honey bee, already adapted to the tropics, might do better in Brazil. He'd heard that it had a nasty streak in it, but he hoped that could be bred out once the bee was removed from its survival-of-the-fittest homeland.[1]

Kerr got it half right. The African bee did indeed take well to the New World. But it showed no signs of controlling its temper.

In 1957 twenty-six African queens escaped into the soft Brazilian air and did what queen bees do best. Soon "Africanized" hives filled the countryside. Not only did they establish feral colonies, but Africanized drones also found European queens on mating flights and planted their little time bombs inside. Africanized bees are slightly smaller than European bees. They take slightly less time to develop and hatch. And since the first thing a virgin queen does upon hatching is to go through the colony and sting to death any other developing queens, commercial hives throughout the tropics became Africanized with shocking swiftness.

Africanized bees are mean, lean, stinging machines. Whereas a threatened European colony will sting once or twice and then go back to business, an Africanized colony piles on. Once a little alarm pheromone fills the air, they sting by the hundreds. And they don't give up easily. Africanized bees will pursue a victim to ridiculous lengths. Don't jump in a pool; they'll outwait you. If you escape indoors, they'll camp out until you poke your nose outside. One beekeeper told me he'd seen an African colony pursue a passing robin, mob it, and kill it.

1. And why wouldn't it be nasty, evolving in Africa? This is the continent, after all, where even the *birds* guide hunters to bee nests.

In Brazil, Africanized bees killed a lot of livestock, as well as a few people. They spread more than one hundred miles a year, reaching Central America and Mexico in the 1980s and Texas in 1990, hitting California by 2000. In 2005 they showed up in Florida, possibly having arrived by ship in Tampa. On average, Africanized bees kill one person per year in the United States. For perspective, this puts them in a tie with circus elephants. Yet they cause enough fear to make beekeepers' jobs extremely difficult.

But here's a funny thing about those Africanized bees. They're ornery little bastards, but they do everything else well. They make lots of honey. They are naturally disease-resistant. They aggressively kill varroa mites. And they are good pollinators. Because the coffee shrub is self-pollinating, people believed that it had no use for pollinators. But David Roubik, a Smithsonian Institution researcher, observed that areas adopting intensive, monocrop-style coffee cultivation suffered declining yields of 20 to 50 percent, while areas practicing traditional shade-grown coffee, which are connected to forest habitat, mostly in Central and South America, show increasing yields. Could the difference be the pollinators? To find out, Roubik encased a branch of flowers on fifty coffee shrubs in fine mesh so they couldn't be pollinated. The non-bagged plants produced 49 percent more coffee berries, and those berries tended to be heavier. Roubik estimates that Africanized bees are responsible for 36 percent of this yield. "From what I see going on in the neotropics, the work of two or three dozen wild African honey bees is in every cup of coffee that you drink."

The Africanized bee arrived at the U.S. border just as the varroa mite was decimating the European bee. Aware of its hardiness, a few rogue beekeepers wondered if the African bee might be their salvation instead of their worst nightmare. The ones who tried working with it gave up once they became human pincushions.

But they kept on thinking about the Africanized bees' ability to control varroa.

Two Arizona beekeepers, Ed and Dee Lusby, suspected that the secret was cell size. Africanized bees are smaller and build slightly smaller honeycomb. Moreover, the Asian honey bee, varroa's original host, is also smaller and is able to control varroa. The Lusbys had pored through nineteenth-century records of Lorenzo Langstroth, M.G. Dadant, and the other pioneers of the modern, movable-frame, mass-produced hive. They discovered the writings of European entomologists who theorized that larger cells would make larger bees, which would produce more honey.

That was the era when the foundation used on frames in Langstroth hives was standardized. Foundation is a thin sheet of wax held in the wooden frame like glazing in a window. It encourages bees to fill out the entire rectangular frame with honeycomb, instead of forming the messy, irregular comb they build if they have no guidelines. By imprinting a hexagonal pattern on the foundation, beekeepers could control the exact size and shape of the comb. The bees dutifully follow the established ridges.

Regimenting bees into rectangular sheets of identical comb in uniform boxes allowed busy beekeepers to manage hundreds of hives a day. Later a wire grid was added to reinforce foundation so it could stand up to multiple honey extractions using mechanized equipment. After experimenting with various sizes of honeycomb, the industry settled on a foundation cell diameter of 5.4 millimeters—and that's what managed bees have been building ever since.

What if that's the problem? asked the Lusbys. What if our bees are Barry Bonds bees and have been warped in the process? To find out, the Lusbys custom-built frames with smaller, killer-bee-sized cells.

Sure enough, some of their bees, when established in the new hives, started detecting and eliminating varroa just like killer bees. That was the good news. The bad news was that 90 percent of their bees died. Bees had a great deal of trouble drawing out 4.9-millimeter comb, sometimes leading to colony collapse, and they suffered poor queen performance, at least for the first few generations. The Lusbys believed this was an unavoidable part of "regressing" bees back to a smaller size. It took a few generations to select for bees with the smaller genes, and in the process all the larger bees that couldn't function on small-cell comb would die. But once you got bees back to their "normal" size, they would become naturally disease and parasite resistant.

The Lusbys kicked off a small-cell movement that is still going strong. Dadant, the leading manufacturer of beekeeping equipment, began selling 4.9-millimeter foundation in 2000. Few commercial beekeepers converted, because they couldn't afford to lose 90 percent of their stock in the process or to buy so much new equipment, but most of the hobbyists who converted found that their surviving bees had no mite problems. Studies continue to show that small-cell hives have less than 10 percent of the mites of large-cell hives.

No one knows why smaller brood cells solve the mite problem. The most convincing theory is that small cells allow the nurse bees to hear the mites. An abnormally large brood cell leaves plenty of room for mites to silently move around the pupa, but a tight cell forces them to scrape against the walls and even push the pupa's legs out of the way. Perhaps the nurse bees hear these scrapings and quickly act to evict the intruders.

Another piece of the puzzle may be development time. Michael Bush, a small-cell proponent, has found that his 4.9-millimeter cells reduce the time elapsed from egg laying to capping of the pupa by one day, and reduce the time it takes the capped pupa to hatch by another day. This gives adult mites less time to slip into a cell after an egg is laid, meaning fewer mites in the cells when they're capped, and less time to reproduce in the cells once they're capped. Simply taking these two days off the normal twenty-one-day development process from egg to adult can reduce overall mite numbers by 75 percent or more.

Dennis Murrell, a Wyoming beekeeper who became a small-cell convert after trying a few small-cell hives and watching them go to work on varroa, came to believe it had nothing to do with genetics and everything to do with environment. "Every bee race I've put on small-cell comb has demonstrated [the ability to detect varroa]. I've tried queens from every major U.S. commercial queen producer. These same bees, when put on large-cell comb, didn't show that behavior. When on small-cell comb, the bees did more than remove the mites. They destroyed them. Over 90 percent of the mite fall had visible damage." The bees would often chew the mites' legs off.

Yet small-cell beekeeping had too many of its own problems, and Dennis Murrell thought that seemed strange. If it was the natural way to keep bees, why was it so difficult?

One day a friend showed Murrell a detailed photograph of a feral hive. These bees, given no foundation and forced to make their own honeycomb from scratch, built a variety of cell sizes. Along the top were a few rows of very large cells nearly 6 millimeters in diameter. Then the comb transitioned to large cells of about 5.4 millimeters, like those in a modern hive, and then at the bottom were small cells of 4.6 to 4.9 millimeters.

Left to their own devices, bees constructed a mixture of cell sizes. This was a revelation. Undoubtedly the developers of the modern hive, when deciding what size to make their foundation, had studied natural hives and observed this. But that was the nineteenth century; the industrial revolution was in full swing and there seemed to be nothing in nature that couldn't be improved by man. The hive pioneers probably thought the bees were just sloppy with their mismatched cells.

Murrell thought otherwise. Maybe the bees had a reason for designing the honeycomb as they did. To find out, he built his own top-bar hives. A top-bar hive has no frames or foundation. Instead, it is an empty box with wooden strips along the top to give bees a place to start their own comb. Its sides narrow as it goes down, like a fitted shirt, because that is the natural shape of honeycomb.

For the next decade, Murrell ran a series of experiments using top-bar hives and standard Langstroth ones, both small- and large-cell. He kept extensive records. And he said he found out that "everything I thought I'd known about beekeeping was wrong. I'd spent decades as what I considered a cutting-edge commercial beekeeper. I stayed on top of new developments and technology. I prided myself that it was my knowledge and intensive management that kept my bees healthy. So it was quite a shock to realize that my bees would have done better without me all along."

Any bees that Murrell put in a top-bar hive, whether from 5.4- or 4.9-millimeter cells, immediately built a natural-cell hive with tapered honeycomb—and completed it much faster than bees working from foundation. Mites disappeared from the hives: he might find one a week in his top-bar hives, versus one hundred or more in his 5.4-millimeter hives. Somehow the colony's collective intelligence had been awoken by the architecture of the hive. Not only did they begin their search-and-destroy missions on the mites, but each generation of bees also got better at it, as if some dormant gene was being switched on after a century of slumber.

Other diseases, especially chalkbrood, disappeared too. The natural-cell hives became extremely vigorous. Spring swarming became a nonissue. They produced an average of 240 pounds of honey per hive, versus 70 for the other hives. The queens laid prolifically. Most commercial beekeepers must requeen their hives every year as the queens fall apart. In Florida, they requeen every six months. Murrell's natural-cell queens invariably lived three years, often longer. He even took failing queens from standard hives, shook them into top-bar hives, and watched them "miraculously" recover.

If natural-cell hives can solve varroa, chalkbrood, and other problems, can they solve CCD? It's a tantalizing idea. If the multiple-stressor theory of CCD is right, then natural hives are one answer. No mites, no miticides, less disease. A low-stress lifestyle in a stimulating, supportive bee environment.

Murrell designed some of his top-bar hives as observation hives, with a glass side that could be exposed for viewing. The more he watched those hives, the more he understood the intelligence behind the architecture. The small cells along the bottom of the comb, near the hive's entrance, form the core of the brood nest. Bees overwinter on the core, where the smaller spaces allow them to cluster more tightly and keep warm. They can tend to the brood, detect pests, and reach food with minimal energy expenditure. When spring arrives, the queen starts laying in these small cells. The bees that emerge are relatively small. Meanwhile, the colony has spent the winter eating the honey stores, so the cells above the core are open, and that's where the queen expands her laying.

As spring progresses, the colony continues eating its way up through the stores, moving to larger cells. The queen follows behind, expanding her laying as cells open up. The population expands, making more foragers. Food comes into the hive and is packed on the periphery. In preparation for late-spring swarming, a colony in a natural-cell hive will start backfilling the empty core with food to be used on the journey. This prevents the queen from laying in those small cells and leaving too many brood for the non-swarmers to care for. In fact, the queen instinctually avoids laying in the small cells of the brood core at that time—which explains the poor midseason performance of queens in small-cell hives.

During summer, queens prefer to lay in the 5.4-millimeter cells that have opened up, then finally in the 6-millimeter drone cells at the top. Large summer bees hatch from the 5.4-millimeter cells. These bees, the draft horses of the colony, power a surge of food gathering in late summer and early fall. The colony packs in resources for the winter, filling the brood chamber—except for the core, which is again empty. There, the last batch of brood for the year is laid. These fall bees will again be smaller, like the spring bees. With high-quality food supplies and few brood to share it with, they become the long-lived winter bees.

Understanding this seasonal cycle of the colony illuminates the problems of both large-cell and small-cell hives. The large-cell hives have no true brood core. Instead, the kids are being raised in warehouse spaces. No wonder they have vermin! The small-cell hives, on the other hand, have nothing but brood core. This solves their mite problems, but it confuses the queens and slows the colony's expansion in summer.

If Murrell is right, then foundation, a basic pillar of modern beekeeping, may be a fundamental problem. The latest trend is toward plastic foundation, which is far cheaper than natural beeswax. The bees don't like it—everyone agrees on that—but it sure is durable, and often the bees can be tricked into accepting it. Yet, if we see the colony as a superorganism, the thought of plastic foundation is unsettling. Wax comes from bees' own bodies. It's as much a part of the living colony as our hair and nails are part of us. Comb is the bones of the colony. When we square off those bones, cut them to fit our needs, and add plastic cores, how can we expect the bees to do anything but fail?

It's important to note that alternative-cell hives are still controversial, which is why I've placed this information in an appendix rather than as part of the main story. Only a minority of beekeepers believe that large-cell hives are unnatural or that natural-cell hives solve things. Natural-cell hives aren't durable enough to stand up to forklifts or industrial honey extractors. They certainly can't help the large-scale commercial beekeepers who have hundreds of thousands of dollars invested in traditional equipment. A natural-cell revolution won't save agriculture.

But it might revitalize hobby beekeeping. Dennis Murrell has had many young beekeepers come to him for advice. Like the new generation of organic farmers, they are open to new ideas and creative solutions and more likely to take their cues from nature. What does he tell these youngsters? "Let the bees show you." If we can do that, then one of our oldest partnerships might be saved after all.

Appendix 2

KEEPING BEES

If you come away from this book with an irresistible urge to get your first beehive, then I couldn't be happier. That's pretty much what happened to me, so we're in the same beginner's boat. It's an ideal, life-affirming hobby. If every rural and suburban household (and even a few urban ones) kept its own bees, as was true once upon a time, then we could make a significant dent in the pollination crisis. We'd enhance the productivity of our vegetable gardens, and we'd have a new attitude. A public no longer fearful of bees, and aware of the role bugs play in our lives, will make better decisions.

Be prepared to throw down a few hundred bucks for bees and equipment. Betterbee (www.betterbee.com), one of the large suppliers of beekeeping equipment, offers a beginner's kit of everything but the bees—hives, veil, gloves, smoker, etc.—for around $230. Bees run about $80 to $150 per nuc, depending on the number of frames in the nuc and the quality of the bees. That's a fairly pricey hobby, but as ranching goes, it's dirt cheap. You get the pleasure of working in partnership with living animals and of seeing the land in a whole new way, and you can do it on a tiny patch of ground.

Still, don't go into beekeeping lightly. It takes a serious commitment of time and mental energy. Bees die—for all the reasons explored in this book, plus many less mysterious ones. I've been amazed by how many beekeepers I know who have lost their colonies to bears. It's entertaining to attend beekeeper meetings and listen to the members brainstorm about solutions. Barbed wire fence? Weak. Electric fence? Bears go through them like water. Sheets of plywood with upright nails in them? Well, maybe.

Bees especially die in the hands of beginners. I'm setting my expectations low as I get started, trying to improve my odds by getting bees that are bred to be mite-resistant and are already adapted to my microclimate, and I'd counsel you to do the same. Get local bees.

Even so, a million things will go wrong, and when they do, you'll need expert advice. Some can come from books. The 930-page bible of beekeeping, in print since 1877 and now in its forty-first edition, is *ABC & XYZ of Bee Culture*. It can be ordered from www.beeculture.com, which also provides an entire supply catalog as well as subscriptions to *Bee Culture*, one of the two venerable beekeeping magazines. (I just wish it had kept its wonderfully archaic original title, *Gleanings in Bee Culture*.) For a smaller, nimbler guide, pick up *Bee Culture* editor Kim Flottum's book *The Backyard Beekeeper*. If you plan on doing things organically—and if you aren't, you must have skipped half this book—then I highly recommend Ross Conrad's thorough and thoughtful *Natural Beekeeping: Organic Approaches to Modern Apiculture*, which came out in 2007. I've found reading *American Bee Journal* priceless in keeping up-to-date with developments in the honey bee world; every issue seems to have an article that changes my understanding of some fundamental beekeeping principle. It can be found, along with all other things bee, at www.dadant.com.

Even better than a book or magazine is a beekeeping club, where lots of seasoned veterans will give you all the amused advice you want. You can find a list of U.S. beekeeping associations by state at www.beesource.com.

If Kirk Webster's Russian bees particularly interest you, then get on his list now. He sells out nearly a year in advance. Pickups are in May. Then you get to alarm people by telling them that you've got a few Russian nucs in your yard. Contact Champlain Valley Bees and Queens, Box 381, Middlebury, VT 05753, 802-758-2501.

If you want to try constructing a natural-cell hive, Dennis Murrell provides lots of guidance at www.bwrangler.com.

And finally, if you can't keep a hive right now but you'd like to see honey bees pull through, you can donate to Project Apis m. (PAm), a nonprofit that raises money for research to improve the health of honey bees, at www.projectapism.org.

Appendix 3

CULTIVATING A POLLINATOR GARDEN

In our minds, we tend to picture a perfect division between human areas and wild ones. Humans live in the cities, towns, and suburbs, while wildlife lives in the national forests. If you want to view wildlife, you have to go visit a national park. But the reality is very different—just ask anyone whose gardens have been decimated by deer. Clear boundary lines appear only on maps; in the real world, wild communities and human ones interlock like clasped hands, giving many opportunities for direct experience of nature. You just have to reset your sights and stop fixating on "charismatic megafauna"—lions and tigers and bears. A hawk moth is every bit as wild as a grizzly bear, and it's a lot safer to feed.

By landscaping your yard with pollinators in mind, you put yourself at that intersection of communities. You invite the wild right up to your door. Not only does that allow you and your family to appreciate wildlife and interact with it—bees rarely sting when in flowers—but it can also make a difference. One lot-sized garden is not going to save an endangered pollinator, but it can be an important emergency food source in times of scarcity, and if it encourages your neighbors to do the same, then you might just transform your area into a de facto nature preserve. If you happen to work with large areas of land, such as golf courses, business or college campuses, or even roadsides, then you have a tremendous opportunity to restore important pollinator habitat.

Not all plants are created equal. Some provide much better sources of nectar and pollen than others. Some attract only certain species, so make sure you plant varieties that appeal to those species you want to see. Here are ten tips to get you started:

- **Avoid "plastic" flowers.** Many modern, showy flower varieties, such as double hollyhocks and sunflowers, provide no nectar or pollen. Bred for garish features, they have lost their basic functionality and are about as wholesome as plastic food. They actually serve to distract pollinators from useful flowers. Tulips, salvia, marigolds, pansies, lilacs, and crape myrtle are all of limited or no use to insects. See the list of good pollinator plants at the end of this appendix.
- **Go native.** Many nonnative flowers provide excellent nutrition, but some don't. Landscaping with native plants is the best way to ensure that your gardens make good forage—if they didn't, those species would no longer exist! On average, native flowers attract four times as many pollinators as nonnative ones. Lists of native plants for any region are available from native plant societies, and often from nurseries. You can also use the resources at the end of this appendix to get started.
- **Think like a bog.** Over the eons, bog flowers have evolved to cooperate with each other to keep their polli-

nators healthy. They don't clump their blooming into one brief period. Instead, they tend to bloom in sequence, with one or two species taking charge for a week or two before handing off the pollen baton to the next species, providing a steady three-season supply of food. Designing your own gardens to extend the blooming season will please your eye and your local bugs' stomachs.

- **Mix it up.** Most pollinators require more than one floral source to get their complete nutritional needs. Planting a variety of colors, shapes, and types of flowers ensures that pollinators can graze from a full buffet.
- **Size matters.** Most pollinators initially spot flowers from a distance, meaning a large block of a single color (three or four feet across) is more likely to catch their eye. Mixed colors won't attract the same attention.
- **Don't poison the food.** Avoid pesticides of all kinds in your garden. Insecticides, fungicides, herbicides—if it says that it kills one type of bug, it probably kills them all. Any kind of lawn-care product is going to seep into your flower beds, too—in fact, consider eliminating as much of your lawn as possible; a mowed lawn is an ecological wasteland.
- **Develop condos.** Pollinators do not live by food alone. They also need homes. For most pollinators, suitable nesting sites are probably scarcer than food. You can help here, too. Don't think of your land as just a pollinator restaurant, but as a whole planned community—a Villages for bugs, minus the golf carts. About one third of wild bee species nest in wood, so you can build your own bee condo by drilling holes into a block of wood, adding a roof to keep them dry,

and affixing the block to a tree or post. The resources at the end of this appendix provide links to instructions for building bee boxes (which can also be bought at some nurseries and garden centers). Better still, develop a new appreciation for nature's condos—snags. Standing deadwood is one of the most ecologically important parts of an ecosystem, as it's home to all manner of bees, beetles, larvae, bats, and birds.

- **Leave it bare.** Two thirds of bee species nest in the ground in old burrows and cavities. Give them small patches of well-drained, exposed ground, preferably facing south for warmth.
- **Go shaggy.** Bumble bees and many other insects often nest in tussocks of tall grass. Various moths, butterflies, bees, and beetles overwinter inside plant stems. Mowing your fields several times a year decimates those communities. Consider mowing in rotation so that the majority of your field is left intact at any one time.
- **Think about the kids.** Bees feed their young, but most other insect pollinators do not. Supporting a viable population of butterflies or moths means catering to the needs of caterpillars as well. Milkweed leaves, for example, are essential to monarch caterpillars.

More Information

Xerces Society

www.xerces.org, 503-232-6639

Named after the Xerces blue, the first butterfly in the United States to go extinct, the Xerces Society is dedicated to the conservation of invertebrates. Its fabulous Web site provides a wealth of publications that can be downloaded as pdf files, including *Farming for Bees: Guidelines for Providing Native Bee Habitat on Farms*; *Pollinator-Friendly Parks: How to Enhance Parks and Greenspaces for Native Pollinator Insects*; *Making Room for Native Pollinators: How to Create Habitat for Pollinator Insects on Golf Courses*; and *Pollinators in Natural Areas: A Primer for Habitat Management*. You can also order its beautiful books *Pollinator Conservation Handbook*, the ideal all-in-one source for individuals and educators, and *Butterfly Gardening*.

Pollinator Partnership
www.pollinator.org

This clearinghouse provides links to every sort of pollinator resource, from articles like "How to Build a Pollinator Garden" to lists of native plants attractive to bees and instructions for building bee boxes.

Bringing Nature Home

Doug Tallamy's 2008 book, *Bringing Nature Home: How Native Plants Sustain Wildlife in Our Gardens*, includes detailed "food webs" showing the interactions between plants, insects, and other wildlife and provides guidance for maximizing the wildlife potential of your land.

BeeSpotter
http://beespotter.mste.uiuc.edu

While you're feeding wild bees with your garden, you can help the experts learn what species are in your area. A project at the University of Illinois spearheaded by May Berenbaum, chair of the National Research Council Committee on the Status of Pollinators in North America, BeeSpotter is addressing the dearth of data on wild bees in the United States by enlisting citizens and their digital cameras. You just head outside, take some good photos of bees, post them to the site, then the pros at UI identify them.

Plants Attractive to Native Bees

GENUS	COMMON NAME	NOTES
Abelia	abelia	
Acacia	acacia	
Acer	maple	
Achillea	yarrow	*A. millefolium* weedy
Aconitum	monkshood	
Agastache	hyssop	
Ajuga	carpet bugle	
Althea	hollyhock	not doubled
Allium	allium	
Amelanchier	serviceberry	
Anchusa	wild forget-me-not	
Anethum	dill	
Aquilegia	columbine	not doubled
Arctostaphylos	manzanita	
Argemone	prickly poppy	
Armeria	sea thrift	
Aster	aster	not doubled
Astragalus	locoweed	
Baileya	desert marigold	

(*Continued*)

GENUS	COMMON NAME	NOTES
Baptisia	false indigo	
Berberis	barberry	
Borago	borage	
Brassica	mustard	*B. kaber* and *B. nigra* weedy
Calamintha	calamint	
Callirhoe	wine cups, poppy mallow	
Calluna	heather	
Camissonia	camissonia	
Campanula	bell flower	
Caragena	Siberian peashrub	
Carpobrotus	ice plant	some weedy
Carthamnus	safflower	
Caryopteris	blue mist spirea	
Cassia	senna	
Ceanothus	buckbrush	
Centaurea	bachelor's button, corn flower	not doubled, some weedy
Cerastium	snow-in-summer	avoid chickweeds
Cercidium	palo verde	
Cercis	redbud	
Cercocarpus	mountain mahogany	
Chaenomeles	flowering quince	
Chilopsis	desert willow	
Chrysanthemum	chrysanthemum	simple flowered
Chrysothamnus	rabbit brush, chamisa	
Citrullus	watcrmelon	
Citrus	grapefruit, orange, lemon	

Coronilla	crownvetch	
Cucurbita	squash, gourd, pumpkin	
Clarkia	clarkia	not doubled
Cosmos	cosmos	
Coriandrum	coriander	
Coreopsis	coreopsis	
Cuphea	false heather	*C. hyssopifolia*
Cydonia	fruiting quince	
Cynara	artichoke, cardoon	
Cynoglossum	comfrey	
Daucus	carrot	some weedy
Delphinium	larkspur	not doubled
Digitalis	foxglove	
Echinacea	cone flower	
Echium	pride of Madeira	*E. fastuosum*
Erigeron	fleabane	
Eriodictyon	yerba santa	
Eriogonum	wild buckwheat	
Eryngium	eryngo, button-celery, coyote-thistle	
Erysimum	wallflower	
Eupatorium	joe pye weed	not *E. capillifolium*
Euphorbia	spurge	some weedy
Ferocactus	barrel cactus	
Foeniculum	fennel	*F. vulgare*
Fragaria	strawberry	
Fremontodendron	flannelbush	
Gaillardia	blanket flower	not doubled
Gaura	gaura	

(*Continued*)

GENUS	COMMON NAME	NOTES
Gentiana	blue gentian	
Geraea	desert sunflower	
Geum	avens	
Gilia	gilia	blue or violet
Glycyrrhiza	licorice	
Grindelia	gumweed	
Hackelia	wild forget-me-not	
Hedeoma	sweetscent, mock pennyroyal	
Hedysarum	sweet vetch, French honeysuckle	
Helenium	sneezeweed	
Helianthella	sunflower	
Helianthus	sunflower	not doubled
Heliotropium	heliotrope	
Hibiscus	rose-of-sharon, hollyhock	not doubled
Hieracium	hawkweed	
Holodiscus	cliff spirea, mountainspray	
Hymenopappus	false cosmos	
Hymenoxys	alpine sunflower	
Hyptis	desert lavender	
Ilex	holly	
Iliamna	mountain hollyhock	
Kallstroemia	Arizona poppy	
Keckiella	bush penstemon	
Lamium	dead nettles	incl. *Lamiastrum*
Larrea	creosote bush	

Lathyrus	everlasting pea	
Lavendula	lavender	
Layia	tidytips	
Lespedeza	bush clover	esp. *L. cuneata*
Lesquerella	bladderpod	
Liatris	blazing star	
Limnanthes	meadowfoam, fried egg flower	
Linanthus	mountain phlox	
Linaria	toadflax	*L. dalmatica* and *vulgaris* weedy
Linum	flax	
Lotus	bird's-foot trefoil, lotus	
Lycium	wolfberry	
Mahonia	mahonia	
Malus	apple	
Malva	mallow	
Medicago	alfalfa, medic	
Melilotus	sweet clover	can be weedy
Mentha	mint	
Mentzelia	blazing star	
Mertensia	bluebells	
Mimulus	monkey flower	
Monarda	bee balm	not red
Myoporum	myoporum	*M. laetum*
Nemophila	blue eyes	
Nepeta	catmint	esp. hybrid *N. x faassenii*
Ocimum	basil	

(*Continued*)

GENUS	COMMON NAME	NOTES
Oenothera	evening primrose	
Opuntia	pear cactus	
Origanum	oregano	
Oxydendrum	sourwood	
Oxytropis	locoweed	
Parkinsonia	Mexican palo verde	
Pedicularis	lousewort	
Penstemon	penstemon	not red, consider *P. strictus*
Perovskia	Russian sage, filigran	*P. atriplicifolia*
Petalostemon	prairie clover	
Phacelia	bluebells, scorpionweed	
Phyllodoce	mountain heath	
Physalis	groundcherry	
Physocarpus	ninebark	
Physostegia	obedient plant	
Pieris	fetterbush	
Platystemon	creamcups	
Polemonium	Jacob's ladder	
Pontederia	pickerelweed	
Prosopis	mesquite	
Prunella	henbit	
Prunus	cherry, plum	not doubled
Psorothamnus	dalea	
Purshia	cliff rose	
Pycnanthemum	mountain mint	
Raphanus	mustard	
Ratibida	Mexican hat	

Rhamnus	buckthorn	
Rhus	sumac	
Ribes	currant	
Robinia	black locust	
Romneya	Matilija poppy	
Rosa	rugosa-type and wild roses	not doubled, some weedy
Rosmarinus	rosemary	
Rubus	raspberry, blackberry, brambles	some weedy
Rudbeckia	black-eyed Susan	
Salix	willow	not weeping willow
Salvia	salvia	blue or violet
Sambucus	elderberry	
Scabiosa	pincushion flower	not doubled
Sedum	sedum, stonecrop	
Senecio	senecio	
Sidalcea	checker mallow	
Silybum	milk thistle	
Solanum	nightshade	some weedy
Solidago	goldenrod	
Sphaeralcea	globe mallow	
Spiraea	spiraea	
Stachys	lamb's ear	
Stanleya	prince's plume	
Sympytum	comfrey	can be weedy
Talinum	flame flower	
Tanacetum	tansy	
Tecoma	yellow trumpet bush	

(*Continued*)

GENUS	COMMON NAME	NOTES
Teucrium	germander	
Thermopsis	false lupine, golden pea	
Thymus	thyme	
Tilia	basswood	
Tithonia	Mexican sunflower	
Trichostema	blue curls	
Trifolium	clover	
Vaccinium	blueberry, cranberry, huckleberry	acid soils required
Valeriana	valerian	
Verbena	verbena	not red
Verbesina	golden crownbeard	
Veronica	speedwell, veronica	
Viburnum	arrowwood, snowball bush	
Vicia	vetch	
Viguiera	showy golden-eye	
Viola	violets	not pansies
Wyethia	mules ear	
Zinnia	zinnia	not doubled

SOURCE: USDA Agricultural Research Service Logan Bee Lab

Plants Hosting Butterfly Larvae

Aspen
Cherry
Clover
Fennel
Grasses
Lupines

Milk vetch
Milkweed
Nettle
Paintbrush
Parsley
Plantain
Plum
Rose willow
Sedges
Spirea
Thistle
Vetch
Violet
Wild carrot (Queen Anne's lace)
Winter cress

SOURCE: Xerces Socicty

Appendix 4

THE HEALING POWER OF HONEY

I once heard Ross Conrad, the author of *Natural Beekeeping*, speak eloquently on the healing nature of bees. "Bees are one of the only animals I know that don't hurt a single thing to survive," he said. "They take nectar and pollen that the plants want them to have and turn it into these amazing healing substances—honey, propolis, bee pollen, even stinger venom. A hive is an incredible pharmacy. And bees are so cooperative. I think they're an integral part of a sustainable future because of their ability to heal."

Every culture that has had access to honey has used it medicinally. Ancient Hindu, Sumerian, Egyptian, Chinese, Greek, and Roman writings all consider honey a basic component of any first-aid kit. It's an intuitive understanding. Only we in the twenty-first-century industrial world seem to need scientists to tell us what humans have always known.

I won't argue that honey can revolutionize medicine, or that the primary reason we need to save honey bees is for apitherapy—the medicinal use of bee products. But I do think that the parallel decline of our agricultural health and apitherapy skills is not purely coincidental. As Kirk Webster says, "We are losing the ability to take care of living things." And one of those things is us. In 2008, however, at the first International Symposium on Honey and Human Health, I saw some encouraging signs that our apitherapy amnesia may be clearing.

All ancient cultures used honey as a wound dressing. It was even the standard choice in modern society until the rise of antibiotics in the 1940s. Its sticky nature makes it ideal to trowel on cuts or burns before bandaging, but that's just the beginning. Honey is one of the great antimicrobial substances on the planet. It kills bacteria, fungi, and other microorganisms.[1] It has several arrows in its quiver. Like other sugars, it is hygroscopic—it draws moisture. Smear a layer of honey on a colony of germs and it sucks the water out of them. They shrivel and die. Any germs that escape dehydration are done in by the acidic nature of honey or by the hydrogen peroxide produced by honey as it absorbs water. In addition, some honeys have mysterious antimicrobial actions that can't be explained by any of these factors. Some of these, such as New Zealand's manuka and Australia's jelly bush, now being marketed around the world as Medihoney, can have one hundred times the antibiotic actions of other honeys.

But so what? Honey may have good antibiotic action, but so do antibiotics, right? Well, yes, but the typical antibiotic creams used on wounds also damage healthy cells. Honey, on the other hand, nurtures new cells, providing the perfect moist environment for vigorous healing. In one study of burn victims, 87 percent of those treated with honey had fully recovered in fifteen

1. It even makes a good spermicide, though the Ancient Egyptian formulation of honey and dried crocodile dung will probably not be making a comeback anytime soon.

days, compared with just 10 percent of those treated with antibiotic creams.

And, as we all know, antibiotics don't always work anymore. Antibiotic-resistant staph infections have become rampant in Western hospitals, killing tens of thousands of people a year, and are now epidemic in Africa and other parts of the developing world. Yet honey works beautifully on many of these infections, as well as being far more affordable and accessible than the rarer antibiotics, and it is once again becoming the wound dressing of choice for many doctors.

That's the honey application I see as most likely to make serious inroads into medicine in the next few years, but a few others are quite intriguing. The highlights:

Cold Medicines

In 2007, the FDA recommended a ban on cold medicines for children under age six. Manufacturers fought that recommendation, but voluntarily withdrew cold and cough medicines for children under age two. They should go further. There's little evidence that cold medicines do anything to alleviate symptoms, and the dangers are chilling: Cold medicines send approximately 750 young children to the emergency room each year. Since 1969 they have killed at least 54. Dextromethorphan (found in Robitussin and most other over-the-counter cough suppressants) is the primary offender; kids can't easily metabolize it.

What do you do instead when the nighttime hacking starts? You're way ahead of me . . . Researchers at Penn State found that a single dose of buckwheat honey was significantly more effective than dextromethorphan or a placebo in reducing kids' cough symptoms and promoting a good night's sleep. Buckwheat honey was chosen because it has one of the highest antioxidant contents of any honey, but the researchers don't yet know whether honey's antioxidant, antimicrobial, or throat-coating properties were responsible.

Diabetes, Obesity, Cardiovascular Disease, and Stress

Then again, maybe the honey just made the kids sleep more deeply. That would be the opinion of Mike McInnes, a Scottish exercise physiologist who is the author of *The Hibernation Diet*. McInnes has spent a decade researching the role of glycogen in enhancing restorative sleep—the type of deep sleep when most healing and growing takes place. Glycogen is brain fuel; the brain needs a steady supply all the time, even during sleep. If it runs out, brain cells begin to die. Yet at any given moment, the brain has only a thirty-second supply of glycogen, which is manufactured by the liver. So the liver steadily feeds glycogen to the brain all day and all night. But the liver itself can store only about eight hours' worth of glycogen, so if you eat an early dinner and then nothing before bed, your liver runs out of glycogen during the night. That's an emergency for your brain, which floods the body with stress hormones, particularly cortisol. Cortisol sounds the alarm, making your body melt down muscle tissue and convert it to glycogen for the brain. This keeps the brain going through the night, so you don't fall into a coma, which is nice, but the stress hormones also shut down restorative sleep. Instead of repairing bone and muscle, building immune cells, and other maintenance projects (which are all fueled by fat-burning), your restless body spends the remainder of the night in a cortisol-fueled "fight or flight" state. The heart beats faster and glucose and insulin levels rise in the blood (to fuel motion that never comes), and fat gets stored instead of metabolized. The results: diabetes, obesity, heart disease, immune breakdown, and accelerated aging.

The key to preventing this chain reaction is to fully fuel your liver before you go to bed. It doesn't take much: just a hundred calories equally divided between fructose and glucose—the liver's two favorites—plus some minerals to act as metabolites. McInnes searched until he found the ideal source. You're way ahead of me again. If McInnes is right, a teaspoon or two of honey before bed promotes deep, restful sleep, weight loss, and long-term health. In children, it promotes learning and growth.

It sounds too good to be true, but studies in other fields are confirming McInnes's theories. Certain honeys, especially tupelo, have always been reputed to be the best sugars for diabetics. Now we know it's true. Honey has a surprisingly low glycemic index—the rate at which a food is absorbed by the bloodstream and produces an insulin response. In other words, diabetics need much less insulin to deal with honey than with corn syrup or sugar. A New Zealand study found that rats fed honey had lower blood-sugar levels than rats on either a sucrose or sugar-free diet. They had a lower percentage of body fat, reduced weight, less anxiety, and improved performance on memory tests. Clearly, something about honey is extraordinarily good for the blood, which makes it good for the brain as well.

There are a few other tantalizing reports out there. Honey in barbecue sauce prevented the carcinogenic effects of grilled meat. Honey's natural anti-inflammatory properties made it as effective as prednisone in treating inflammatory bowel disease. Forty percent of cancer patients fed honey needed no colony-stimulating factor (which costs thousands of dollars a day) to boost their immune systems following chemotherapy. Honey is an effective probiotic, boosting the populations of good bacteria in the gut (as it does in bees themselves).

You get the idea. When we work in harmony with bees, the benefits go way beyond bountiful blueberry crops. To stay apprised of the latest research on the health benefits of honey, visit the Committee for the Promotion of Honey and Health at www.prohoneyandhealth.com. And remember that all these studies used raw honey in as natural a state as possible. Honey is an active, living food. When you heat it, you kill it.

ACKNOWLEDGMENTS

I live in an old Vermont farmhouse surrounded by fields of wildflowers and gnarled apple trees sloping gently southward to a pond. One day my friend Carter Stowell, who used to keep bees in San Francisco, took a look at my landscape and said, "You should have some hives." So in the fall we placed a deposit on two hives with a beekeeper in New Hampshire, to be picked up in the spring. Yet in early spring, the beekeeper sent a clipped e-mail to his clients. There would be no bees this year. They had all died. He returned everyone's deposit. I didn't get my bees, but I did get an inkling of how dire the situation was for bees and beekeepers, and I couldn't stop thinking about it. So I thank Carter for getting me interested, and for mentoring me on my new and, I hope, more successful bee endeavors.

Annik LaFarge was way ahead of the curve on this project and was the key to making the book happen. Thanks, Annik. Kathy Belden showed preternatural grace under pressure and Stephany Evans was thoroughly enthusiastic from day one. It's not every agent that will send her author catclaw honey from Texas. Thanks to Mary Elder Jacobsen for her fine hand and careful eye, and to Erick Jacobsen for knowing his tupelo from his gallberry.

Many beekeepers and researchers were incredibly generous with their time and information. I've developed tremendous appreciation for this hardworking industry. I'd like to single out Dave Hackenberg, Bill Rhodes, and Kirk Webster for patiently answering a beginner's questions for hours and hours, and Jerry Hayes for profound insights and perspective. If anybody can make the bee thing work, it's guys like these.

SOURCES

Chapter 1: Breakfast in America

A fair amount of the reason we are all thinking about pollinators now is because of Stephen L. Buchmann and Gary Paul Nabhan's seminal 1996 book, *The Forgotten Pollinators*. As important as *Silent Spring*, it should be required reading for everyone. I have no doubt that it will come to be thought of as one of the most important works of the past quarter century.

Buchmann, Stephen L., and Gary Paul Nabhan. *The Forgotten Pollinators*. Washington, D.C.: Island Press, 1996.

Carson, Rachel. *Silent Spring*. New York: Houghton Mifflin, 1962.

Chapter 2: How the Honey Bee Conquered the World

Most of the information on honey bee communication and feedback systems comes from Thomas Seeley's wonderful book *The Wisdom of the Hive*. Though heavily scientific and by no means light reading, Seeley's book is remarkably entertaining for his elegantly precise experiments, his observations, and his sheer enthusiasm that occasionally peeks through the science. The gold standard on honey bee history, and my main source, is Eva Crane's *World History of Beekeeping and Honey Hunting*. Other good books on honey bee basics include Holley

Bishop's *Robbing the Bees*, Bill Mares's *Bees Besieged*, and Ross Conrad's *Natural Beekeeping*. The pithiest information on bee nutrition is Randy Oliver's "Fat Bees" series of articles, published in *American Bee Journal*. Oliver is a California beekeeper with an astoundingly engaging and active mind. Everything he writes is worth reading, and much of it can be found on his Web site: www.scientificbeekeeping.com.

Bishop, Holley. *Robbing the Bees: A Biography of Honey*. New York: Free Press, 2005.

Conrad, Ross. *Natural Beekeeping: Organic Approaches to Modern Apiculture*. White River Junction, VT: Chelsea Green, 2007.

Crane, Eva. *World History of Beekeeping and Honey Hunting*. New York: Routledge, 1999.

Lovell, John Harvey. *The Flower and the Bee*. London: Constable, 1919.

Mares, Bill. *Bees Besieged: One Beekeeper's Bittersweet Journey to Understanding*. Medina, OH: A. I. Root, 2005.

McGee, Harold. *On Food and Cooking: The Science and Lore of the Kitchen*. New York: Scribner, 2004. Source of the Washington Irving quote.

Mangum, Wyatt. "Moving Beehives in Times Before Bobcat Loaders, Tractor Trailers, and Pickup Trucks (with Cup Holders)." *American Bee Journal*, February 2008. Quotes M. G. Dadant.

Oliver, Randy. "Fat Bees." Pts. 1–4. *American Bee Journal*, August 2007–December 2007.

Seeley, Thomas D. *The Wisdom of the Hive: The Social Physiology of Honey Bee Colonies*. Cambridge, MA: Harvard University Press, 1995.

University of Illinois at Urbana-Champaign. "Honey Bee Chemoreceptors Found for Smell and Taste." Press release, October 27, 2006.

Wilson, E. O. *Success and Dominance in Ecosystems: The Case of the Social Insects*. Oldendorf/Luhe, Germany: Ecology Institute, 1990.

Chapter 3: Collapse

An invaluable source of information on beekeeping basics, bee biology, and honey bee diseases is the Mid-Atlantic Apiculture Research and Extension Consortium (http://maarec.cas.psu.edu). It's the best clearinghouse on scientists' current understanding of CCD.

Barrionuevo, Alexei. "Honeybees Vanish, Leaving Keepers in Peril." *New York Times*, February 27, 2007.

Boecking, Otto, and Kirsten Traynor. "Varroa Biology and Methods of Control." Pt. 1. *American Bee Journal*, October 2007.

Chong, Jia-Rui, and Thomas H. Maugh II. "Suddenly, the Bees Are Simply Vanishing." *Los Angeles Times*, June 10, 2007.

Kolbert, Elizabeth. "Stung." *New Yorker*, August 6, 2007.

Laurenson, John. "Plight of France's Honey Bee." BBC News, October 14, 2003.

Pennsylvania State University. "Bee Mites Suppress Bee Immunity, Open Door for Viruses and Bacteria." Press release, May 18, 2005.

Vidal, John. "Threat to Agriculture as Mystery Killer Wipes Out Honeybee Hives." *Guardian*, April 12, 2007.

Chapter 4: Whodunit

American Bee Journal. "Questions and Answers About Colony Collapse Disorder and Israeli Acute Paralysis Virus." November 2007.

Cameron, Craig, and Ilan Sela. "Characterization of Bee Viruses and an Investigation of Their Mode of Spread." BARD US-3205-01R, Final Scientific Report, March 31, 2005.

Chen, Yanping, and Jay Evans. "Historical Presence of Israeli Acute Paralysis Virus in the United States." *American Bee Journal*, December 2007.

Chong, Jia-Rui, and Thomas H. Maugh II. "Experts May Have Found What's Bugging the Bees." *Los Angeles Times*, April 26, 2007.

Christian Newswire. "Missing Bees, Cell Phones and Fulfillment of Bible Prophecy." April 27, 2007. http://christiannewswire.com/news/27552961.html.

Cox-Foster, Diana, et al. "A Metagenomic Survey of Microbes in Honey Bee Colony Collapse Disorder." *Science Express*, September 6, 2007.

Dayton, Leigh. "Bee Acquittal Stings Journal." *Australian*, November 21, 2007.

Fischer, James. "A Beekeeper Reads the Paper." *Bee Culture*, September 2007.

Harst, Wolfgang, Jochen Kuhn, and Hermann Stever. "Can Electromagnetic Exposure Cause a Change in Behaviour? Studying Possible Non-Thermal Influences on Honey Bees—An Approach within the Framework of Educational Informatics." *Acta Systemica* 6 (1), 2006.

Hayes, Jerry. "Colony Collapse Disorder: Research Update." *American Bee Journal*, December 2007.

Information Liberation. "No Organic Bee Losses." May 10, 2007. www.informationliberation.com/index.php?id=21912.

Johnson, Chloe. "Widespread Die Off May Be Affecting Area's Bees." *Foster's Daily Democrat*, April 22, 2007.

Milius, Susan. "Not-So-Elementary Bee Mystery." *Science News*, July 28, 2007.

Nikiforuk, Andrew. "Is the Bee Virus Bunk?" *Toronto Globe and Mail*, November 3, 2007.

Oldroyd, Benjamin P. "What's Killing American Honey Bees?" *PLoS Biology*, June 2007.

Oliver, Randy. "The Nosema Twins." Pt. 1. *American Bee Journal*, December 2007.

Wall Street Journal. "Bee Mystery: Virus Linked to Colony Deaths." August 6, 2007.

Chapter 5: SLOW POISON

Bonmatin, J. M., et al. "Quantification of Imidacloprid Uptake in Maize Crops." *Journal of Agriculture and Food Chemistry* 53 (13), 2005.

Bortolotti, Laura, et al. "Effects of Sublethal Imidacloprid Doses on the Homing Rate and Foraging Activity of Honey Bees." *Bulletin of Insectology* 56 (1), 2003.

Chauzat, M. P., et al. "Survey of Pesticide Residues in Pollen Loads Collected by Honey Bees in France." *Journal of Economic Entomology* 99 (2), 2006.

Comité Scientifique et Technique de l'Etude Multifactorielle des Troubles des Abeilles. *Imidaclopride utilisé en enrobage de semences (Gaucho®) et troubles des abeilles.* Final report, September 18, 2003.

Cox, Caroline. "Imidacloprid." *Journal of Pesticide Reform* 21(1), Spring 2001.

Fishel, Frederick M. "Pesticide Toxicity Profile: Neonicotinoid Pesticides." University of Florida Extension Service, October 2005.

Frazier, Maryann. "Protecting Honey Bees from Pesticides." *Crop Talk*, May 2007.

Greatti, Moreno, et al. "Presence of the A.I. Imidacloprid on Vegetation Near Corn Fields Sown with Gaucho® Dressed Seeds." *Bulletin of Insectology* 59 (2), 2006.

Maus, Christian M., Gaëlle Curé, and Richard Schmuck. "Safety of Imidacloprid Seed Dressings to Honey Bees." *Bulletin of Insectology* 56 (1), 2003.

Medrzycki, P., et al. "Effects of Imidacloprid Administered in Sub-Lethal Doses on Honey Bee Behaviour." *Bulletin of Insectology* 56 (1), 2003.

Newark (NJ) Star-Ledger. "Possible Culprit Identified in Decline of Honeybees." May 28, 2007.

Preston, Richard. "A Death in the Forest." *New Yorker*, December 10, 2007.

Ramirex-Romero, Ricardo. "Effects of Cry1Ab Protoxin, Deltamethrin and Imidacloprid on the Foraging Activity and the Learning Performances of the Honeybee *Apis mellifera*, a Comparative Approach." *Apidologie* 36, 2005.

Rortais, A., et al. "Modes of Honeybees Exposure to Systemic Insecticides: Estimated Amounts of Contaminated Pollen and Nectar Consumed by Different Categories of Bees." *Apidologie* 36, 2005.

Schneider, Franklin. "Buzz Kill." *Washington City Paper*, June 14, 2007.

U.S. Environmental Protection Agency. "Reregistration Eligibility Decision for Tau-fluvalinate." September 2005.

Chapter 6: FLORIDA, NOVEMBER 2007

Barboza, David. "In China, Farming Fish in Toxic Waters." *New York Times*, December 15, 2007.

Ezenwa, Sylvia. "Contaminated Honey Imports from China: An Ongoing Concern." Pts. 1 and 2. *American Bee Journal*, July 2007 and August 2007.

Lee, Don. "Cleaning Up China's Honey." *Los Angeles Times*, May 3, 2007.

McKay, Rich. "Beekeepers Stung by Imports." *Orlando Sentinel*, July 8, 2000.

Pollan, Michael. "Our Decrepit Food Factories." *New York Times Magazine*, December 16, 2007.

Sanford, Malcolm. "Pollination of Citrus by Honeybees." University of Florida Extension Service, 1992.

Chapter 7: THE ALMOND ORGY

Agnew, Singeli. "The Almond and the Bee." SFGate.com, October 14, 2007.

Almond Board of California. *Almond Industry Position Report*. May 2007.

Blue Diamond. "A Historical Reference of the Almond." www.bluediamond.com/almonds/history.

Burke, Garance. "Beekeepers Get Stung by Hive Heists as California Nut Trees Bloom." *North County (CA) Times*, March 11, 2008.

Cline, Harry. "Almond Growers Facing Bee Crisis." *Western Farm Press*, May 27, 2005.

McGregor, S. E. *Insect Pollination of Cultivated Crop Plants.* Agriculture Handbook No. 496. Washington, D.C.: U.S. Government Printing Office, 1976.

Nachbaur, Andy. "SAD and BAD Bees." www.beesource.com, January 1989.

Traynor, Joe. "Improved Pollination Will Improve Yields." *Pacific Nut Producer*, February 2004.

Chapter 8: Bees on the Verge of a Nervous Breakdown

Excellent histories of the Africanized bee and the small hive beetle can be found in Bill Mares's 2005 book, *Bees Besieged*. Florida's Department of Agriculture and Consumer Services maintains a wealth of current information on both critters: www.doacs.state.fl.us/pi. Information on Tobias Olofsson and Alejandra Vásquez's study of lactic acid bacteria in bees (not yet published, as this book went to press) can be found at www.prohoneyandhealth.com. More information on the Tucson Bee Diet is available at www.megabeediet.com. Randy Oliver's articles on bee nutrition and vitellogenin are available at www.scientificbeekeeping.com. For a comprehensive approach to the subject, see Doug Somerville's book *Fat Bees, Skinny Bees*, available as a free download at www.rirdc.gov.au/reports/HBE/05-054.pdf.

Ferrari, Thomas. "When Bees Carry Dead Pollen." *Bee Culture*, December 2007.

Llauener, Paul, and Marie-Laure Combes. "French Beekeepers Brace for Asian Sting." Associated Press, April 13, 2007.

Mares, Bill. *Bees Besieged: One Beekeeper's Bittersweet Journey to Understanding*. Medina, OH: A. I. Root, 2005.

Oliver, Randy. "Fat Bees." Pts. 1 and 2. *American Bee Journal*, August 2007 and September 2007.

Salon.com. "Who Killed the Honeybees?" May 29, 2007. Quotes Eric Mussen.

Somerville, Doug. *Fat Bees, Skinny Bees*. Barton, Australia: Rural Industries Research and Development Corporation, 2005.

Tingek, Salim, et al. "A New Record of a Parasite of Honey Bees in Sabah, Malaysia, Borneo: An Additional Danger for Worldwide Beekeeping?" *American Bee Journal*, December 2007.

Chapter 9: Resilience and the Russians

Kirk Webster was first brought to my attention by Bill McKibben, who has a nice piece on him in the July–August 2006 issue of *Orion*. Webster's articles were published in *American Bee Journal* (www.dadant.com). They provide a good introduction to Sir Albert Howard's work; Michael Pollan's *The Omnivore's Dilemma* contains a more in-depth profile. For a chronology of the Russian Honey Bee Queen Breeding Project, go to www.ars.usda.gov. The bible of the resilience movement is *Resilience Thinking*, by Brian Walker and David Salt. A superb introduction to the subject is Chip Ward's article "Diesel-Driven Bee Slums and Impotent Turkeys: The Case for Resilience."

Burley, Lisa Marie. "The Effects of Miticides on the Reproductive Physiology of Honey Bee (*Apis mellifera L.*) Queens and Drones." Master of science thesis, Virginia Polytechnic Institute, 2007.

Chang, Kenneth. "Mathematics Explains Mysterious Midge Behavior." *New York Times*, March 7, 2008.

Flottum, Kim. "Cold Country Queens." *Bee Culture*, December 2007.

Garreau, Joel. "Honey, I'm Gone." *Washington Post*, June 1, 2007. Quotes Barry Lopez.

Harder, Ben. "Powerful Pollinators, Wild Bees May Favor Eco-Farms." *National Geographic* news, October 28, 2004.

Kremen, Claire, et al. "The Area Requirements of an Ecosystem Service: Crop Pollination by Native Bee Communities in California." *Ecology Letters* 7, 2004.

McKibben, Bill. "Of Mites and Men." *Orion*, July–August 2006.

North Carolina Cooperative Extension Service. "A Comparison of Russian and Italian Honey Bees," May 2005.

Pollan, Michael. *The Omnivore's Dilemma*. New York: Penguin, 2006.

Richard, Freddie-Jeanne, David R. Tarpy, and Christina M. Grozinger. "Effects of Insemination Quantity on Honey Bee Queen Physiology." *PLoS One* 2 (10), 2007.

Romanov, Boris, "Russian Bees in USA and Canada." www.beebehavior.com.

Surowiecki, James. "Bonds Unbound." *New Yorker*, February 11 and 18, 2008. He's paraphrasing the sociologist Charles Perrow.

Walker, Brian, and David Salt. *Resilience Thinking: Sustaining Ecosystems and People in a Changing World*. Washington, D.C.: Island Press, 2006.

Ward, Chip. "Diesel-Driven Bee Slums and Impotent Turkeys: The Case for Resilience." www.TomDispatch.com, July 30, 2007.

Webster, Kirk. "A Beekeeping Diary." *American Bee Journal*, January–December 2007.

Chapter 10: THE BIRTH OF BEAUTY

The spirit of Michael Pollan has flitted through several chapters of this book, and here he swoops close. His chapter on the tulip in *The*

Botany of Desire is a brilliant meditation on flowers, beauty, and desire. I read it many years before starting work on this book, but the ideas must have worked their way deep into my brain. I thought I came up with my chapter title all on my own, but when I went back to reread *The Botany of Desire* while editing my manuscript, there it was, gosh darn it: "The birth of beauty goes back further still, to a time . . . before human desire, when the world was mostly leaf and the first flower opened." For a dazzlingly entertaining explanation of flower strategy and evolution, see Bastiaan Meeuse and Sean Morris's *The Sex Life of Flowers*. Two other excellent sources on the topic are *The Forgotten Pollinators* and Bernd Heinrich's *Bumblebee Economics*.

Buchmann, Stephen L., and Gary Paul Nabhan. *The Forgotten Pollinators*. Washington, D.C.: Island Press, 1996.

Heinrich, Bernd. *Bumblebee Economics*. Cambridge, MA: Harvard University Press, 1979. Heinrich's clover quote can be found here.

Meeuse, Bastiaan, and Sean Morris. *The Sex Life of Flowers*. New York: Facts on File, 1984.

Pollan, Michael. *The Botany of Desire: A Plant's-Eye View of the World*. New York: Random House, 2001.

Raine, Nigel, and Lars Chittka. "The Adaptive Significance of Sensory Bias in a Foraging Context: Floral Colour Preferences in the Bumblebee *Bombus terrestris*." www.plosone.org, June 20, 2007.

University of Chicago. "Amino Acids in Nectar Enhance Butterfly Fecundity: A Long Awaited Link." Press release, February 23, 2005.

Chapter 11: Fruitless Fall

The best source of information on the plight of all pollinators is *The Forgotten Pollinators*. It was published in 1996, so for more updated information, try the Xerces Society (www.xerxes.org).

Berenbaum, May. "The Birds and the Bees: How Pollinators Help Maintain Healthy Ecosystems." Written testimony before the Subcommittee on Fisheries, Wildlife and Oceans, Committee on Natural Resources, U.S. House of Representatives, June 26, 2007.

Biesmeijer, J. C., et al. "Parallel Declines in Pollinators and Insect-Pollinated Plants in Britain and the Netherlands." *Science*, July 21, 2006.

Bodin, Madeline. "A Mysterious Nighttime Disappearance." *Times Argus*, July 15, 2007.

———. "The Plight of the Bumblebee." *Times Argus*, August 5, 2007.

Buchmann, Stephen L., and Gary Paul Nabhan. *The Forgotten Pollinators*. Washington, D.C.: Island Press, 1996.

Goddard Space Flight Center. "Tropical Deforestation Affects US Climate." Press release, September 20, 2005.

Harder, Ben. "Powerful Pollinators, Wild Bees May Favor Eco-Farms." *National Geographic* news, October 28, 2004.

Harrar, Sari. "Bee Crisis." *Organic Gardening*, November–January 2007–2008.

Klein, Alexandra-Maria, et al. "Importance of Pollinators in Changing Landscapes for World Crops." *Proceedings of the Royal Society B* 274, October 27, 2006.

Levine, Ketzel. "Rock Star Botany 202." NPR.org, January 2, 2008.

Losey, John, and Mace Vaughan. "The Economic Value of Ecological Services Provided by Insects." *Bioscience*, April 2006.

National Research Council. *Status of Pollinators in North America*. Committee report. Washington, D.C.: National Academies Press, 2007.

Partap, Uma, and Tej Partap. "Declining Apple Production and Worried Himalayan Farmers: Promotion of Honeybees for Pollination." *Issues in Mountain Development* 1, 2001.

Raver, Anne. "To Feed the Birds, First Feed the Bugs." *New York Times*, March 6, 2008.

Science Daily. "Flowers' Fragrance Diminished by Air Pollution, Study Indicates." April 11, 2008.

———. "Wild Bees Make Honeybees Better Pollinators." September 24, 2006.

Tang, Ya, et al. "Hand Pollination of Pears and Its Implications for Biodiversity Conservation and Environmental Protection: A Case Study from Hanyuan County, Sichuan Province, China." College of the Environment, Sichuan University, 2003.

Xerces Society. "Bumble Bees in Decline." www.xerces.org .bumblebees/index.html.

Appendix 1: The African Paradox

Dee Lusby's writings on small-cell hives can be found at www .beesource.com. Dennis Murrell's extensive studies involving natural-cell hives are available at www.bwrangler.com.

Roubik, David. "The Value of Bees to the Coffee Harvest." *Nature* 417, June 13, 2002.

Appendix 4: The Healing Power of Honey

Most of the studies cited in this appendix were still awaiting publication when this book went to press. For updates on them, visit www .prohoneyandhealth.com.

Harris, Gardner. "FDA Panel Urges Ban on Medicine for Child Colds." *New York Times*, October 20, 2007.

McInnes, Mike, and Stuart McInnes. *The Hibernation Diet*. London: Souvenir Press, 2006.

Pifer, Jennifer. "Child Deaths Lead to FDA Hearing on Cough, Cold Meds." CNN.com, October 17, 2007.

INDEX